The Determination of a Lifespan

The Determination of a Lifespan:

A 400-Year-Old Shark and a 40,000-Year-Old Plant

By

Yasumi Ohshima

Cambridge Scholars Publishing

The Determination of a Lifespan:
A 400-Year-Old Shark and a 40,000-Year-Old Plant

By Yasumi Ohshima

This book first published 2023

Cambridge Scholars Publishing

Lady Stephenson Library, Newcastle upon Tyne, NE6 2PA, UK

British Library Cataloguing in Publication Data
A catalogue record for this book is available from the British Library

ISBN (10): 1-5275-0158-2
ISBN (13): 978-1-5275-0158-4

CONTENTS

PREFACE

Recent developments in our understanding of the lifespans of organisms have been really outstanding. About a decade ago, the longest recorded lifespan of an animal was said to be less than 200 years, but now it is known that the longest records for vertebrates and invertebrates are about 400 years and 4,000 years, respectively. Likewise, in the plant kingdom, the longest recorded lifespan was extended from about 5,000 years to more than 40,000 years. Elsewhere, molecular and statistical studies on lifespans, mainly in humans and animals, have been developing extensively, and will help us to live longer. This book describes the present states of actual lifespans of animals, plants and humans; important factors for their lifespans, especially for humans; and surprising facts and secrets of centenarians, based on many scientific papers and books.

This book is basically an English version of the book "４００年生きるサメ、４万年生きる植物　生物の寿命はどのように決まるのか", published in 2020 by Kagaku-Dojin. However, Chapter 9, "Biological significance of a lifespan", which was lacking in the Japanese book but is important, has been newly written and added for this English book.

The author knows of no other similar comprehensive book on lifespans like this. He wishes that this book will be read by scientists and students in the field of biology as a textbook, and by many general readers for their interests and for the further extension of their lifespans.

Yasumi Ohshima
March 8, 2022

PROFILE OF THE AUTHOR

Professor Emeritus from Kyushu University, Japan, Yasumi Ohshima obtained his PhD from the Graduate School of Science, University of Tokyo in 1969, and since then has studied molecular biology in Japanese universities and at the Carnegie Institution in the USA. His main study areas are the biology of the nematode *C. elegans*, and the molecular biology of RNA. He has published several books in Japan, the most recent one translated here, and another recent one on the body sizes of organisms (published in 2013).

CHAPTER 1

A 400 YEAR OLD SHARK, 4,000 YEAR OLD CORALS: THE LIFESPAN OF AN ANIMAL

1-1 Lifespan ranking of vertebrates

1st: Greenland shark

The longest lifespans of some animals of each of the vertebrate classes are presented in **Table 1-1**. For each group, the lifespans are listed in order from shortest to longest. Among all the animals listed, the one with the longest lifespan is a shark known as the **Greenland shark** (*Somniosus microcephalus*) (**Fig.1-1**), the long lifespan of which was reported quite recently in 2016. This shark lives widely in the North Atlantic Ocean and the Arctic Ocean. The females are larger than the males, and they are said to grow up to 4~5m long (Nielsen et al. 2016, 702-704).

Its longest lifespan was reported to be 392+/-120 years as shown in the table. This lifespan belonged to the biggest (~5m long) of the 28 female sharks studied, and is a value estimated from the **radioactivity of the carbons** in the eye lens (+/-120 years represents 95% confidence interval or 2σ). This suggests that their longest lifespan may be up to about 500 years, or even longer in bigger specimens. The Greenland shark is thought to have the longest lifespan among all vertebrates. This record is twice or three times as long as the longest lifespan of the Galapagos or Aldabra giant tortoise which was previously thought to be the longest, and therefore is an epoch-making discovery.

Fig.1-1: Greenland shark (https 8).

Table 1-1: The longest lifespans of animals in each class of vertebrates.

Class	Species	Longest lifespan (years)
Fish	guppy	5
	salmon	13
	whale shark	70
	carp	70~100
	eel	88
	sturgeon	152
	Greenland shark	392+/-120 (Nielsen et al. 2016,702)
Amphibian	toad	40
	giant salamander	55
Reptile	boa	40

	American alligator	66
	sphenodon	100
	Galapagos giant tortoise	177 (大島 2013, 27)
	Aldabra giant tortoise	183 (Nat. Geo. News 2016)
Bird	hummingbird	8
	chicken	30
	crane	62
	ostrich	62
	owl	60~70
	stork	70~100
	cockatoo	100
	griffon vulture	118
Mammal	shrew	1.5
	mouse	4
	pig	27
	dog	34 (under breeding)
	cat	35
	chimpanzee	59 (鈴木 2002, 22)
	horse	61 (under breeding)
	Indian elephant	69 (鈴木 2002, 22)
	donkey	100
	finback whale	116 (鈴木 2002, 22)
	human	122 (https 6)
	Arctic whale	211+/-35 (George et al. 1999, 574)

Abstracted from Table 1.1.2 of Flindt et al. 2007, 7-9, if not indicated otherwise.

Estimation of a lifespan is a difficult task

In the case of the Greenland shark, its lifespan is an estimation and has a wide range of confidence. Likewise, as for other data in Table 1-1, there are a wide range of confidence intervals such as 70~100 years for carp and stork. The cases in which precise lifespan data were obtained are those of animals under breeding such as dogs and horses (as shown in the table). The lifespans of the guppy, chicken and cat in the table are probably those obtained under breeding, and so they are thought to be exact, too (the longest lifespan of a cat is shown to be 34 years in the Guinness Book of World Records). Many of the data in Table 1-1 may not be exact but are estimated values.

It is easy to imagine that the exact determination of the lifespan of an animal may be difficult especially for a long lifespan, except when there is a precise record under breeding. The methods used to measure or estimate an animal lifespan will be described in Chapter 10. Table 1-1 is an important one in this book, but readers should be cautious with its findings as stated above.

2nd: Arctic whale

The second longest lifespan in Table 1-1 is that of the **Arctic whale** (also called the **Greenland whale**, *Balaena mysticetus*), at 211+/-35 years (George et al. 1999, 574). The Arctic whale (**Fig. 1-2**) is a kind of giant whale belonging to the suborder Mysticeti, lives in the cold Arctic Ocean (likely with the Greenland shark), and grows up to 20m long (https 9). The longest lifespan of the Arctic whale shown in the table is the longest one among the 48 individuals studied. It is based on the racemization rate of amino acid aspartic acid in the nuclei of cells in the eye lens (as described in Chapter 10).

By the way, a carp named Hanako bred in the Japanese village of Higashishirakawa was said to be 226 years old based on annual rings of the scales. This lifespan record is included in the Guinness Book of World Records, but its reliability is said to be in question, and so it is not listed in Table 1-1.

Fig. 1-2: Arctic whale (https 9).

3rd and 4th: Tortoises

The third and the fourth places in the longest lifespan records in Table 1-1 both belong to reptiles. The **Aldabra giant tortoise** (also called as the Seychelle giant tortoise) has been known to live for 183 years while the **Galapagos giant tortoise** has reached 177. Both are terrestrial big tortoises, and the Aldabra giant tortoise named Johnathan (**Fig.1-3**) was 183 years old and fine in 2016 (大島 2013, 27) and therefore now, in 2022, is 189. Based on another reference (http: 11), Johnathan was 182 years old in 2014, and was the oldest among the living individuals of the same or similar species. It is said that the Aldabra giant tortoise Adoweicha, raised in a zoo in India, lived for 255 years, but the veracity of this is questionable (http 11).

The longest lifespan on record for a Galapagos giant tortoise is 177 years, written in the book *On Size and Life* (MacMahon and Bonner 2000, 12), but the evidence for it is missing. Another data suggests that a Galapagos giant tortoise in an Australian zoo was 176 years old.

Fig. 1-3: The Aldabra giant tortoise Johnathan (http 11).

5th and 6th: Sturgeon and human

In fifth place of the longest lifespans in Table 1-1 is 152 years for a **sturgeon**, after which in sixth comes a human at 122 years. This human record of 122 years is based on the lifespan of a French woman, Jeanne-Louise Calment (**Fig. 1-4**). There are records indicating that she was born on February 21, 1875, and died on August 4, 1997, and she is believed to have the longest human lifespan on record for which the evidence is certain (https 6; https

13). Meanwhile, **the longest lifespan recorded among Japanese** has recently increased. Mrs Kane Tanaka living in Fukuoka prefecture has been assigned as the oldest person in the Guinness Book of World Records, and it was recently reported in the newspaper *The Mainichi* that she became 117 years old and was fine (as of January 6, 2020). This news is exciting for us Japanese as a symbol of Japanese longevity.

Fig. 1-4: Jeanne L. Calment (https 6).

In seventh place among the longest lifespans in Table 1-1 is the **griffon vulture (Fig. 1-5)**, a bird which has been recorded to live up to 118 years. It is one of the birds of prey of the order Falconiformes, and is big enough that its wings are 2.6m wide when open (https: 14). In eighth place is a lifespan of 116 years for a finback whale.

Fig. 1-5: Griffon vulture (https 14).

Animals with a short lifespan

On the other hand, the shortest lifespans shown in Table 1-1 are 1.5 years for a shrew, 4 years for a mouse, 5 years for a guppy, 8 years for a hummingbird, and so on. All these animals are very small in terms of bodily size, and their body weights are several grams or less, except for the mouse (~20 g). In contrast, all the long-lived animals are big, and lifespan seems to be proportional to body weight for vertebrates in general (see Chapter 7).

The average lifespan of dogs in Japan is 14.36 years, based on "The studies of dogs and cats under breeding in Japan in 2016" (https 15). This represents about 40% of the longest lifespan of 34 years for dogs.

If you're interested in finding out more information on animal lifespans, there is a list of lifespans for more than 50 birds and one for about 200 fish freely available on the web (https 16; https 17).

1-2 The average lifespan of the human being

While the longest human lifespan is around 120 years, as stated above, how long is the average lifespan? Based on a report by the WHO (World Health Organization) from 2018, the worldwide average was 72.0 years for men and women together, 69.8 years for men and 74.2 years for women in 2016. This indicates that women live more than 4 years longer than men.

The average lifespan in each country

Average lifespans differ among the countries of the world. **Table 1-2** shows the data for the top 10 countries and the bottom 10 countries abstracted from the WHO report. The table shows that the highest is 84.2 years for Japan and the lowest is 52.9 years for Lesotho, with the difference between them more than 30 years. The countries showing very long lifespans are in Europe or Asia, but those showing very short lifespans are all located in Africa, which is telling. For us Japanese, it is fortunate that our country belongs to the top long-living countries. On the other side, the main reason for the very short average lifespans in the African countries may be their poverty due to their history of being colonies of the European countries. The races, climates and environments in Africa may also be related. Swaziland in the table changed its name to Eswatini in 2018. This country and Lesotho are kingdoms while all the other African countries in the table are republics.

Table 1-2: The top ten and bottom ten countries of the world in terms of average lifespan

The top ten countries			The bottom ten countries		
Order	Country	Average lifespan (years)	Order	Country	Average lifespan(years)
1	Japan	84.2	183	Lesotho	52.9
2	Switzerland	83.3	182	Central African Rep.	53.0
3	Spain	83.1	181	Sierra Leone	53.1
4	Australia	82.9	180	Chad	54.3
4	France	82.9	179	Côte d'Ivoire	54.6
4	Singapore	82.9	178	Nigeria	55.2
7	Canada	82.8	177	Somalia	55.4
7	Italy	82.8	176	Swaziland	57.7
9	Korea	82.7	175	Mali	58.0
10	Norway	82.5	174	Cameroon	58.1

Abstracted from the report in The WHO World Health Statistics, 2018

As for the average lifespan of males in each country, Switzerland came first (81.2 years), Japan second (81.1 years), and Australia third (81.0 years). As for that of females, Japan was first (87.1 years), and joint second were France and Spain (85.7 years).

In the WHO statistics, in addition to the 183 countries for which average lifespan values are shown, the names of 12 countries or districts were listed without any lifespan data. Hong Kong is not included in these 12 countries/districts, the reason for which may be that Hong Kong is a part of China and not a member of the WHO. However, in the statistics by The World Bank, Hong Kong was top in terms of the average lifespans for both men and women. *The Mainichi* (July 21, 2018) reported that the Japanese average lifespans were 87.26 years for women and 81.09 years for men. Both numbers had increased since the previous year, with the female value ranking second globally (as it had done the year before) and the male value ranking third. In first for both men and women was Hong Kong, and in second place for men was Switzerland. Even at present, Japan may have the longest average lifespan for men and women combined across the globe.

Extension of the average human lifespan

The average human lifespan is a great deal longer today than for most of human history. *A Concise History of World Population* (Fifth Edition) by M. Livi-Bacci states that the estimated average human lifespan was 20 years in 10,000 BC, 22 years in 1 BC/1 AD, 27 years in 1750 (in the middle of Edo era in Japan), 35 years in 1950 and 56 years in 2,000. In recent years the elongation of the average has become especially remarkable, and is now more than twice what it was in 1950. This situation is likely to be due to the recent development of medicine, food, economic state etc., in the world. Clearly, the average human lifespan has extended significantly based on the advances of civilization. The recent value of 72 years in the world is about

60% of the longest human lifespan of about 120 years, and thus is a higher percentage than the one for dogs mentioned above (about 40%).

The extension of the average human lifespan has been continuing in both Japan and the world at large. In Japan in 2017 it was 0.1 year longer than it was in 2016. The extension in Japan may continue for the time being, but it is difficult to say when it will stop.

1-3 Factors for the long lifespan of a vertebrate

In general, the mechanisms determining the lifespan of an animal are very complex, and the related factors are various. The mechanisms including those at the molecular level will be explained in Chapter 7. Here, I would like to pick up the probable factors that are supposed from the contents described above.

The factors for a long lifespan can be classified into environmental factors and those inherent to the animal. Table 1-1 shows that very long-lived animals are all considerably large. Namely, **big body size** is likely a factor for a long lifespan. This seems true for both homoiotherms (mammals and birds) and poikilotherms (such as fish and reptiles), whether they live on land or in water.

The reason that big body size is a factor for a long lifespan may be that big size is favorable to bear an environmental change, such as that in temperature or food, and an unfavorable environment. For example, both the Greenland Shark and Arctic whale, the first and the second in the lifespan ranking, live in the cold seas. However, the temperatures in their body's centers are high enough due to their big body sizes, and therefore they can hold a fairly active metabolic activity to support their lives and growth.

As for environmental factors, both the Greenland shark and Arctic whale stated above live in cold seas, which suggests that the **cold temperature of the environment** is thought to be a factor for their long lives. In low temperatures, growth is slow and a long time is needed to grow to an adult, from which we can understand their long lifespans. The low temperature of an environment leads to the slow growth of an animal, which is a characteristic of that animal, and a big body size leads to a very long lifespan.

Living in a cold sea is an ability which likely derives from the characteristics of the organism that are basically determined by its genes. Therefore, the reason for a long lifespan of an animal resides ultimately within the body of the animal. The **average lifespans** for human beings and dogs, for example, depend greatly on their living environments. This is clear from the large differences in human lifespans among countries or across history.

1-4 Lifespan ranking of invertebrates

As in the case of vertebrates, **Table 1-3** shows the longest lifespans of invertebrates classified into groups. In this table, the groups are phyla, such as Porifera, Cnidaria and Mollusca, which are the largest units in biological classification. Studies on lifespan have greatly developed for invertebrates too, and several lifespans of more than 1,000 years have been reported.

Table 1-3: Longest lifespans of invertebrates

Phylum	Species	Longest lifespan (y=years)
Porifera	glass sponge	9000 y? (Kenny 2019, 50)
Cnidaria	beadlet anemone	15 y
	hard coral	>28 y
	Octocorallia coral (*Geradia* sp.)	2740+/-15 y (Roark et al. 2009, 5204)
	black coral (*Leiopathes* sp.)	4265+/-44 y (Roark et al. 2009, 5205)
	Yamato hydra (*H. magnipapillata*)	>3572 y (Schaible et al. 2015, 15702)
	immortal jellyfish	eternal? (Piraino et al. 1996, 302-312)
Platyhelminthes	tapeworm	35 y
Rotifera	saline rotifer (*B. plicatillis sp.*)	14 days
Nematoda	*C. elegans*	36 days (Kenyon et al. 1993, 462)
	roundworm	5 y
Annelida	earthworm	10 y
Mollusca	golden cuttlefish	5 y
	oyster	12 y
	winkle (*L. littorea*)	20 y
	nautilus (Nautilidae)	60~100 y
	Hyriopsis schlegelii	100 y
	ocean quahog (*A. islandica*)	507 y (https 26; Nat.Geo. News 2013)

Arthropoda	fruit fly (*D. melanogaster*)	46 days
	bed bug (*C. lectularius*)	6 months
	stone centipede	5~6 y
	mantis	8 y
	crayfish	20~30 y
	lobster	45 y
	termite queen (*N. triodae*)	100 y (https 28; http 29)
Chordata	nudibranchi	7 months

y = years. Abstracted from Table 1.1.2 of R. Flindt (2007), 7-9, except for the cases stated otherwise.

1st and 3rd: Corals

Among the lifespan values in Table 1-3 that are likely to be relatively reliable, the first and the third ranks are both for corals in Cnidaria. **Figure 1-6** shows a community of a few kinds of corals. The Cnidaria phylum is a group of animals to which jellyfish, corals, sea anemones and hydras belong, and it was previously called as Coelenterate. A cnida or nematocyst is an organ used for injection of a toxin or for catching food, and is a common characteristic among Cnidaria animals.

Fig. 1-6: A community of a few kinds of corals (https 30).

As for the two corals, *Octocorallia* coral and black coral, the ages were estimated based on the carbon radioactivity of living corals from the sea near Hawaii (Roark et al. 2009, 5204). The black coral ranking 1st with the age 4,265 +/-44 years is a member of the order Antipatharia in the subclass Hexacorallia. The coral in third place with the age 2,740+/-15 years belongs to the subclass Octocorallia, and therefore differs much from black coral in its classification. In the slices of a semi-fossilized or calcified branch of each of these corals, the radioactivity of the carbon was measured at various depths, which indicated that the examined parts were essentially not metabolized. Therefore, the time of formation of each part of the coral branch was estimated. For example, the ^{14}C level of the deepest part of the coral ranked 1st was about 40% lower than that of the surface. Since the half-life of ^{14}C radioactivity is 5,730 years, we can understand that the age of the coral is 4~5,000 years near the half-life of ^{14}C.

2nd: Hydra?

The second rank of the estimated longest lifespans, which are thought to be relatively reliable in Table 1-3, is 3,572 years (or longer) of a kind of Yamato hydra (*Hydra magnipapillata*) (Schaible et al. 2015, 15702). **Figure 1-7** shows a similar hydra in the same genus. Hydras belong to Cnidaria like corals, but live in fresh water, have unique forms, and are small (less than 2.5 cm). *H. vulgaris*, the hydra shown in Fig. 1-7, is also well studied, and the age of the oldest among the studied individuals is estimated to be 1,893 years. These hydras showed little ageing in breeding experiments for several years and have a very low mortality rate. Their lifespans were estimated from these mortality rates, and there is no solid evidence for them (Schaible et al. 2015, 15701-706).

Fig. 1-7: ***Hydra vulgaris*** (https 31).

Is the jellyfish immortal?

The immortal jellyfish in Table 1-3 also belongs to Cnidaria, but to the order Anthomedusae in the class Hydrozoa, and is a kind of jellyfish (**Fig. 1-8**). This jellyfish is said to be possibly immortal (Piraino et al. 1996, 302-12).

This possibility is based on the observations of the abilities of its adult body for repeated rejuvenation by contraction of the tentacles, followed by turning over its umbrella-shaped bell, reduction of its body size, settling on a rock and becoming a polyp. This was first discovered for the Mediterranean immortal jellyfish (*Turitopsis dohrnii*) in 1991, which led to a sensation, and was then confirmed for another jellyfish (*T. nutricula*) (Piraino et al. 1996, 302-312). Examples of rejuvenation of an adult animal capable of sexual reproduction are quite rare among multicellular organisms, and have been reported otherwise only for another kind of jellyfish. In Japan, M. Kubota, an associate professor in the Marine Experimental Station of Kyoto University, succeeded up to 10 times in rejuvenation of an immortal jellyfish picked from the Kagoshima Bay (https 23). These results indicate that an immortal jellyfish can really be immortal. However, its solid record for a long lifespan seems to be much shorter than those for corals, and so I have written "eternal?" in the table.

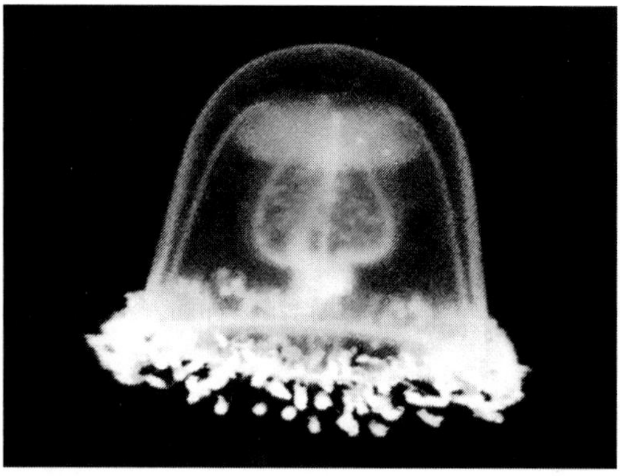

Fig. 1-8: A kind of immortal jellyfish, *Turitopsis. sp* (https 32).

Colony

Many members of Cnidaria such as corals described above live in a characteristic form called a "**colony**". A colony is defined as "an assembly of individuals which is produced by uniting individuals newly born by division or budding using a body part or a structure secreted outside such as a shell, and there are many examples among organisms, from the protozoan to the sea squirt (八杉 et al. 1996, 376)". Also for plants, most of the very long-lived species living for 10,000 years or longer are the examples of this colony. The very long lifespans of the corals are probably due to the formation of colonies. A colony is formed based on the production of new individuals by cell division or budding, as presumed by the above definition, and therefore the lifespan of the colony as a whole is elongated even if the lifespan of an individual is not long. In principle, a colony could be as immortal as the immortal jellyfish. An adult of a jellyfish such as the immortal jellyfish is not a colony, however a polyp, as a developing form, is a colony, and this may be related to the long lifespan of the immortal jellyfish.

Porifera

The animals belonging to Porifera are the animals of the most primitive group. They live in the sea, as corals and jellyfish do, and form colonies. The glass sponge, which is able to live for 9,000 years, is a giant assembly formed by three kinds of sponges *Aphrocallistes vastus*, *Farrea occa* and *Heterochone calyx* near the Pacific coast of Canada (Kenny, 2019, 50). The above lifespan of 9,000 years, if true, would mean it ranked first. But solid evidence for it has not been found, so a question mark was added in the table. The glass sponge is also a kind of colony, and a long-lived individual in the colony is estimated to have a lifespan of 200~250 years.

4th: Clam

The 4th longest lifespan in Table 1-3 is 507 years for the ocean quahog (*Arctica islandica*, **Fig. 1-9**). This is an edible bivalve shell and a kind of general food in the coastal areas of the North Atlantic Ocean. It also goes by the name ocean hard clam. Its shell size is larger than 5cm at its biggest. It is believed that the clam has a striped pattern like that of a tree on the surface of the shell and therefore its age can be estimated by counting the number of stripes.

In 2007, the researchers Scourse and Butler of Bangor University in Wales collected 200 individuals of this clam and examined their ages in order to study changes in climate. Then, the age of the individual supposed to be the oldest was estimated to be 405~410 years old, and this clam was named Ming. However, the age of this clam was re-estimated to be 507 years by the second examination including ^{14}C radioactivity measurement in 2012. It is said that the growth of this clam is slowed when it grows to a certain age, therefore many individuals show similar sizes and their age cannot be supposed by size alone (Nat. Geo. News, 2013).

As to this clam, the reason for its longevity was studied, and its increased resistance to oxidative stress was reported (Munro and Blier 2012, 845-855; Ungvari et al. 2011, 741-750). In one of these studies (Munro and

Blier 2012, 854), the paper on the estimation of the age of the clam, 507 years (Butler et al. 2012) was cited.

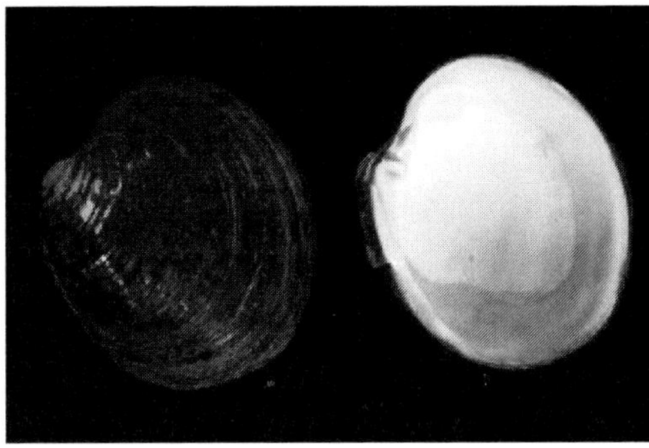

Fig. 1-9: Shells of an ocean quahog (https 26).

Arctica islandica belongs to the phylum Mollusca that includes many shells, cuttlefish and octopuses. Mollusca is a considerably advanced group of animals among invertebrates, and the members do not form a colony like that of a coral. *Arctica islandica* lives longer than any vertebrate listed in Table 1-1, and is believed to have the longest lifespan record among non-colony forming animals. It is interesting that *Arctica islandica* is much smaller than the Greenland shark and Arctic whale which carry long lifespan records of vertebrates and are very big in terms of bodily size.

Nautilus and *Hyriopsis schlegelii* listed in Table 1-3 live up to about 100 years old. Therefore, shells or clams may live long in general, which suggests the possibility of finding a shell or clam with a longer lifespan than that of *Arctica islandica*. *Arctica islandica* lives in a rather cold sea and grows slowly like the long-lived shark and whale, which may be a reason for its long lifespan.

Short-lived invertebrates

The shortest lifespan in Table 1-3 is 14 days for the saline rotifer (*Brachionus plicatillis sp.*). It is a member of rotifers belonging to the phylum Rotifera. Rotifers are actively moving animal planktons, abundant in fresh water, and more than 1,500 species are known in the world (椎野, 1969, 95-97). Most of us are not familiar with this group of animals. However, saline rotifer (**Fig. 1-10**) is a plankton living in brackish water, and is raised in large amounts for feeding salt water fish. Fig. 1-10 shows a female of about 0.2 mm in size. It has a fairly complex body system, whereas the male is lacking a digestive organ and is smaller.

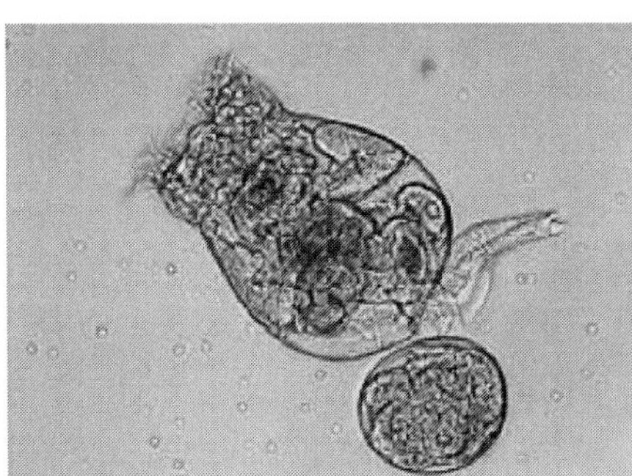

Fig. 1-10: Saline rotifer (https 24).

The second shortest span in Table 1-3 is 36 days for the nematode *C. elegans*. *C. elegans* is a small and liny worm of about 1mm in length. This worm is said to be abundant in the soil and on fallen leaves in nature. It has been used for scientific studies for about 50 years, and is now used as an important model animal worldwide (like the fruit fly). It is a very useful animal for studies since it is small in size, its lifecycle is very short, around 3 days, and since more than 200 littermates are born in a cycle, among other reasons. I myself used *C. elegans* as the major experimental organism for a long time. While its average lifespan in a laboratory is around 2 weeks, it can be extended about 10-fold by genetic mutations (Kenyon 2010, 510). Though I will not go into detail here given the specialist nature of the subject and my desire not to alienate the general reader, *C. elegans* has provided much to studies on animal lifespans. I can describe the details of such studies.

The 3rd shortest rank in Table 1-3 is 46 days for an insect: the fruit fly (*D. melanogaster*). The class Insecta includes about half of all animals, around 800,000 species, is the largest animal group, and belongs to the phylum Arthropoda. It is well known that insects are short-lived in general. However, the mantis in the table is said to live for up to 8 years. Surprisingly, it is said that there is a lifespan record of 100 years for a termite queen bee (*N. triodae*). As for this record, I could find information only on the web, and am not sure of its reliability.

For its part, the stone centipede is classified in the class Chilopoda, and crayfish and lobster are classified in the class Crustacea. Details of lifespan studies of the fruit fly (*D. melanogaster*) may be important, but have been omitted for the same reason as a discussion of *C. elegans*.

1-5 The secrets of the super long-lived invertebrates

Ocean quahog

It was explained in the previous section that the longest lifespan among animals except colony-forming animals (507 years) belongs to the ocean quahog (*Arctica islandica*, **Fig. 1-9**), a member of the phylum Mollusca. On this clam, at least two studies for the reason of its long lifespan have been published. In one of them to be described here (Ungvari et al. 2011,741-750), old and young groups of the ocean quahog and of another, less long-lived clam *Mercenaria mercenaria* – its longest recorded lifespan being 106 years – were compared in various aspects. Based on the results, production of hydrogen peroxide (H_2O_2), a kind of active oxygen molecule which promotes ageing, in the gill and the heart was much lower in the ocean quahog than in *M. mercenaria*. The production of hydrogen peroxide in *M. mercenaria* noticeably increased when the animal became old, while it did not change in the ocean quahog compared to its younger ages.

When they were exposed to an oxidizer, TBHP (*tert*-butyl hydroperoxide), the mortality rate of the ocean quahog was much lower than that of *M. mercenaria* (**Fig. 1-11**). Also, the caspase 3 activity that induces cellular apoptosis (programmed cell death) increased significantly in *M. mercenaria*, but did not increase in the ocean quahog, which suggested that cell death did not occur in the ocean quahog. The activities of several antioxidant enzymes and those of proteases involved in protein regeneration, were also examined, and no difference was found between the two. Based on these results, a lower level of active oxygen production, no increase of it in old age and a high resistance to oxidation stress were suggested to be the reasons for the long lifespan of the ocean quahog.

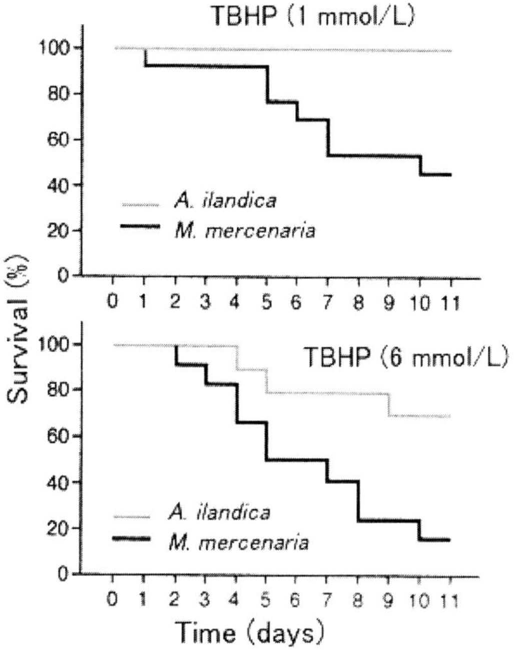

Fig. 1-11: Survival curves of *A. islandica* and *M. mercenaria* exposed to TBHP (adapted from Fig. 3A, B of Ungvari et al. 2011, 745).

In another study (Munro and Blier 2012, 845-855), the degree of super oxidation (super oxidation index or PI) of the lipids in the cell membrane was the target. In a comparative study between mammals and birds, the PIs in the skeletal muscles and mitochondria had been reported to be inversely related to the lifespans (the lifespan is longer when the PI is lower). In this study, the PIs of the mitochondria of the four kinds of bivalves, which lived in the same place ocean quahog did and had the longest lifespans of 28, 37, 92 and 106 years old, were measured and compared. The result was that these PIs decreased logarithmically as the longest lifespans increased, and in ocean quahog they were much less than in the four clams. The paper concluded that these are the reasons for the super long lifespan of ocean quahog. Both of the papers suggest that a low oxidation level of biomolecules is important.

Hydra

Animals called hydra belong to the class Hydrozoa of the phylum Cnidaria, and one third of the Hydrozoa members likely correspond to these hydras (八杉 et al., 1996, 1582). In the ranking of longest lifespans among invertebrates (Table 1-3), the 1st was that of a coral and the 2nd was that of a hydra (>3,572 years). The name of this hydra, the Yamato hydra, is the Japanese name for hydras belonging to the genus *Hydra*.

Here, let me first introduce a review (Martinez and Bridge 2012, 479-487) on the mechanisms of development and ageing of these hydras. **Fig. 1-12** shows the adult body structure and the cells making the body of *H. vulgaris* which has been studied most extensively. The completely differentiated cells in the adult body are shown in dark gray. The adult body stacks to something in the water by the basal disc, is suspended by the peduncle, and has the tentacles and hypostome at the top. Sometimes, a bud comes out of the budding zone in the center and it can multiply asexually. The central body is mainly composed of ectodermal epithelia (outside) and endodermal epithelia (inside), both of which can multiply indefinitely and are multipotent stem cells. These stem cells differentiate into tentacle cells and basal disk cells etc., move, and constantly regenerate these tissues. Also, there are stem cells mixed with the epithelial cells in the body, which are also multipotent and differentiate into various somatic cells and germline cells (sperms and ova). The remarkable characteristics of this hydra include the epithelial cells being multipotent stem cells capable of indefinite multiplication, the interstitial cells also being multipotent stem cells and differentiating also into germline cells, and the body multiplying asexually by forming buds. Based on these characteristics, these hydras are said to be ageless and immortal.

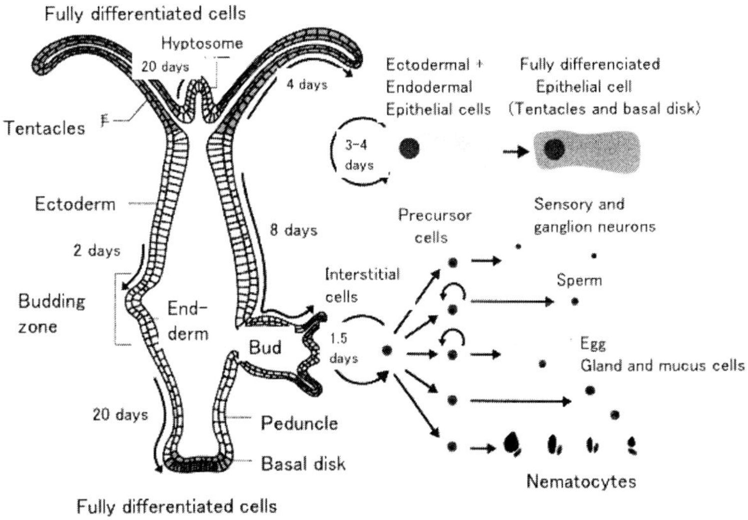

Fig. 1-12: Body structure and body-forming cells of *H. vulgaris*

(adapted from Fig.1 of Martinez and Bridge 2012, 480).

In the same genus *Hydra*, another species (*H. oligactis*), in which ageing and death are observed after sexual reproduction, is also observed. **Fig. 1-13** compares the population survival curves of the two hydras, *H. vulgaris* and *H. oligactis*. During the four years of the observation, *H. vulgaris* continued both sexual and asexual reproduction, showed an extremely low level of mortality, and there were only a few dead individuals. In contrast, the surviving period of *H. oligactis* after induction of sexual reproduction was examined, and it was less than a year in the longest case. Under conditions when only asexual reproductions occur, this species is said to continue living for years, too.

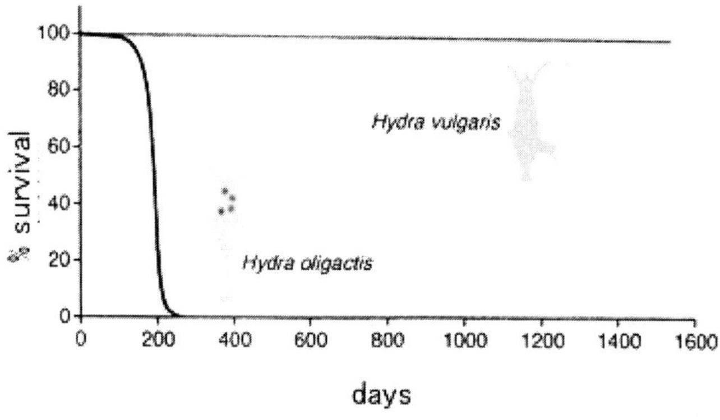

Fig. 1-13: Survival curves of *H. vulgaris* and *H. oligactis* (adapted from Fig. 2 of Martinez and Bridge 2012, 481).

Next, the study on the longevity factors using two hydra species (*H. magnipapillata* and *H. vulgaris*) is described (Schaible et al. 2015, 15701-706). In this study, the seven groups of *H. magnipapillata* maintained in a German institute (204 individuals in each group) and the three groups of *H.*

vulgaris maintained in an American institute (150 or 120 individuals in each group) were used, and the observation was made for 8 years. The rates of natural death of these groups were 0.0008~0.0080 per year and very low. The lowest value 0.0008 was for a group of *H. magnipapillata*. If this rate continues, the age of the group should be 3,572 years when the survival rate is 5%. The lowest death rate for *H. vulgaris* groups was 0.0016 per year, from which the age for the lowest group was estimated to be 1,893 years when the survival rate is 5%. These values were described as the estimated longest lifespans for the two hydra species in Table 1-3 and in the previous section.

In this chapter, a collection of long-lived animals was shown. That a vertebrate can live up to about 400 years and that a colony-forming invertebrate can live more than 4,000 years became clear recently. The author is glad if the readers felt that these long lifespans were surprising and that recent advancement in biology is remarkable.

CHAPTER 2

A PLANT LIVING FOR MORE THAN 40,000 YEARS: THE LIFESPAN OF A PLANT

2-1 Lifespan ranking of plants

Table 2-1 shows the longest lifespans of various plants, especially those of long living plants. The plants in the table are classified into large groups, as in the previous tables for animal lifespans. The largest plant groups are **algae**, **mosses** and **vascular plants**, and vascular plants can be further classified into **pteridophytes**, **gymnosperms** and **angiosperms** (八杉 et al. 1996, 1549-1559). Algae are thought to be the most primitive and contain many species, but no very long living one seems to have been found. As for mosses, there is a description indicating that a 5,500 year old moss on Elephant Island in the Antarctic Ocean (Sussman 2014, 242-249), but both its species name and age are uncertain. In Table 2-1, the plants with a relatively reliable lifespan estimated by ^{14}C radioactivity or annual rings are mainly listed. Most of them belong to gymnosperms or angiosperms in the vascular plants carrying vascular bundles.

Vascular bundles are the differentiated tissue systems which run through the organs such as stems, leaves and roots, and are the moving routes for water and bodily substances. Among the seed plants, those in which the ovules are not covered with carpels are called gymnosperms, and those in which the ovules are covered with carpels and form ovaries are called angiosperms.

Fig. 2-1: *Lomatia tasmanica*, the plant with the longest lifespan in the world. (a) shows it in the wild and (b) shows its flowers. From the website of the Royal Tasmanian Botanical Garden (https 48). The man in (a) is A. Macfayden, and the photograph (a) was taken by N. Tapson.

1st, 2nd and 3rd: Colony-forming plants

The plant in the table with the longest lifespan is a kind of dicotyledon known as ***Lomatia tasmanica***, which belongs to the subclass Rosiatae, order Proteales and family Proteaceae. The wild plant of this species has been found only at a single place on the island of **Tasmania** (**Fig. 2-1a**), and therefore it is a very precious plant. This plant sometimes has flowers (**Fig. 2-1b**), but no seed has ever been found. Therefore, it is thought to multiply asexually by means of roots. In fact, several hundred plants of this species on the earth form a continuous, great plant body extending over 1.2km in distance (Lynch et al. 1998, 25).

Table 2-1: Longest lifespans of various plants

Classification and species	Longest lifespan (y=year, m=month)
Bryophyta	
haircap moss	10 y (Flindt, 2007, 133)
Vascular plants: Pteriophyta	
oak fern (*G. dryopteris*)	7 y (Flindt, 2007, 133)
Botrychium lunaria	30 y (Flindt, 2007, 133)
Vascular plants: Gymnosperms	
Sakhalin spruce (*P. glehnii*, Hokkaido, Japan)	586 y (鈴木, 2002, 19)
Japanese hemlock (Yakushima Island, Japan)	794 y (鈴木, 2002, 19)
spruce fir (S. Alps, Japan)	800 y (鈴木, 2002, 19)
Japanese cypress (Yakushima Island, Japan)	1065 y (鈴木, 2002, 19)
Jomon cedar (Yakushima Island, Japan)	1920±150 y (https 39)
Alaska cedar (USA)	3500 y (鈴木, 2002, 19)
Patagonian cypress (Chile)	3620 y (鈴木, 2002, 19)
bristlecone pine (USA)	5062 y (Sussman, 2014, 10-17)
spruce (Sweden)	9550 y (Sussman, 2014, 142-149)

Angiosperms	
Dicotyledonopsida	
wall cress (*A. thaliana*)	~3 m (大島, 2013, 31)
blueberry	25 y (Flindt, 2007, 133)
grape	130 y (Flindt, 2007, 133)
apple	200 y (Flindt, 2007, 133)
beech（Nagano pref.）	435 y (鈴木, 2002, 19)
Mongolian oak（Hokkaido）	444 y (鈴木, 2002, 19)
Barringtonia sp. （tropical Amazon）	1400 y (鈴木, 2002, 133)
*Jacaranda decurrens**	≧3801 y (Alves et al. 2013, 671)
creosote bush* (*L. tridentata*, USA)	11,700 y (Witte and Stocklin 2010, 860; Vasek 1980, 246)
*Lomatia tasmanica**（Australia）	43,600 y (Sussman, 2014, 208-213; Witte and Stocklin 2010, 860; Lynch et al. 1998, 25)
Monocotyledonopsida	
*Carex curvula** (USA)	5000 y (de Witte et al. 2012, 1081)
saw palmetto*(*S. repens*, the USA)	~10,000 y (Takahashi et al. 2011, 3730)

*: colony plant.

L. tasmanica looks like a conifer or a herb at a glance, but is broad-leaved as seen in Fig. 2-1b, although the leaves are small, and the tree grows up to 8m high (Sussman, 2014, 210). Also, it grows in a mixed state like a bush with other plant-species as seen in Fig. 2-1a.

Based on a comparison of the chromosomes in this plant and a closely related plant of the same genus, this plant is likely to be **trisomic**. For this reason, this plant does not form seeds, and so it is likely that it has not extended its habitat. Furthermore, the chromosomes of the wild plants isolated from 78 different parts and 16 kinds of isozymes (enzymes exhibiting plural genetic types) were examined, and no genetic diversity was found. Such an assembly of genetically uniform plants is called a "**clone**" or "**genet**". Such a plant assembly is also called a "**colony**" in terms of shape or morphology, like a colony of an animal such as a coral. The relationship between a clone and a colony will be described later.

As for *Lomatia tasmanica*, a fossil of the plant was found and its lifespan was estimated as 43,600 years or longer based on the measurement of the radioactive carbon (^{14}C), as indicated in the table (Lynch et al. 1998, 25-33). In the Royal Tasmanian Botanical Garden, many plants of this species were grown by planting the cuttings.

Ranking second among the longest lifespans in Table 2-1 is the **creosote bush** (11,700 years old, *Larrea tridentata*, **Fig. 2-2**), which was found in the Mojave Desert in the State of California in the USA.

This plant is a small, ever-green tree which belongs to Dicotyledonopsida, of the order Sapindales and family Zygophyllaceae. This plant also forms a colony, which is an irregular and nearly circular community with a diameter up to over 20m. There are several colonies of this plant in the Mojave Desert. The age of the biggest colony estimated from its growing speed is 11,700 years, and it is reported that this age is nearly the same as that estimated from the carbon radioactivity (Vasek 1980, 246).

Fig. 2-2: Creosote bush, a colony plant (https 49).

Ranking third among the longest lifespans is ~10,000 years for a monocotyledon **saw palmetto** (*Serenoa repens*). It is a basic plant of the ecological system in the southeastern part of the USA. However, it is regarded as a harmful plant invading farms, and is said to be being exterminated. For the 263 saw palmetto samples collected in a $20m^2$ wooded region in the State of Florida, the genetic types were examined by the length of restriction fragments amplified by PCR (Polymerase Chain Reaction). The results were that the genetic types of most samples belonged to one of several groups, indicating that most of the plants were forming colonies. Also, many of the ages of the colonies were estimated to be about 10,000 years old (Takahashi et al. 2011, 3730). If this estimation is correct, their longest lifespan is more than 10,000 years.

Many long-lived conifers

The fourth rank among the longest lifespans in Table 2-1 is for **spruce** (**Fig. 2-3**, *Picea sp.*). This spruce tree was found in Dalarna, Sweden in northern Europe, and its age was estimated to be 9,550 years based on the carbon radioactivity (Sussman, 2014, 142-149; https 41; https 50 describes as 9,561 years). Around this tree, there are other 20 spruce trees the ages of which were estimated to be more than 8,000 years.

Fig. 2-3: A spruce tree in Sweden (https 50).

Most **gymnosperm trees** have thin needle-like leaves and are known as **conifers**. The spruce is an ever-green conifer in the order Taxodiales and family Pinaceae. The *Picea abies* species of this tree can form a colony (de Witte and Stocklin 2010, 860; https 50). Online information on Old Tjikko (https 50) confirms this, and the tree seen in Fig. 2-3 is 600 years old. Since this tree looks rather young, that seems true. A variety of Yezo spruce grows naturally also in the Japanese mountains above 1,500m (高橋 et al. 2018, 98).

Fig. 2-4 shows a **bristlecone pine** (*Pinus longaeva*) tree, a species with the fifth longest lifespan in Table 2-1. It is also a conifer, and is a kind of pine belonging to the order Taxisodiales and family Pinaceae. The photograph (Fig. 2-4) is that of a tree growing at heights over 3,000m (White Mountains), and many trees of the same species are found near here and in the mountains of the State of Nevada.

Fig. 2-4: A bristlecone pine tree, about 5,000 years old, in the State of California, USA (https 52).

The ages of these trees were examined based on the annual rings or the radioactivity of carbons of the excised pieces, and the oldest of them is said to be 5,062. There is another example of a previously cut-down tree of 4,844 years old (Sussman, 2014, 10-17 for the descriptions so far). There seemed to be another example estimated to be 4,862 years old (鈴木, 2002, 19). Thus, it is likely that there are many bristlecone pine trees around 5,000 years old in this region. This bristlecone pine is likely to have the longest lifespan record among non-colony trees.

In sixth and seventh place are *Carex curvula* (~5,000 years) and for *Jacaranda decurrens* (≧3,801 years), respectively, both of which are colony plants belonging to angiosperms. Eighth, ninth and tenth are occupied by conifers belonging to gymnosperms: a 3,620 year old Patagonia cypress, 3,500 year old Alaska cedar and a Jomon cedar estimated to be 1,920±150 years. The **Jomon cedar** on **Yakushima Island** in Japan (**Fig. 2-5**) is famous in the country and may be familiar to many Japanese. It is said that there are many Japanese cedars older than 1,000 in the highlands of Yakushima Island. Among them, the Jomon cedar shown in the image is 25m tall, has a 16m trunk circumference at 1.3m height, is a representative giant tree in Japan, and was believed to be about 7,000 years old (渡辺, 1999, 421). However, the real age has been estimated to be 1,920±150 years (as shown in the table) and no older than 2,170 years, based on the measurement of radioactive carbons (http 39). It is still alive and so its lifespan is unknown, as with other living trees.

Besides the Jomon cedar, there are two other giant Japanese cedars on Yakushima Island, the Daio cedar and Kigen cedar, which are said to be about 3,000 years old, though these ages have not been proven. As with the lifespans or ages of the plants other than the Jomon cedar and listed in Table 2-1, they should have error ranges, but these error ranges are not known.

Fig. 2-5: Jomon cedar on Yakushima Island in Japan (https 53).

Japanese cedar trees

The order Taxisodiales includes the cedar and pine and is a big group of conifers or gymnosperms. **Japanese cedar** (*Cryptomeria japonica*) trees are abundant in Japan and since it has a botanical name containing the name of the country, they may be endemic to Japan. The book on giant trees in Japan (渡辺, 1999, 1-451) cited above includes 15 giant cedars in Japan. The definition of a **giant tree** by the Department of Environment in Japan is a tree with a circumference over 3m at 1.3m above the earth. In the lists of the above book, the Japanese cedar is one of the species with the most giant trees, alongside camphor and cherry trees. The 15 giant cedars listed include 11 trees with an estimated age over 1,000 years, and 6 trees assigned as **natural monuments**. This may be because the Japanese cedar is a long-lived species and since they are the most populous trees in Japan. There are 4.48 million hectares of artificial Japanese cedar forests in the country, which occupy over 40% of the area for all the artificial forests and 18% of the area for all the forests in Japan. This ranks top in terms of area covered (web 55). I do not know the area of the natural Japanese cedar forests, but the sum of it and that of the artificial forests probably occupies over 20% of all the country's forests. Japanese cedar trees grow fast, and are useful as lumber. However, they cause hay fever for which I hate them. Also, artificial forests of conifers such as cedar and pine are said to be ecologically poor and to include only a few animals.

Other plants possibly long-lived

In the book *The Oldest Living Things in the World* by Rachel Sussman, from which several descriptions on long-lived plants are cited above, and in the review on colony plants (de Witte and Stocklin 2010, 859-870), several plants with potentially an extremely long lifespan are introduced. Since their long lives are not certain, they were not listed in Table 2-1. Among them, Posidonia Sea Grass (*Posidonia oceanica*) was assigned the longest estimated lifespan of 100,000 years. It spreads in the sea between the Balearic Islands Ibiza and Formentera. UNESCO defines it as an important species which is specific to the Mediterranean Sea. Studies have been carried out on this species which show that the genetic types are the same in a large area and suggest that the whole plants likely form a very old colony. Although the plants grow in the sea, they are not so-called seaweeds, but are like grasses on the ground and thought to be rare. However, I do not know the evidence for the age described above.

Besides this, long lifespan examples such as ≧13,000 years for *Gaylusaccia brachycerium*, ≧12,000 years for *Populus alba*, 12,000 years for *Populus tremuloides* and 10,000~12,000 years for spruce (*Picea abies*) are listed in the review (de Witte and Stocklin 2010, 859-870). They are all colony plants, and these estimated lifespans seem to be the upper limits of the values based on the mutation frequencies which have quite wide ranges, and therefore thought to be uncertain. Possible factors for the longevity of plants, including those for long-lived conifers and colony plants will be described later.

2-2 Herbs, trees and their varieties

The shortest of the maximum known lifespans listed in Table 2-1 is about 3 months for wall cress (*Arabidopsis thaliana*, **Fig. 2-6**). *A. thaliana* belongs to order Capparales of Dicotyledonopsida plants, which are mostly common plants. It grows naturally in many districts in Japan. It is a so-called annual plant, and its whole plant body dies in winter under usual conditions.

Fig. 2-6: ***A. thaliana*** (from Fig. 5・1 of 大島, 2015, 129).

Plants are classified into herbs (grasses) and trees. **Herbs** can be further classified into annual, biennial and perennial plants. **Annual plants** grow, flower, fruit, die and leave seeds within a year after germination (八杉 et al. 1996, 71; https 57). Examples of plants which are universally annual based on their inherent nature are morning glory, sunflowers, cones and pumpkins. Besides these, there are plants which are perennial in warm areas such as tropical zones but annual in Japan because of their difficulty in surviving the winter, such as the rice plant, tomato, Madagascar periwinkle and red pepper. Also some annual plants have difficulty surviving hot summers in Japan, such as the daisy and pansy (https 57).

Biennial plants pass the winter in a dormant state, leaving the stems, leaves and roots in the first year. They flower, fruit, leave seeds and die in spring or summer in the second year. The life cycle of a biennial plant covers two adjacent years and it dies within two years. Examples of biennials are **wheat**, parsley, beet, baby's breath, evening primrose, ornamental cabbage, lupin and so on, including important crops, vegetables and garden flowers (八杉 et al. 1996, 1040 and others).

In contrast, in the case of **perennial plants**, the plant bodies over the ground die in winter, but the roots, underground roots or bulbs remain alive and the plant bodies grow again in the next or a later year. Also, there are ever-green perennial plants which live for two or more years. Chrysanthemums are representative perennials in which the plant bodies over the ground die in winter. Examples of ever-green perennials are mint and *Lampranthus spectabilis,* and examples of bulb plants are lilies, tulips, narcissus, dahlias and so on (八杉 et al. 1996, 872).

Among annuals, biennials and perennials, there is some overlap between the groups depending on the environmental conditions. For example, some herbs which were originally perennial are thought to adapt to more severe environments and grow as annual or biennial plants (https 57). As stated above, the **rice plant**, the most important crop plant for Japanese people, is such an example. It is interesting that wheat, which is also important and lives only within a year, fruiting and dying after the year of planting seeds, is classified as biennial.

One very long-lived perennial is the colony plant *Carex curvula* which has a maximum lifespan of 5,000 years, making it the sixth longest in our standings. This and related species belong to the order Cyperales and class

Monocotyledonopsida, as do the Poaceae family of plants including rice and wheat. Some of them grow naturally in Japan. *C. curvula* is surely a herb because of its appearance and characteristics, and it has thin and long leaves (佐竹 et al., 2005, PL. I, 135). The reason for its very long lifespan is likely to be its formation of colonies, similarly to *Lomatia tasmanica*.

In contrast to herbs, **trees** are defined as plants in which the stems and roots grow fat and form much **xylem**, which makes most of the cell walls hard (八杉 et al. 1996, 1403). The reason for this difference between herbs and trees is whether or not they have the tissues called **cambium**. In general, annual and biennial plants are short-lived, and trees are of course much more long-lived. Only wall cress is listed as an example of short-lived herbs, but there are many of them.

Trees can be classified into lower trees or **shrubs** and higher trees. Higher trees tend to be long-lived. The blueberry, showing a longest lifespan of 25 years is a kind of shrub belonging to the Ericaceae family and so its lifespan is not long, but is a tree (https 59). As for trees, there are other classifications such as those between **broad-leaved trees** and **conifers**, and between **ever-green trees** and **deciduous trees**. As stated above, there are many long-lived trees among conifers which are abundant in cold areas.

It is believed that there are no fundamental differences between herbs and trees. Besides, that is, bamboo, which lacks a cambium and so should be called a perennial herb, but is classified as a tree as an exception. Therefore, the situation is complex.

2-3 What are long-lived colony plants?

Examples of colony plants

As written in Section 2-1, *Lomatia tasmanica*, the creosote bush, saw palmet and spruce, which rank first to fourth in terms of longest lifespans, are all colony forming plants. A "**colony**" is a morphological term and can be assigned mainly by sight. In contrast, a "**clone**" is an assemblage of genetically uniform plants which have multiplied asexually from a single parental plant and have been connected together. Actually, *a colony is a single clone in most cases*, as with the above four cases, since two or more clones cannot connect together to form a single colony. If a colony is found to contain two or more clones, in fact there should be two or more colonies instead of a single clone.

Even if the parental plant is a herb, a derived colony can be very long-lived, as with *Carex curvula*. Therefore, **colony plants are very interesting with regard to lifespan**. I will describe what such interesting colony plants are, and what other plants are included.

A colony or clone can also be defined as an assemblage of several or many plants which are connected together by roots, underground roots or stems above the ground and seem to be independent from one another at a glance. The plant unit for the assembly is called "**ramet**". **Fig. 2-7** shows a model for colony formation in which a colony of **poplar** (*Populus tremuloides*) is formed by the spreading of roots. The poplar forest shown in **Fig. 2-8** is comprised of Pando, residing in the State of Utah in the USA, and since the genotypes of all the trees are the same, the trees are considered to be united together as a clone. The heights of these trees are up to 30m, the growing area is 43 hectares ($430,000m^2 = 0.43km^2$), the total number of the trees and their total weight are estimated to be 47,000 and 5.8 million kg, respectively. The lifespan of each tree (ramet) and the total colony are estimated to be 100~150 years and 11,000~80,000 years, respectively (Kenny, 2019, 74; Sussman, 2014, 55).

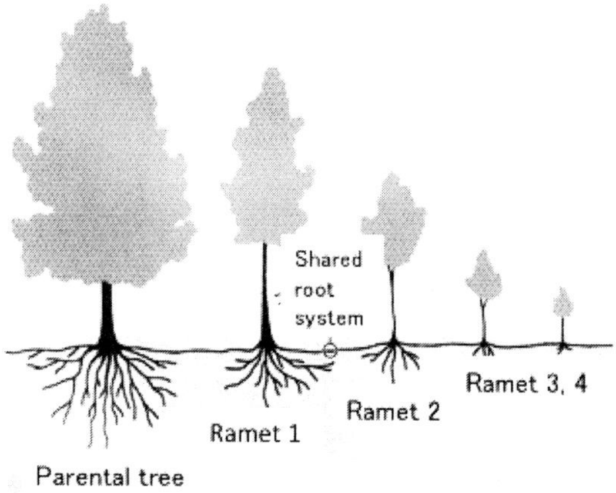

Fig. 2-7: A schematic figure of a poplar colony (re-drawn from the figure in Kenny, 2019, 73).

Fig. 2-8: Poplar trees in Fishlake National Forest in The State of Utah in the USA (https 61).

However, the evidence for the colony's lifespan is not clear, and it was not described in Table 2-1 or Section 2-1. This poplar colony seems to have the highest total weight among the known colonies. Also, colonies of tall trees are comparatively rare.

Other plants which can form a colony are listed below (de Witte and Stocklin 2010, 860-861; Liu et al. 2016, 1-11).

- Trees: spruce, Japanese red pine, elm, false acacia, Japanese lacquer, hazel nut, willow, fig, wisteria, kerria and blueberry
- Herbs: tall goldenrod, sweet potato, strawberry, German iris, clover, dandelion and cattail
- Pteriophyta: club moss and bracken

Here, only species which are considerably familiar to us are listed, and many more colony plants are known. Gymnosperms, and Dicotyledonopsida and Monocotyledonopsida of Angiosperms all include colony plants.

Among the colony plants listed above, the name of fig in Chinese letters means no flower, and the varieties grown in Japan produce flowers and fruits but no seeds because they lack pollination (高橋 et al., 2018, 49). So, fig is unique, and likely forms colonies owing to the lack of seeds. As for wisteria, it climbs up trees with its vines.

Though not listed above, the most remarkable colony around us Japanese may be a **bamboo** thicket or grove. Surprisingly, bamboos belong to the family Poaceae in Monocotyledonopsida as does the rice plant, and the plants in a subfamily of the family Poaceae are called bamboos in a wide classification. Furthermore, the species in which the barks surrounding a bamboo shoot fall off as the shoot grows is classified as a bamboo, and that in which the barks do not fall is classified as bamboo grass.

The number of bamboo species in Japan is said to be over 150, including the giant timber bamboo, thick-stemmed bamboo, henon bamboo, medake bamboo (grass), golden bamboo, and Chishima bamboo grass. Most of the bamboo shoots eaten by the Japanese are those of thick-stemmed bamboo or henon bamboo. Thick-stemmed bamboo is most familiar to us in Japan, and its thicket is shown in **Fig. 2-9**.

Fig. 2-9: A forest of thick-stemmed bamboo (photographed by the author in Kitakyushu in 2019).

Thick-stemmed bamboo is the biggest among the bamboos in Japan. It grows up to 20m high and 18cm in diameter, and is said to have been imported from China in the early 18th century (高橋 et al. 2018, 513; https 64). So, the ages of its thickets or bushes in Japan should be less than 300 years.

Bamboo is an ever-green herb in the classification of plants, but is unique in several senses. As shown in **Fig. 2-10**, it spreads underground roots widely, from which bamboo shoots grow here and there and become bamboo stems. That bamboo shoots appear at many places in a bamboo bush and grow to new bamboo stems is the evidence for its forming colonies. A bamboo stem has a firm structure which carries knots and is different from the stalk of a herb, and therefore can grow up to 20m high. The structure is, however, different from that of a tree.

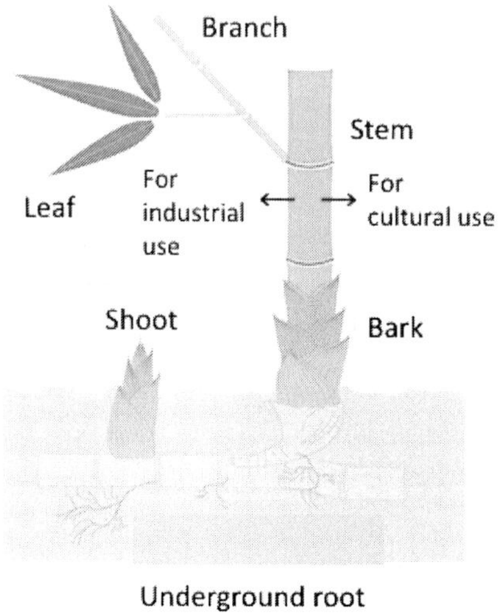

Fig. 2-10: A schematic structure of a bamboo tree (http 65).

It is said that the flowers of a bamboo are rarely seen, that bamboo flowering occurs in a part or all parts of a bush, and that when flowering occurs everywhere in a bush it continues for several years and all the bamboos die thereafter. There is a theory indicating that bamboo flowering has a cycle of 60 or 120 years. It is said that flowering occurs once per 120 years for giant timber bamboo, that only two cases of flowering of a 67 year-cycle are known for thick-stemmed bamboo, and that some flowering results in no seed. Thus, further research is needed about bamboo flowering (https 62; http 65). Bamboo spreads roots and forms a colony probably because of these situations. There is a henon bamboo (hachiku)-like bush near my home which has several thousands of stems and for which I suppose all the stems form a colony. If DNA is taken from 20-30 stems at different points and the genotypes are analyzed, my supposition may be proven.

Characteristics and advantages of colony plants

The ratio of colony forming plants among all plants is not clear, but they may be minor. What characteristics and advantages, then, do colony plants have? They are described in a review by Liu et al. (2016, 1-11), and are introduced here.

The basic characteristics are that unit plants or ramets are physically linked via roots, stems or underground stems, and that nutrients, hormones etc. are exchanged among the parts by the vascular bundles within them. The second characteristic was proven by experiments using a radioactive isotope or a dye. Based on these physiological connections, each ramet can absorb nutrients, photosynthesizes and synthesizes metabolites taking advantage of its conditions. From these, the characteristic by which the plant functions are divided to some extent among the ramets is derived. The ramet at an end of a colony can help spread the colony to a new land.

The advantages of a colony are described below in numbered sections.

1) As for bamboo, fig and *Lomatia tasmanica* (first in the table), they produce few or no seeds, and therefore colony formation is essential for them to survive. The reasons for the no flowering or producing no seeds are genetic changes during evolution such as a mutation. Such genetic changes can happen in general.

2) To a ramet in a land poor in nutrients, nutrients are supplied from a ramet in a rich land, and therefore the entire colony becomes richer. This was demonstrated by the fact that, when a ramet in a poor land is connected to

another ramet in a rich land, its weight, the number of newly produced ramets from it and the number of produced seeds are all increased. If the connection between ramets under different nutritional conditions is lost the total ramet weight decreases, but if the conditions are the same the weight does not change.

3) When a part of the ramet is damaged by salt, buried under sand, faces strong wind or stress, or is damaged by an animal pest, the stress is ameliorated by a ramet under weak stress, which is also the case under different nutritional conditions.

4) Several advantages of colony formation for competition between species are known, especially in competition with non-colony forming plants. This may not be general, but may depend on the species involved or the conditions. If colony formation is advantageous in competition among species, it is likely to be because of its faster invasion into a new land in general rather than a direct victory in competition with another species.

CHAPTER 3

STUDIES ON THE LIFESPAN OF A MAMMAL SUCH AS A MOUSE

Experimental studies of an animal lifespan, which are not simple surveys of a lifespan, likely began with the study on rats reported in 1935 (McCay 1935, 63-79). After that, studies using the **fruit fly** (*Drosophila melanogaster*) began around 1960 and many studies have been done on them since. Also, studies on the lifespan of a **nematode** (*C. elegans*) began around 1980, and many cutting-edge studies were published due to its advantage on lifespan studies.

When I searched for papers on an animal lifespan which include the word "lifespan" in the title, the number of them was enormous – significantly above my expectation. The numbers of papers on the lifespan of humans, mammals such as mice, fruit flies and nematodes numbered about 900, over 1,000, over 800 and about 300, respectively. This gives us a combined figure of over 3,000.

In this chapter, I will introduce several of the representative studies on the lifespan of mammals, focusing mainly on mice. In the following chapter, studies on human lifespan will be introduced.

3-1 Characteristics of the studies on the lifespan of mice

The body weight of an adult mouse is around 20g, making it one of the lightest mammals. Since a mouse is small, it is easy to breed or use for experiments, and therefore used most frequently as a model mammal. As for other mammals, rats which are bigger by about one order and monkeys which are closely related to humans are used. The average lifespan of a mouse under breeding is around two years, and it is in a considerably short lifespan group. However, it is 20~50 times as long as the average lifespan of the nematode (2 weeks) or fruit fly (30-40 days). Therefore, studies on the lifespan of a mouse take at least four years and so are not easy.

Knock-out (KO) mice, in which the function of a specific gene is lost, have been made recently and are used as important materials for studying the gene function for lifespan control. Over-expression of a gene by introducing a second gene into a mouse's body besides the inherent gene, and the expression of such a gene only in some specific organ or tissue are also carried out.

In a review from 2009 (Ladiges et al. 2009, 346-352), which evaluated various aspects of about 20 studies on lifespan extension by these genetic manipulations, six important points were described. These points represent the characteristics of studies on mouse lifespan, and I will describe them below:

1) The mice used for the experiments have various genetic backgrounds, and the use of those with a homogeneous genetic background is necessary.
2) A sufficient number of mice should be used. In general, more than 20 individuals in a group are needed to get statistically significant results.
3) Adequate managements to prevent an infection by a pathogen are needed.
4) Since the lifespan differs between males and females, males and females should be examined in different groups.
5) Observations should be done every day and an exact lifespan in the unit of days is needed.
6) Always observe and grasp the state of health of each mouse. Especially, when a mouse dies, determination of whether it is because of a specific disease or not is important. Among the 20 or so studies included in the above review, few pass all the standards, which indicates the difficulty of mouse lifespan studies.

Among the many studies on the lifespan of mice, those which have different features from experiments on invertebrates may be those on the relationship between lifespan and the pituitary gland or cancer gene MYC. Many studies on the effects of diet restriction on lifespan, which are in common with those on the nematode or fruit fly, are also done. Lifespan extension by adding a specific substance to food is possible to some extent, and is noticeable in its applicability to humans. I will introduce several representative studies which discuss such matters.

3-2 The lifespan extension of a knock-out mouse

Among the lifespan extensions of knock-out mice described in the review from 2009 which was introduced in the previous section, the case showing the longest extension was that of the Ames Dwarf mouse (Brown-Borg et al. 1996, 33). **Fig. 3-1** is the result, and it shows the survival curves for males and females of Ames Dwarf and wild type mice (34 Ames Dwarf and 28 wild type mice were used, both male and female). The average lifespans were 723 and 718 days for males and females, respectively, amongst the wild type mice, and 1,076 and 1,206 days for the Ames Dwarf mice. These results indicate 49% and 68% (average ~60%) extension in Ames Dwarf mice for the average lifespan in males and females, respectively. Two of the Ames Dwarf females lived for more than 4 years.

An Ames Dwarf mouse lacks by nature all or most of the anterior lobe of the pituitary gland which secretes growth hormones, prolactin and thyroid stimulating hormones. As a result, while the body size at birth is normal, growth thereafter is severely inhibited. The final body size is 1/3 of that of a normal mouse and therefore the Ames Dwarf is a dwarf. This paper states that the level of insulin-like growth factor 1 (IGF-1), which mediates growth stimulation by the growth hormone, is very low. The paper supposes that this is the major factor for the lack of growth and in turn the extension of the lifespan of the Ames Dwarf mouse, and the decrease in the metabolic rate due to the lack of thyroid hormones may also be another factor. Besides this, the Snell Dwarf mouse, which has defects in the same three hormones due to a mutation on another chromosome, has also been studied and its lifespan extension has been reported (Ladiges et al. 2009, 346-352). In spite of the lifespan extension, the extended lifespans of Ames Dwarf or Snell Dwarf mice are far from ideal since they are very abnormal given their much smaller body size.

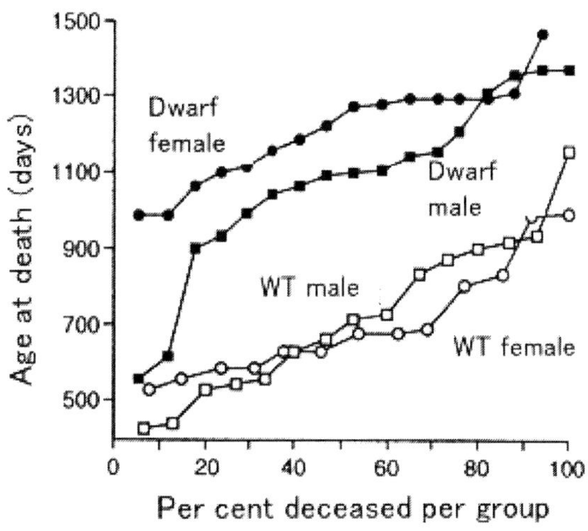

Fig. 3-1: Survival curves for Ames Dwarf and wild type mice (adapted from the figure in Brown-Borg et al. 1996, 33).

As for Ames Dwarf mice, further lifespan extension by **caloric restriction** has been reported (**Fig. 3-2**, Bartke et al. 2001, 412). By 70% caloric restriction, the lifespan was extended both in wild type and Ames Dwarf mice. This result applied to both male and female mice.

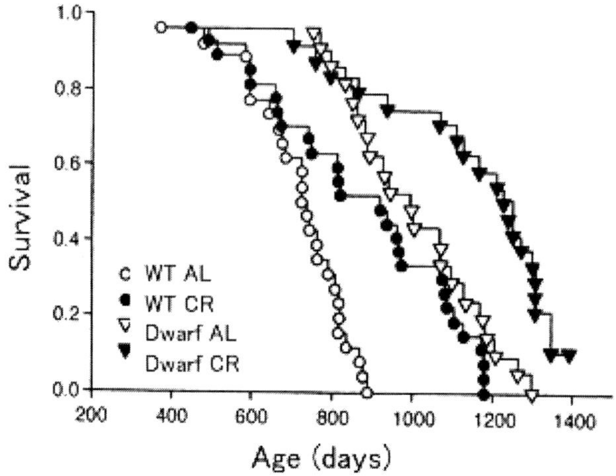

Fig. 3-2: Survival plots of wild type (○, ●) and Ames Dwarf (▽, ●) mice under normal (AL) or 70% caloric restriction (CR) conditions
(adapted from Fig. 1 of Bartke et al. 2001, 201).

The breeding conditions in this experiment probably differed from those in Brown-Borg et al. (1996, 33) stated before, and the average lifespan of the Ames Dwarf mouse was about 1,000 days for males and females combined in contrast to over 1,100 days in Bartke et al. (2001, 412). Since further lifespan extension of a long-lived mutant animal by caloric restriction had not been found in the nematode or fruit fly, these results are evaluated as valuable.

The other examples of lifespan extension by genetic manipulation stated in the review by Ladiges et al. (2009, 346-352) include a knock-out of the gene for the growth hormone receptor; overexpression of the gene for catalase, which hydrolyzes hydrogen peroxide in mitochondria (Shriner et al. 2005,

1909-1911); overexpression of the gene for hormone klotho; and overexpression of the uncoupling protein UCP2, which uncouples oxidative phosphorylation and breathing in the mitochondrial membrane, in the orexin-expressing neurons of the hypothalamus. The last example (Conti et al. 2006, 825-828) lowered the body temperature of a homoiotherm mouse by 0.3~0.5℃, and the authors concluded that this small difference in the body temperature was the reason for the lifespan extension. Therefore, this study is a quite unique example of a lifespan extension.

Also, as for similar studies after 2009, knock-out of the angiotensin receptor II gene (Benigni et al. 2009, 524-530), knock-out of the gene for the pain-sense receptor TRPVI (Riera et al. 2014, 1023-1036), and others were reported.

3-3 Cancer gene product MYC and lifespan

MYC is a transcription factor highly conserved among Metazoa (multicellular animals). The gene for MYC was first discovered in the avian myelocytomatosis virus, and later identified as a cellular proto-oncogene which is activated in Burkitt lymphomas. Overexpression of the MYC protein has been reported strongly to activate cell multiplication and to occur frequently in many human cancers. In addition, MYC directly regulates the expression of 15~20% of all the genes, including important genes such as those involved in ribosome formation, the cell cycle, cellular differentiation and the metabolism. Because of these functions of MYC, knock-out mice for MYC are embryonic lethal.

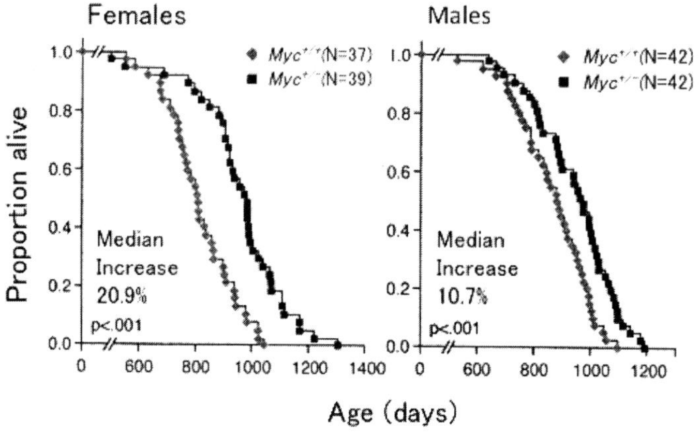

Fig. 3-3: Survival curves for Myc$^{+/+}$ (wild type) and Myc$^{+/-}$ mice

(adapted from Fig. 1B of Hofmann et al. 2015,478).

MYC overexpression also enhances ageing by producing **reactive oxygen species (ROS)** and DNA damage. Therefore, reduction of MYC expression may possibly inhibit ageing and extend the lifespan in mice. In fact, heterogeneous mice in which the MYC gene in one of the chromosomes was knocked-out became smaller, but were healthy and their median lifespans increased by 20.9% in females and 10.7% in males (**Fig. 3-3**, Hofmann et al. 2015, 478). These heterogeneous knock-out mice and normal mice were compared in various ways: in the heterogeneous mutant the metabolic activities were higher in total, rejuvenation of lipid metabolism was found, and healthy lifespan was increased. Also, protein synthesis decreased as a result of decreased ribosome synthesis. Since a decrease in protein synthesis is known to be inversely related to the lifespan, it is thought to be the main reason for the lifespan extension. The entire effects of the decrease in MYC expression are shown in **Fig. 3-4**.

MYC is expected to exist also in the nematode and fruit fly, and so decrease in MYC expression is expected to cause an increase in their lifespans. However, since both of them are short-lived, cancers are not found in them. In contrast, cancers cause important problems in mammals, and this situation may have led to this study.

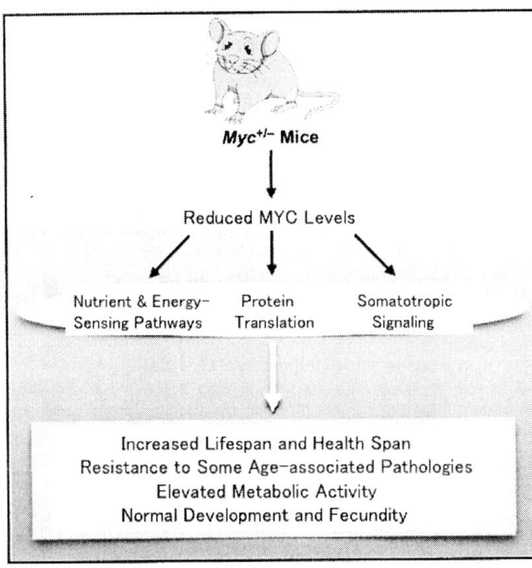

Fig. 3-4: Various effects of decreased expression of MYC on lifespan extension and other factors (adapted from Hofmann et al. 2015, Graphical Abstract).

3-4 Lifespan extension by diet restriction

Restriction of diet or food is said to be the only common factor to extend lifespan in various studied organisms, from yeast and nematodes to fruit flies to primates. Many studies have been done also in mammals such as mice. How the diet is restricted is varied, but the simplest way is to decrease the amount of food in a fixed way every day for a certain period. This type of diet restriction is called caloric restriction.

Let me first introduce a review from 2012 (Swindell 2012, 254-270) which compared and examined such studies in mice and rats since 1934. **Fig. 3-5** compares the median and maximum lifespans of males and females separately for mice and rats. Based on this result, lifespan extension due to diet restriction in rats is much larger than that in mice except for the maximum in females. The extension of the median lifespan of males and females combined was about 30% in rats and about 15% in mice (based on the evidence cited in Fig. 3-5). The above paper states that 14~45% increases were found in half of the rat experiments, but that 4-27% extension was found in the mouse experiments. As for mice, the effect of diet restriction is smaller in inbred strains than in hybrids, and no extension or reverse shortening was found in certain inbred mice.

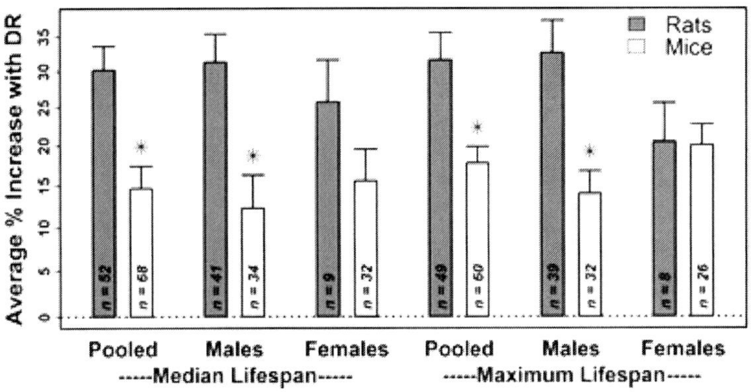

Fig. 3-5: Increases in the median and maximum lifespans in rats and mice by diet restriction. The results of 53 rat experiments and 72 mouse experiments since 1934 were summarized. The numbers in the bars represent the numbers of the experiments used for the graph (Fig. 1 of Swindel 2012, 254-270).

The reasons for these differences in the results among different genetic backgrounds are thought to include the fact that mammals are complex higher animals with large genomes. Also, only a study using native and caught mice was cited, which indicated no extension of the median lifespan by caloric restriction. In all the other studies, strains which had been studied for a long time were used, and it was stated that the obtained results were affected by this situation.

Several studies on the **effects of caloric restriction on the lifespan and ageing of primates** were also reported. It is possible that similar results in mice or rats can be applied to humans, but these rodents are considerably far from humans in terms of biological classification. For example, the average human body weight is about 3,000 times that of mice, and the average human lifespan differs by about 30 times (70 years and 2 years). Therefore, studies on primates, which are closely related to humans, are needed. Here, maybe the most important study (Colman et al. 2009, 201-204) can be introduced. It was done in the Wisconsin National Primate Research Center (WNPRC) over 20 years, which shows how extensive and laborious studies on a primate lifespan are. This study used rhesus monkeys (*Macaca mulatta*) originating from Southwestern Asia. This primate is one of the monkeys often used for biological and medical studies. Its average lifespan and longest lifespan are about 27 years and 40 years, respectively, and the average body weight of adults is around 10kg. Therefore, they are much closer to humans than rodents are. Naturally, any study of primate lifespan – given this longevity – must itself take a long time.

In **Fig. 3-6**, photographs A and B on the left are those of a 27 years old rhesus monkey which did not receive caloric restriction. Its age is near the average lifespan, and it has lost a large part of its hair. In contrast, C and D on the right hand side are the photographs of another monkey of the same age which received caloric restriction for a long time, and the monkey seems much younger. The experiments were begun in 1989 using 30 male monkeys 7~14 years old, with 30 females and 16 males being added 5 years later. The caloric restriction group and the control group of 38 monkeys were each observed and compared for 20 or 15 years (depending on when they arrived).

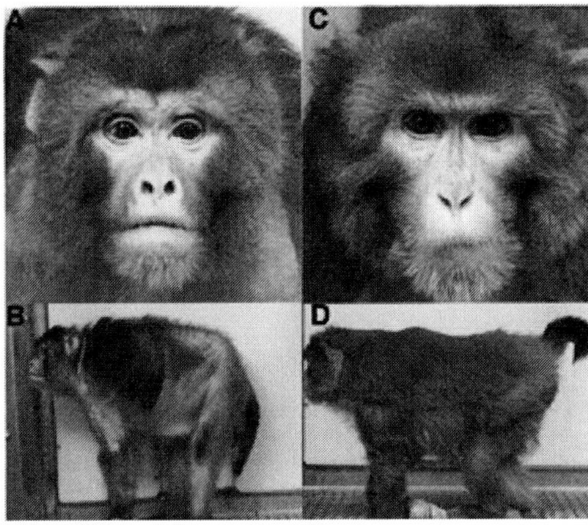

Fig. 3-6: A typical, control rhesus monkey of 27.6 years old (A, B), and one of about the same age which had been calorie-restricted (C, D)
(Fig. 1 of Colman et al. 2009, 202).

The monkeys were divided into the two groups cautiously to prevent an imbalance, based on the data of the age, body weight, and average diet (calorie/day) observed before the beginning of the experiment. For the caloric restriction group, the amount of food was reduced by 10% per month from that of the beginning, and after 3 months a 30% reduction was continued.

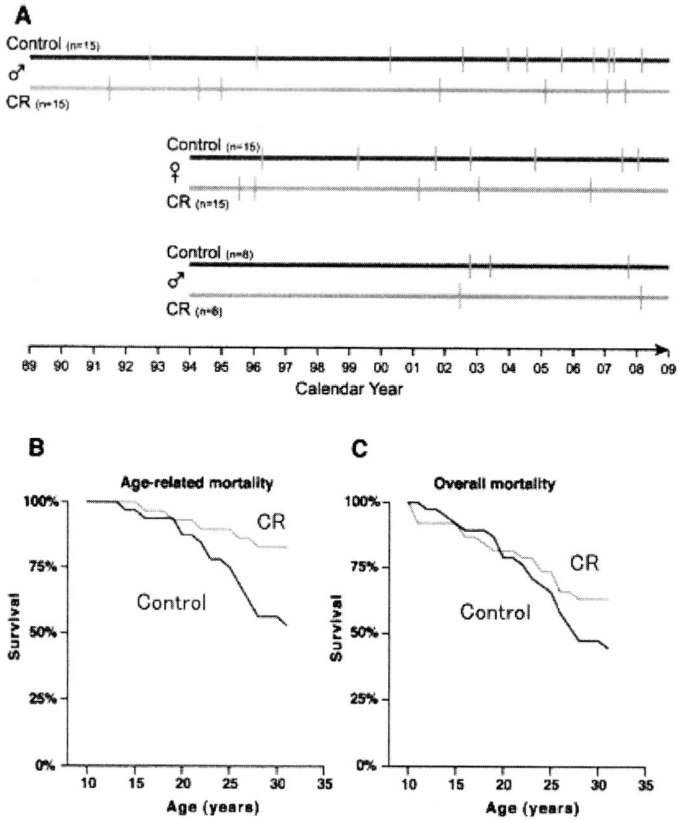

Fig. 3-7: Studies on the lifespan of rhesus monkeys. (A) Study design. The upper lines are for the control group and lower lines for the calorie-restricted (CR) group. The vertical lines (hash marks) represent deaths. (B) Age related mortality. Animals that died from non-age related causes are excluded. (C) Overall mortality (adapted from Fig. 2 of Colman et al. 2009, 202).

Fig. 3-7 (A) depicts the entire plan of the experiments, in which the death of each monkey is shown as a vertical line. The total number of dead monkeys was 21 in the control group and 14 in the caloric restriction group; the survival rates were 45% and 63%, respectively, and they differed clearly from each other. As for the dead monkeys, a detailed dissection of the body was done, the cause of the death was specified, and the causes were classified into diseases due to ageing and others. Based on these results, there were 14 deaths related to ageing (37%) in the control group and 5 (13%) in the caloric restriction group, with the latter figure clearly much smaller.

Fig. 3-7 (B) shows the relationship between the age of death and the mortality rate. The causes of deaths unrelated to ageing (7 in the control group and 9 in the caloric restriction group) were anesthesia, stomach expansion, endometritis and external injuries. For all the deaths (including these), the relationship between the dying age and the mortality rate is as shown in **Fig. 3-7 (C)**, and there is no significant difference between the two groups.

The diseases of rhesus monkeys related to ageing were well studied in the WNPRC, which showed that diabetes, cancer and a heart/blood vessel disease were the most frequent. These are all so-called adult diseases or lifestyle-related illnesses, and so rhesus monkeys are good models for humans. Thus, the effects of caloric restriction on the incidences of these diseases were also examined. The results are shown in **Fig. 3-8 (A)**, indicating fewer incidences of all the diseases in the caloric restriction group.

The incidences of cancer were halved. Sixteen monkeys suffered from diabetes or a pre-diabetic stage in the control group, however abnormality highly related to diabetes, such as that in the blood sugar, was not at all found in the caloric restriction group. **Fig. 3-8 (B)** shows the relationship between the total rate of all these incidences and the monkeys' age, and the effect of caloric restriction is clear.

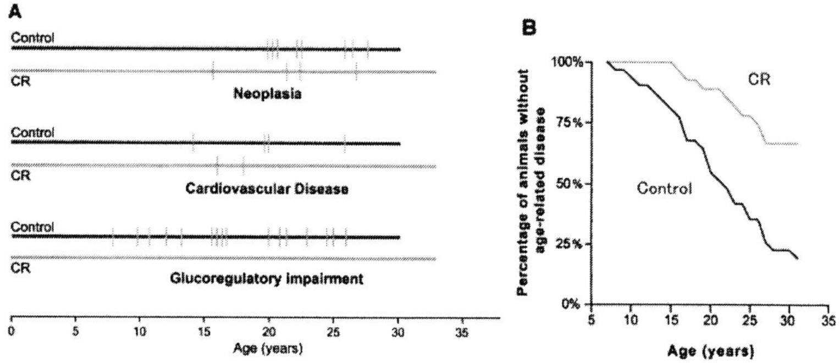

Fig. 3-8: Studies on the lifespan of rhesus monkeys (continued). (A) The effects of caloric restriction (CR) on the incidences of neoplasia (cancer), cardiovascular disease and glucoregulatory impairment. The vertical lines show the ages of diagnosis (occurrence). (B) The curves show the percentage of animals without an age-related disease (adapted from Fig. 3 of Colman et al. 2009, 202).

As for the other effects of caloric restriction, a decrease in body weight mainly due to a decrease in fat, amelioration of muscle decrease, and an improvement in the metabolism (such as that in insulin sensitivity) were observed. For the entire experiments, it was concluded that *an adequate caloric restriction by 30% begun in an adult stage reduced ageing-related diseases and extended the lifespan in primates.* This is likely to be very helpful to us human beings.

3-5 The effects of nutrients

A decrease in the size of a diet or a meal is called caloric restriction as above. The extension of a lifespan by caloric restriction may mean that a decrease in the amount of the calories consumed is important in itself, but it is not necessarily true. Obviously, the effects of the contents of a meal, namely those of the kinds of nutrients and their ratios should be examined. Based on the results of such examinations, the contents of a meal are now thought to be more important than the total calorific value itself.

Likely the first research into such diet contents was done on a kind of fly (Fanson et al. 2009, 514-523). In this study, 28 kinds of diets including carbohydrates and proteins at various ratios but at a constant calorie level were given. The results showed that the higher the ratio of carbohydrate/protein, the longer the lifespan was extended. Indeed the longest lifespan was at a 21:1 ratio between them. Also, a lower calorie diet led to a shorter lifespan overall.

Next, a more advanced study on mice (Solon-Biet et al. 2014, 418-430) will be described in detail. In this research, mice were raised throughout their lives by being fed with 25 different kinds of feeds containing proteins (5~60%), fats (16~75%), carbohydrates (16~75%) and calories (8, 13 or 17 kJ/g feed), and the relationships between the diets versus the amounts taken, lifespans, diseases and so on were measured. This study was done on a very big scale and released as a paper by 18 researchers. It employed a method using multi-parameters known as the Geometric Framework.

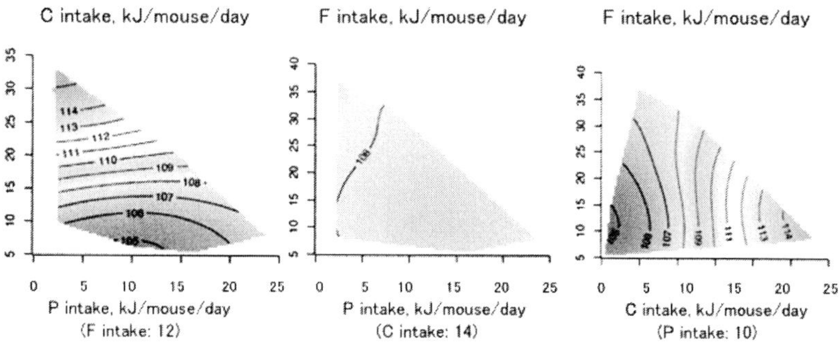

Fig. 3-9 (A): Relationships between the median lifespan in weeks and intakes of protein (P), carbohydrate (C) and fat (F). For each graph, the third nutrient is fixed at its median value as indicated in the parentheses (adapted from Fig. 2A of Solon-Biet et al. 2014, 422).

Fig. 3-9 (A) shows the median lifespans in week units by the numbers and lines in the figures. In the left-hand side graph, the horizontal axis and the vertical axis represent the amounts of protein intake and carbohydrate intake, respectively. In this experiment, the fat intake was made constant (at 12 kJ/mouse/day). In this graph, the lifespan lines are nearly horizontal, which shows that lifespan determination almost depends on the carbohydrate/protein ratios or the carbohydrate amounts, and not on the protein amounts. Also, this result is thought to indicate that a higher carbohydrate/protein ratio leads to a longer lifespan in the range examined. In the right-hand side graph showing the relationship between carbohydrate intake, fat intake and lifespan at a constant protein intake (10 kJ/mouse/day), the lines representing lifespans are almost vertical, which indicates that the amount of carbohydrate intake is important and its higher value leads to a longer lifespan in the range examined. In the middle graph showing the relationship between protein intake, fat intake and lifespan at a constant carbohydrate intake, the lifespans are almost constant for all the combinations of the two nutrients.

In another study related to Fig. 3-9 A, the survival curves of mice fed with nine classes of diets containing varied protein/carbohydrate ratios (0.07~3.01) were examined. The shortest lifespan was observed in the cases of high ratios (3.01 or 1.65) and the median lifespans in these cases were about 95 weeks (665 days). In contrast, in the cases of the lowest ratios (0.07 or 0.1), the median lifespan was 125 weeks (875 days), and longer by 30% than in the high ratio cases (the evidence is not shown pictorially here because of the difficulty in understanding a black and white graph made from the original color figure).

Next, **Fig. 3-9 (C)** compares the survival curves at the three energy densities of the diet (Low=8, Med=13 and High=17 kJ/g). This graph shows the effect of the total caloric intake, namely that the lifespan is the longest for the medium calorie diet and the shortest for the low calorie diet. Based on these results, it was concluded that diets of a low protein/carbohydrate ratio are more important than low caloric diets.

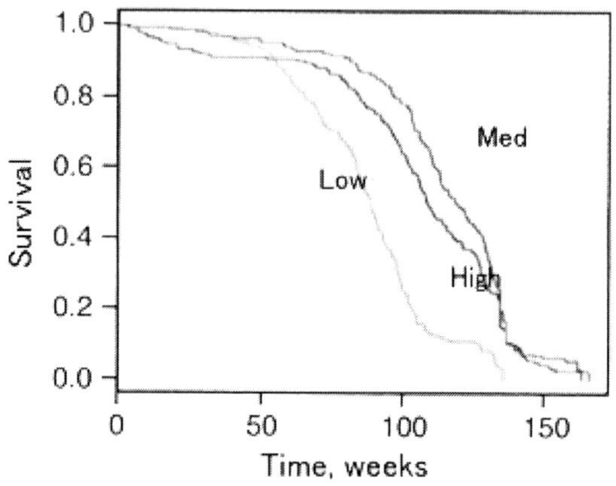

Fig. 3-9 (C): Survival curves at three dietary energy densities (adapted from Fig. 2C of Solon-Biet et al. 2014, 422).

This study examined not only lifespans but also the effects of the nutrients in the diet on body conditions such as weight and blood pressure, and on body components in 15 month (about 60 week) old mice. The results were that the body weights of the mice consuming a smaller amount of protein were lower (**Fig. 3-10**) and that the mice fed with a diet of a higher carbohydrate/protein ratio showed a lower blood pressure (**Fig. 3-11** shows systolic blood pressures; diastolic pressures are similar). Besides, a diet with a higher carbohydrate/protein ratio led to an increase in high-density lipoprotein (HDLc) and a decrease in low-density lipoprotein (LDLc). These results indicate not only that a diet of a lower protein ratio extends a lifespan but also that it improves body conditions for various indices.

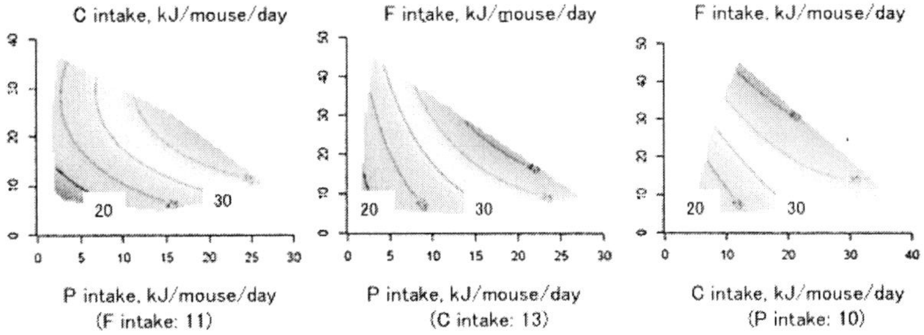

Fig. 3-10: The relationships between body weight in grams and protein (P), carbohydrate (C) and fat (F) intake in mice (adapted from Fig. 5A of Solon-Biet et all. 2014, 426).

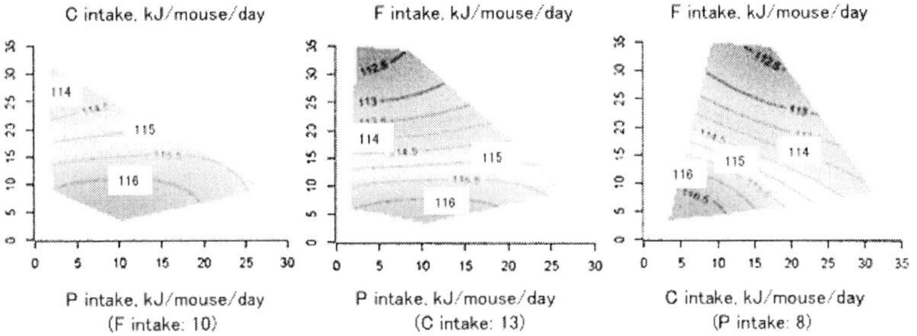

Fig. 3-11: The relationships between systolic blood pressure (mmHg) and protein (P), carbohydrate (C) and fat (F) intake in mice (adapted from Fig. 5C of Solon-Biet et al. 2014, 426).

The next problem to solve was the reason for these effects or mechanisms. In relation to this problem, this paper showed that the **mTOR** (mammalian target of rapamycin) – which is activated by an amino acid – was somewhat activated (phosphorylated) in the liver by protein intake, and that only the branched chain amino acids (valine, leucine and isoleucine) in the blood increased in response to protein intake. It is known that activation of mTOR represents an early stage of ageing. It is thought that a lower protein intake inhibits mTOR activation and thereby inhibits ageing.

If a diet with a lower protein content extends lifespan, it is possible that some amino acid derived from protein shortens lifespan. Related to this possibility, papers showing that a decrease in the amino acid **methionine** extended lifespan were reported in the 1990s after studies with rats. In one of them (Richie et al. 1994, 1302-1307), in which the methionine content was restricted for the animals' entire lives, the average lifespan and the longest lifespan of the rats were extended by 42% and 44% respectively, from the control rats. Some extension of the longest lifespan by methionine restriction was reported for mice, too (Miller et al. 2005, 119-125). A few possibilities and their reasons for the mechanisms of the effects of methionine were shown in another paper (Kitada et al. 2019, 632-640).

In contrast to the ideas stated above, it was reported that addition of the three proteinogenic branched-chain amino acids (valine, leucine and isoleucine) to a diet extended the median lifespan of male mice (D'Antona et al. 2010, 362-372). This addition of the branched chain amino acids resulted in stimulation of the mitochondria formation and the expression of the lifespan control factor sirtuin 1 in specific cells and tissues, and this fact was supposed to be the reason for the extension of the lifespan. As for the branched chain amino acids, there are reports indicating that they are both good and bad for the health of mice and humans. It is stated that taking an adequate amount of them may be necessary for humans (D'Antona et al. 2010, 362-372).

3-6 The effects of meal frequency and hunger on the lifespan

When the human history of meals is recalled, rather constant meals had been taken after the onset of agriculture. More recently, three meals per day have been a general custom. In the last 50 years, high caloric foods such as sugar and oil have been added to our diets, and people whose lifestyles include sitting for most of the day have increased. According to Mattson et al. (2014, 16647-16653), the fact that obesity and obesity-related diseases, which are major causes of various diseases and death, have increased is likely to be due to such meals and lifestyles.

Fig. 3-12 showing these relationships is a graph from this study. Based on this figure, the average caloric intake in the USA increased from 2,100kcal to 2,800kcal/day, and the rate of obese adults increased from 13% to 35% in the 60 years from 1950 to 2010. Also, it is shown that the numbers of families owning a car or a computer have increased.

In general, this situation is the basis for the studies on the effects of calorie or diet restriction on lifespan. However, the main themes of the above study are the effects of meal frequency and hunger etc. on health. In this relation, it was shown in the nematode that intermittent hunger with a two-day interval extended the lifespan, and a similar study was done on the fruit fly. Meanwhile, the results in rodents were various in another article (Longo and

Panda, 2016). For example, while hunger every other day was effective for lifespan extension in rats, it had no effect or sometimes shortened the lifespan in mice. That mice which are hungry rapidly lose body weight may be the reason for the negative effect of hunger.

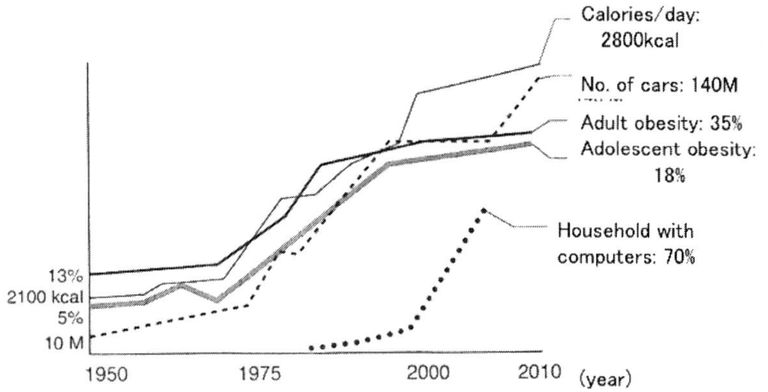

Fig. 3-12: The changes in caloric intake (kcal/day), adult obesity (%), adolescent obesity (%), households with computers (%) in the USA, and automobile production (in millions) worldwide (adapted from Fig. 1 of Mattson et al. 2014, 16648).

Therefore, a fasting-mimicking diet (FMD) was developed. This FMD contained fewer proteins and sugars, more lipids and 10~50% of the usual calories, and was given for 4 days continually in a cycle. The FMD resulted in the same indices as those when only water was given for 2~3 days.

Another example of a study using FMD by Brandforst et al. (2015, 86-99) merits introducing here. In the mouse groups for which the above FMD was given for 4 days once every 2 weeks, the average lifespan extended by 11.3% from that of the control group, and the longest lifespan did not change (**Fig. 3-13**). Also, the amount of fat in the internal organs, cancer incidences and skin injuries decreased, and immunity was rejuvenated. In the old mice, the IGF-1 (insulin-like growth factor) level and the activity of protein kinase A (PKA) decreased, and cognitive activity was improved. In this study, a clinical examination of FMD on humans was also done, and a good result was reported.

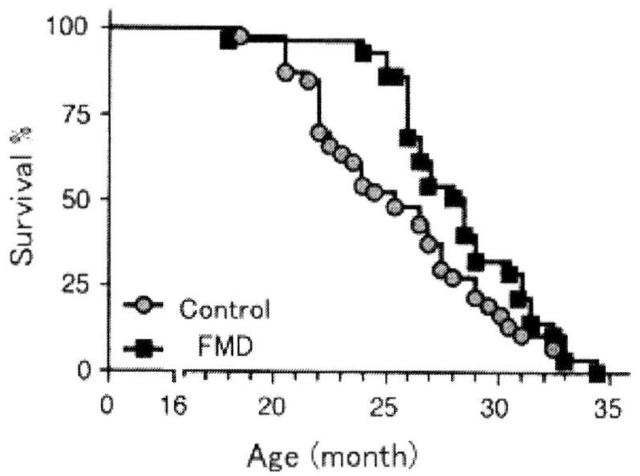

Fig. 3-13: Extension of lifespan in mice fed with fasting-mimicking diet (FMD) (adapted from Fig. 5A of Brandforst et al. 2015, 93).

3-7 Extension of the lifespan by a drug

Some research has confirmed that a drug called **resveratrol** (3,5,4'-trihydroxystilbene) extended the lifespan of yeast, nematodes and fruit flies. Also, it was shown that the addition of this drug into the diet of mice extended their lifespan (or suppressed lifespan shortening) when they were raised with high calorie diets (Bauer et al., 2006, 337-342).

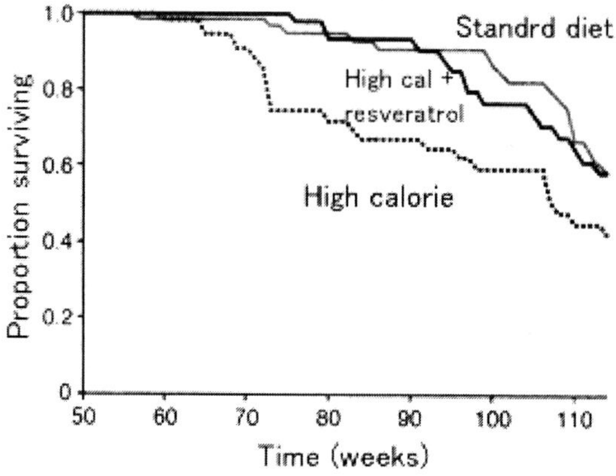

Fig. 3-14: Survival curves of mice fed with a standard diet, a high calorie diet or a high calorie + resveratrol diet (adapted from Fig. 1 of Bauer et al. 2006, 338).

Fig. 3-14 shows the results of such an experiment in which one of three kinds of diet was given to one year old male mice. The graph shows that their lifespan was shorter when fed with the high calorie diet, in which lipids provided 60% of the total calories, than when fed with the standard diet, and that addition of resveratrol reversed the lifespan to almost the same level as that observed for the standard diet. At the end of the experiment, 114 weeks (2 years and 2 months) after the birth, while 58% of the high calorie group mice were dead, the mortality rates of the high calorie + resveratrol group mice and standard diet group mice were 42%. A statistical analysis of the results shows that resveratrol decreased the mortality rate of the high calorie-fed mice by 31%.

It has been proven that the lifespan extension of the nematode and other species by resveratrol is due to the action of the deacetylating enzyme Sir 2, as in the extension by caloric restriction, and therefore it must be true also in the case of mice. Besides this, in the experiments on mice, the effects of resveratrol on increasing insulin sensitivity, decreasing IGF-1 level, increasing mitochondria and improving physical activity were observed, which are thought to be related to lifespan extension. No results on female mice were described, so it is thought that no clear effect was observed.

Another drug known for extending the lifespan of some species is **rapamycin**. This is a compound carrying a complex structure (as shown in **Fig. 3-15**) and a molecular weight of 914, and was developed as an antibiotic. Later, rapamycin led to the discovery of the TOR (target of rapamycin).

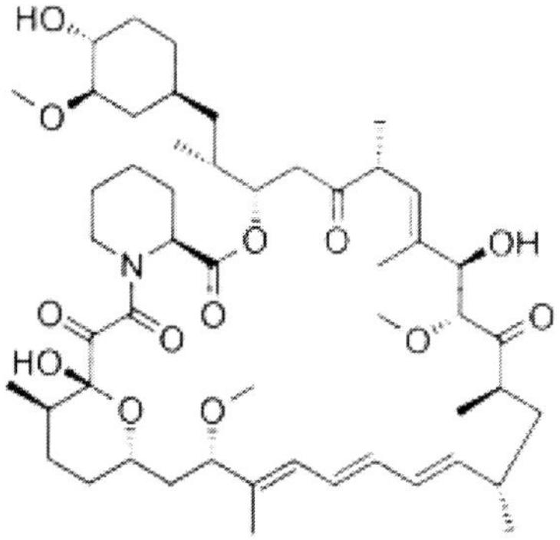

Fig. 3-15: Chemical structure of rapamycin (https 87)

Now, the TOR in a mammal is called mTOR and is an important factor related to human diseases and lifespan. Rapamycin is known to act by binding to mTOR and inhibiting its activity.

Let me introduce here the paper that first reported the extension of mouse lifespan by rapamycin (Harrison et al. 2009, 392-395). **Fig. 3-16** shows the graphs representing the results. The graphs are the results of carefully planned studies on a very big scale. Specifically, the results of studies done in three separate institutions were combined, with each study using very genetically diverse groups of mice from 600 days after birth. The subjects were generated by secondary crossing of the first-generation hybrids generated by crossing two genetic groups of males and females. The reason for using genetically very diverse mice is that a difference among the genetic strains may lead to different results. The results indicate that rapamycin extended their lifespan by 9% and 14% in males and females respectively, if the data are calculated on the basis of the ages of mice at the time of their death.

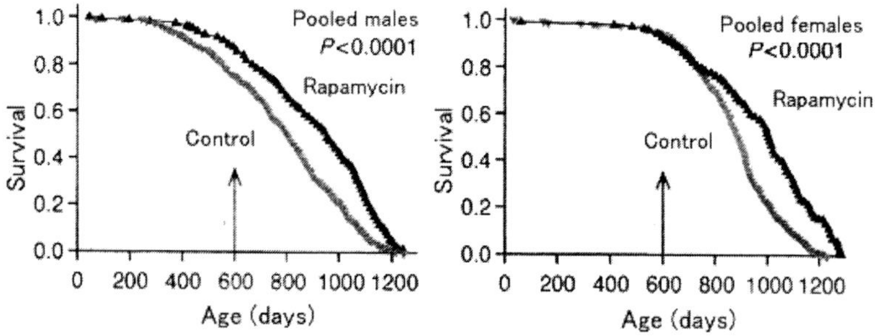

Fig. 3-16: Survival curves of male or female hybrid mice showing lifespan extension by addition of rapamycin into the diet (adapted from Fig. 1 of Harrison et al. 2009, 392).

Also, in the experiments started from 270 days after birth, rapamycin extended the lifespan of both males and females.

Although a branched chain amino acid is not a drug but a nutrient, it is possible to extend lifespan as stated in the previous section. **Resveratrol, rapamycin and a branched chain amino acid are the substances with which it is possible to extend human lifespans when added to our diet.**

CHAPTER 4

STUDIES ON THE HUMAN LIFESPAN BASED ON EXPERIMENTAL DATA

Since the lifespan of a human being is considerably long, experimental studies to identify factors determining the lifespan need a very long time. In spite of this difficulty, many studies on the effects of obesity, caloric or protein restriction, sleeping duration, physical activity, smoking, diabetes and high blood pressure on mortality during a considerably long period, up to 32 years, have been done. Statistical studies on the relationships between the indices for lifespan or ageing and their possible factors have also been done. Among them, there are studies on super-old people such as centenarians. These kinds of statistical studies have been done on various people around the world many times. Quite comprehensive statistical studies which integrate such studies (meta-analyses) have also been done. These may be representative characteristics of human lifespan studies. I will introduce representative studies of these kinds on human lifespan. Studies on centenarians will be described later, in Chapter 5.

4-1 Effects of obesity on the lifespan

While it is generally said that obese persons don't live as long, how much is this true in fact? Let me introduce the new and most comprehensive paper

(The Global BMI Mortality Collaboration, 2017, 76-786). It is stated in the introduction of this paper that there are more than 1.3 billion people with a BMI of 25~30 (overweight) and 0.6 billion people with a BMI of 30 or more in the world, and that both groups are growing in number, based on reports by the World Health Organization (WHO). BMI (Body Mass-Index) is the value obtained by dividing a body weight in kg by the square of the body height in m, and is used generally as an obesity index. For example, the BMI of a person whose weight and height are 60kg and 170cm, respectively, is 20.8. A person with a BMI near this value is neither fat nor slim, and is considered a standard in the obesity index.

This paper describes the results which were obtained by Cambridge University in England after statistically integrating 239 individual search results about the people in Asia, Australia/New Zealand, Europe and North America. The search periods for deaths were 5~18 years, and the total number of target people was more than 10.62 million. **Table 4-1** shows the classification of these people into six classes by BMI and the WHO criteria of obesity, and shows the number of people, its percentage, the number of dead people and the mortality hazard ratio (HR) of each group.

The group at a normal weight (BMI 18.5~25.0) includes most (52.5%) of the total participants, and the hazard ratio for the mortality of this group is taken as the standard (1.00). The second largest group is that of overweight people (BMI 25.0~30.0, 32.6%), and the third is that of obesity grade 1 (BMI 30.0~35.0, 8.9%). The total percentage of people belonging to the obesity grades 1~3 is about 12%. A person with a BMI of 40, which separates obesity grade 2 from grade 3, and 170cm tall, would be 116kg in weight and classed as super-obese. The table shows that people more obese than such a person comprise nearly 1%.

Table 4-1: Hazard ratios for the mortality of each obesity category in all the participants.

Obesity category	BMI (kg/cm^2)	Partici-pants	Rate	Deaths	Hazard Ratio (95% CI)
Underweight	15.0~18.5	292,003	2.7%	68,455	1.82 (1.74~1.91)
Normal weight	18.5~25.0	5,586,892	52.5%	810,838	1.00 (0.98~1.02)
Overweight	25.0~30.0	3,467,671	32.6%	526,098	0.95 (0.94~0.97)
Obesity grade 1	30.0~35.0	946,257	8.9%	144,871	1.17 (1.16~1.18)
Obesity grade 2	35.0~40.0	237,223	2.2%	36,113	1.49 (1.47~1.51)
Obesity grade 3	40.0~60.0	92,458	0.87%	15,399	1.95 (1.90~2.01)

Abstracted from Table I of The Global BMI Mortality Collaboration 2017, 778. CI: Confidence Interval.

As for the mean hazard ratios for mortality, that of obesity grade 1 is 1.17, which means that the mortality of this group is 17% higher than that of the standard (normal weight) group. The hazard ratio of the obesity grade 3 group is 1.95, about twice that of the standard value.

Table 4-2: Hazard ratios for the mortality of people who are non-smoking and without a chronic disease, classified into nine obesity grades.

Obesity category	BMI (kg/cm^2)	Partici-pants	Ratio (%)	Deaths	Ratio (%)	Hazard Ratio (95%CI)
Under-weight	15.0~18.5	114,091	2.9	12,726	11.1	1.51 (1.43~1.59)
Standard	18.5~20.0	230,749	5.8	20,989	9.1	1.13 (1.09~1.17)
	20.0~22.5	838,907	21.2	72,701	8.7	1.00 (0.98~1.01)
	22.5~25.0	1,075,894	27.2	98,833	9.2	1.00 (0.99~1.01)
Over-weight	25.0~27.5	821,303	20.8	84,952	10.3	1.07 (1.07~1.08)
	27.5~30.0	428,800	10.9	45,341	10.6	1.20 (1.18~1.22)
Obesity grade 1	30.0~35.0	330,840	8.4	37,318	11.3	1.45 (1.41~1.47)
Obesity grade 2	35.0~40.0	80,827	2.0	9,179	11.4	1.94 (1.87~2.01)
Obesity grade 3	40.0~60.0	30,044	0.76	3,840	12.8	2.76 (2.60~2.92)

The ratios were calculated by the author. The other data are from Table 2 of The Global BMI Mortality Collaboration 2017, 778. CI: Confidence Interval.

Interesting points of Table 4-1 include that the hazard ratio of the underweight group (BMI 15.0~18.5) is 1.82 and very high, higher than those for most of the overweight people, and that the hazard ratio of the overweight group (BMI 25.0~30.0) is 0.95.

The important points of the paper are that smoking and chronic diseases are body weight decreasing factors and therefore statistical results including such people do not give an effective suggestion for lifespan, and that the classification of obesity grades by the WHO standard is too rough. Based on these ideas, the target people were refined as non-smokers and those without chronic diseases, and obesity was classified into nine grades. The paper takes the ensuing results as important. Among all the searches surveyed, 189 searches were done on 3.95 million people in total who were non-smokers, free of any chronic disease and lived for at least 5 years. The results on these people during at least 5 years are summarized in **Table 4-2**.

In this table, the standard and overweight categories are divided into three and two classes, respectively. As for the simple mortalities for the entire search period, the lowest is 8.7% for a BMI of 20.0~22.5, and the highest is 12.8% for obesity grade 3, and they do not differ much. However, the means of the survival periods and of the lifespans (ages at death) differ among the classes, and the hazard ratios for mortality were calculated considering these factors. The hazard ratios for obesity grades 1, 2 and 3 are 1.45, 1.94 and 2.76, respectively, compared to 1.00 for the standard two classes. These values for the obesity groups are much higher than those in Table 4-1. Also, the hazard ratios for the overweight classes are 1.07 and 1.20, higher than

1.00, which clarifies the risk of being overweight hidden in the rough classification in Table 4-1. In contrast, the hazard ratio of the underweight category is lower than that in Table 4-1 (1.82→1.51). A simple summary of these results is that **the hazard ratios for the people with a BMI of 18.5~27.5 are not high (1.13~1.20), but that the ratios for people fatter or slimmer than those are by 20%~three-fold as high as those with a BMI of 18.5~27.5, for those who are non-smokers and have no chronic diseases.**

When the results in Table 4-2 are classified by regions, the average hazard ratios for highly obese people are the highest in Europe, and low in Australia/New Zealand, East Asia and South Asia. Also, when the results are classified by age into three groups, the increase in the hazard ratios by obesity is higher in the younger group. As for the relationship to sex, the increase of the hazard ratio in a higher grade obesity is higher in males than in females. These results may be very important for us.

Why does obesity shorten one's lifespan? First, as a direct effect, if the body weight of a person is high, an increase in the blood pressure is needed to send blood to his/her whole body. A high blood pressure induces arteriosclerosis and so results in a higher possibility of death by a bad condition in the cardiovascular system. Also, a high blood pressure results in the excitation of sympathetic nerves and stress for the body. Being overweight is a burden on the knees, and induces osteoarthritis in them, as well as difficulty in walking and a higher frequency of bone fracture.

Secondly, obesity accompanies an increase in body fat and thereby affects the body badly and indirectly, which is considered more serious. In many obese people, the number of adipocytes and the amount of stored fat per cell increase. These increases happen either in the whole body or mainly in the internal organs, and the latter has a deeper relation to a disease. The reason is that an increase of fat in adipocytes in the internal organs results in an increase in the production of substances with anti-insulin activity. The body then increases insulin production against this situation, which results in the earlier exhaustion of insulin production and leads to high blood pressure and diabetes. Diabetes is a cause for many diseases and shortens the lifespan. Also, an increase in fat storage leads to a decrease in the appetite-depressing hormone leptin and in the secretion of the arteriosclerosis-depressing factor adiponectin from adipocytes, which further promotes obesity and arteriosclerosis. Thus, obesity affects health badly and in complex ways, and ultimately shortens the lifespan (大島、2013, 113-115). I hope that obese people counteract their obesity by decreasing the calories in their diets and by adequate physical exercise.

By the way, the author feels that only BMI being used as the index for the analyses of the effects of obesity may be a problem. For example, even if BMI is at 25 (the boundary between the standard category and overweight category in Table 4-2), the body weight of a person 160cm high and that of another person 180cm high are 64kg and 81kg, respectively, and differ by 26%. Both the burden on the heart and that on the bones increase in response to the body weight and not to BMI, and so body weight itself should also be an index in the related studies.

4-2 Statistical studies on many factors related to human lifespan

A worldwide study

A paper written by about 100 authors and published in 2017 (Joshi et al. 2017, 1-13) is a worldwide study of the largest scale. This paper studied the relations between the genes of about 300,000 people of the ages $\geqq$ 40 years old, their health statuses and the lifespans of their parents of about 600,000. Of the parents, about 270,000 people were alive and about 330,000 people were dead at the search point, and the ages at the search point or at death were taken as the lifespans. The birth places of the target people were mainly Europe, Australia and North America. This study provides the results of a meta-analysis which integrated the results of 24 searches by UK Biobank and others. Another unique feature of this study is that the relations between the genetic types of the people and not their lifespans but the lifespans of their parents, were studied. By this feature, the relations between the two are less direct, but such relations can be estimated to some extent by the searches in rather short periods. As for the parents, the average lifespans of the dead were 71 years in men and 75 years in women, and those of the living were 63 years in men and 66 years in women.

In this study, strong relations between specific mutations (genotypes) in the four genes and the lifespans of the parents were found. The four genes are 1) a gene for the human major histocompatibility antigen system (HLA-DQA1/DRB1), 2) the gene for lipoprotein (a) (LPA), 3) the gene for neuronal nicotinic cholinergic receptor α (CHRNA3/5), and 4) the gene for apolipoprotein E (APOE).

1) The **human major histocompatibility antigen system** is composed of the antigens that induce a strong rejective reaction in the transplantation of an organ, tissue or cell between individuals of the same species (humans). The related antigens are classified into **class I antigens** (A, B, C), **class II antigens** (DPα, DPß, DQα, DQß, DRα, DRß) and **class III antigens** (TNF, C2, C4). While the class I antigens are expressed in most somatic cells, the class II antigens including the products of DQA and DRB genes (DQα, DRß) which were found to be related to the lifespan are expressed only in some cells such as B cells, macrophages and sperms etc. in the immunological system. These genes are important for the expression of human personality. There are various genetic types in each of these genes, and A1 and B1 are members among them. Also, these genes exist in a site of the sixth human chromosome as a group.

2) **Lipoprotein (a)** is a complex of low-density lipoproteins (LDL), which are made of apolipoprotein B, lipid and apolipoprotein (a), and exist in the blood. LDL is a risk factor for arteriosclerosis, and its concentration is increased in diabetes and kidney diseases (伊藤 et al., 2003, 2528).

3) Cholinergic receptors in general are proteins which bind specifically with the neurotransmitter acetylcholine. A **nicotinic cholinergic receptor** is a cation channel which opens/closes in the presence or absence of acetylcholine, and nicotine, a major component of a cigarette, stimulates its function. This receptor is composed of five protein subunits, α, β, γ, δ and ε, and only subunit α is related to lifespan. There are 10 kinds of α subunit

and 5 kinds of β subunit. Also, nicotinic cholinergic receptors are classified into skeletal muscle type, neuronal type and sensory epithelium type, and they are composed of different sets of subunits and so are members of a complex group of molecules (今堀 and 山川, 2003, 29).

4) **Apolipoprotein E** is a protein that has an important function in lipid metabolism. It binds with a low-density lipoprotein (LDL), exists widely on blood plasma lipoproteins, stimulates lipid movement and controls lipid metabolism (伊藤 et al., 2003, 45).

Among the four kinds of genetic mutations, mutations in HLA-DQA1/DRB1 (rs34831921) were found in 9% of the participants, and it was concluded that a copy of this mutation extended the lifespans of their parents by 0.6 year/copy. In contrast, mutations in LPA (rs55730499), CHRNA3/5 (rs8042849) or APOE (rs429358) were found in 8.3%, 35.6% and 14.2 %, respectively, but all of them reduced the lifespans of their parents, and those in LPA reduced by 0.7 year per copy. The fact that two of the factors found are related to lipids indicates that they are important for the lifespan. However, the effects of the identified **genetic factors on lifespan** are not significant, given that the effects of all genetic factors on lifespan are estimated to be at most 25% is described in the preface of this paper. The review on centenarians which will be described later (赤木・神出 2018, 554-561) states that the contribution of genetic factors to longevity is estimated to be 15~25% based on studies on twins.

In the paper which describes these results (Joshi et al. 2017, 1-13), the other important results on the relations between the **lifestyles** or **health parameters** of the participants and the lifespans of their parents are reported. Based on them, the **periods during which they received education**, their **non-smoking**, their **positivity** for a new experience and the **level of high-density lipoprotein (HDL)** showed a high correlation with longevity. Also, a high incidence of coronary artery diseases, high numbers of cigarettes smoked per day, high **insulin-resistance** and high **BMI** or **amount of body** fat showed a high correlation with mortality or a reduced lifespan. The results suggest that **if BMI is higher by 1, the lifespans of the parents are reduced by 7 months, and that if the education period is longer by a year the lifespans are extended by 11 months**. That a longer education period leads to a longer lifespan is mainly due to the fact that it strengthens the tendency of non-smoking. The results as a whole are quite interesting. As for obesity, there is a correlation between a BMI increase by 10 and a reduction of the lifespans of the parents by 6 years, which is similar to the results described before. It is not described to what extent this result affects the lifespans of the participants themselves. In general, the effect may be about half of that on the parents.

Studies on a Chinese region

Here, let me introduce a unique study on a Chinese region (Deng et al. 2018, 938-953). The target of this study was Guangxi Zhuhang, a large autonomous region of 240,000 km^2 located at the most southern part of China between latitude 22° and 26°N with a population of 51 million. **Fig. 4-1** shows a topographical map of the region cited from the paper. This region is a subtropical area with a mild climate, consisting of rather flat land in the south and central parts, and a mountainous region in the northwest.

The main reason for this region being selected as the target of the study was its high rate of centenarians. The city of Hechi located in the north part of the region was recognized as having the highest rate of centenarians in China (17.9/population of 100,000) in 2016 by an international organization (International Expert Committee on Population Aging and Longevity). As will be described in the centenarian chapter, the overall rate of centenarians in China is about 2/100,000, and so this rate in Hechi is about 10 times as high. The other reasons for the selection of this region as the target were the large differences in the levels of economy and education among the different parts of the region, and that the statistics on the population of the old people were favorable.

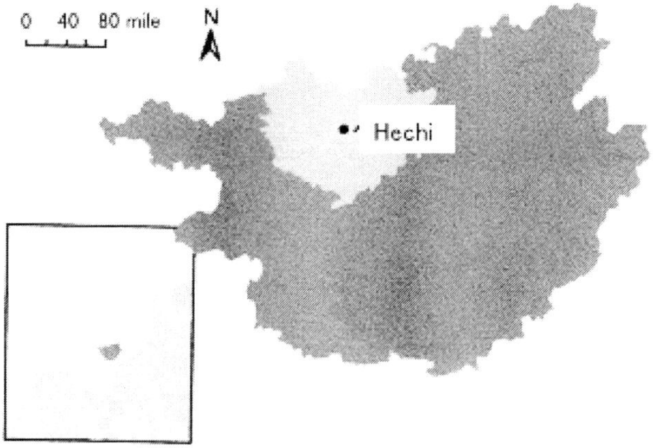

Fig. 4-1: A topographical map of Guangxi Zhuhang Autonomous Region (adapted from Fig. 1 of Deng et al. 2018, 940).

In these contexts, the relationship between the longevity and various indices were explored in 109 selected counties and towns. As longevity indices, the rates of centenarians and the rates of the population over or equal to 90, 80 or 60 years old etc. were searched. As for longevity-related indices, the items listed in **Table 4-3** and related to **natural environments, economical indices, education levels, infrastructures** and **medical facilities** were also incorporated. The average temperatures for a year in these selected areas ranges from 18.7~22.7℃, their altitudes stretch from 15~1,118 m, and the rainfall levels are 1,084~2,677 mm/year.

As for the ratio of centenarians per 100,000 inhabitants, the highest and the lowest were 36 and 0.6, respectively, thus there was a big difference of 60-fold between them, which is interesting. The top three areas with a very high ratio of centenarians are concentrated in the city of Hechi (17.9 on average). The rates of people 60 or older were 8.4~17.7%, and the difference was about two-fold.

Table 4-3: The indicators used for the search of the factors related to longevity in Guangxi Zhuhang Autonomous Region.

Classification	Indicators
Natural indicators	atmospheric pressure, difference in temperature, humidity, rainfall, radiation, temperature, water vapor, altitude
Economic indicators	primary industry, secondary industry, tertiary industry, government revenue, GDP, output of gain, urban registration employment rate
Educational indicators	population with primary school education, population with secondary school education, number of primary schools, number of secondary schools

Local infrastructural indicators	number of resident buildings, number of mobile telephone subscribers, annual electricity consumption
Health care facilities	number of hospitals, number of hospital beds

Adapted from Table 2 of Deng et al. 2018, 942.

It is a pity that the average lifespan data are not shown. Perhaps the authors did not have access to good lifespan data. The conclusion that seems to be the most important is that the **annual temperature difference** and the **altitude** (as natural indicators) and the **GDP** as an economic indicator are highly correlated with the lifespans of 60~90 year olds. As for the annual temperature difference and the altitude, they mean that lifespans are longer in the areas with a mild climate where the indicators are smaller.

The details of this research are not described here, however the following three points are some of its representative features: 1) The division of the target region into many small areas leads to rather special factors of lifespan characteristics in each area; 2) The correlations between the indicators of the natural environment, the economic status, educational levels etc. and lifespan were studied; and 3) An area which is still under development, considerably large and rich in variety was selected as the target region of the research. This study is thought to have a characteristic value different from that of the research for the common and worldwide factors introduced in the previous section.

4-3 Effects of meals on the lifespan

In the first of the papers introduced here (Ravussin et al. 2015, 1097-1104), diet restrictions which were done in mice were tried also in humans, and their effects on the health parameters related to lifespan are examined. In this paper, the results on the effects of caloric restriction were measured for two years by an international research team called CALERIE (**C**omprehensive **A**ssessment of **L**ong term **E**ffects of **R**educing **I**ntake of **E**nergy). The subjects were non-obese males and females 21~51 years old, and they were divided randomly into two groups. One group was subjected to caloric restriction (CR) and the other was a control group, and their results were compared. It's probable that all the subjects were Americans, or Americans and Italians. Their BMI was between 21.9~28.0, and the average was 25.1. This BMI range corresponds to the standard 2nd group to the overweight 2nd group in Table 4-2 and does not include obese or underweight people. Thus the target people are likely to be average American residents.

The study was started with 143 CR people and 75 control people, giving 218 in total. Among them, 69.7% people were females and 77.1% were Caucasian (white). Their blood pressures, blood sugar levels, insulin and lipids in hunger were normal at the start point, and there was no difference for these indicators between the two groups. As such, we can understand that to make a study meaningful is laborious. 117 from the CR group and 71 from the control group completed the study, in total of 188 participants.

The everyday amount of calorie intake of each subject was strictly measured by the method known as Total Daily Energy Expenditure (TDEE) using double-labeled water. At the start point, those of the CR group and the control group were 2,390±45 and 2,467±34 kcal/day, respectively, and there was no meaningful difference between them. For the CR group, an average reduction of calorie intake of 19.5% (480 kcal) for the first half year, 9.1% (234 kcal) for the later period and by 11.7% overall was implemented.

Fig. 4-2 shows some of the main results, the changes in body weight for both groups. There was little body weight change in the control group. In contrast, there was around an 8% (7.1~8.3kg) reduction in the body weight for the CR group.

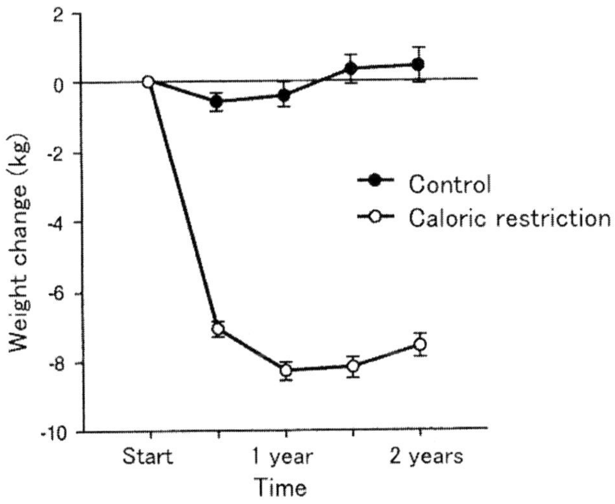

Fig. 4-2: Body weight changes of the CR group (-○-) and control group (-●-) for two years (adapted from Fig. 2B of Ravussin et al. 2015, 1101).

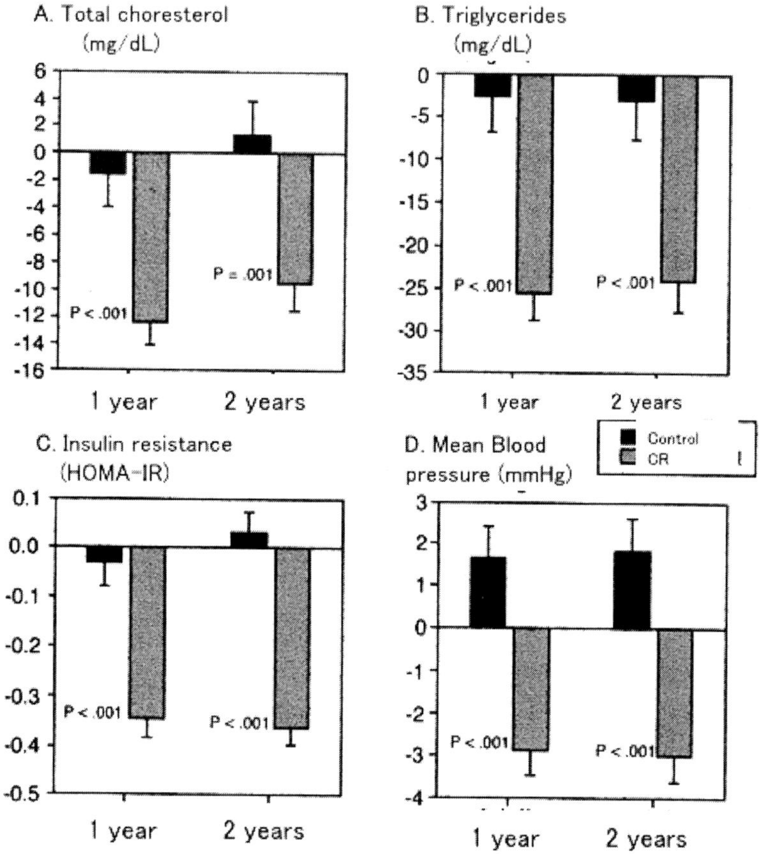

Fig. 4-3: Changes of health parameters by caloric restriction (CR). Gray bars for CR group and black bars for control group (adapted from Fig. 4 of Ravussin et al. 2015, 1103).

It is thought that this result strictly showed body weight reduction by caloric restriction in humans for the first time. **Fig. 4-3** presents the other major results of the study: the changes in the levels of cholesterols and triglycerides in the blood and in average blood pressure (A, B and D). The

HOMA-IR shown in C is an indicator for insulin resistance, or insulin concentration in hunger (μg/ml) x blood glucose level in hunger/405. All these indicators decreased due to CR after a year or 2 years. These results shown in Fig. 4-3 mean that the hazard factors in the cardiovascular system, which are significantly related to the human lifespan, are reduced by CR and therefore the results seem to be important.

A study which directly studied the effects of general diet restriction on the lifespan was not found, but several papers which studied the effects of protein amounts in the diet were published. There are three important ones among them which I shall introduce in turn.

The study by Levine et al. (2014, 407-417) was done as part of a larger study called NHANESIII which had carried out similar research on mice. The subjects of this study were 6,381 people whose ages at the start were 50 years or older and 65 on average. They were representative or average American residents in terms of their racial traits, educational levels and health. The subjects ate meals of 1,823 kcal/day on average: 51%, 33% and 16% of the energy came from carbohydrates, lipids and proteins, respectively, on average, and more than half of the proteins (11% of the total calories, 2/3 of the total proteins) were of animal origins. The people were divided into three groups based on the protein contents: a high protein group (≧20% of the total calories from proteins), medium protein group (10~19% from proteins) and low protein group (less than 10% from proteins). By comparison of the mortalities and the causes of the deaths, the effects of the protein intakes were examined during a period of 18 years. Some people died during the research period, and the average survival period after the start was 13.1 years.

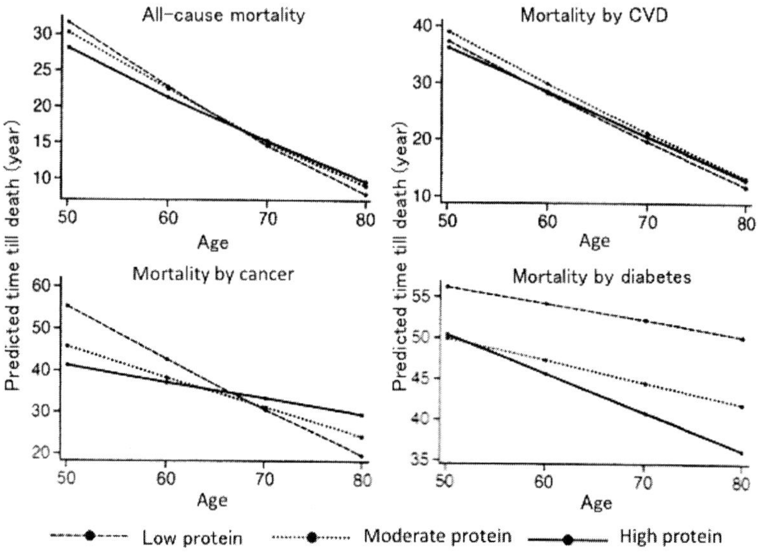

Fig. 4-4: Association between protein intake and all-cause mortality, mortality by cardiovascular diseases (CVD), mortality by cancer and mortality by diabetes. The ordinates represent predicted time till death or remaining life expectancy. The data were obtained by using the Cox proportional hazard model (adapted from Fig. 1 of Levine et al. 2014, 409).

Fig. 4-4 shows the main results of this study. The graphs in the figure show how many years later on average all the deaths and those deaths caused by a cardiovascular disease (CVD), cancer or diabetes will occur (average residual lifespans) on the ordinates. The graphs are somewhat difficult to understand, but the lines are a kind of survival curve and their slopes represent mortality and the differences in the slopes depending on the protein intake levels are important.

The main conclusions to be taken from these results are as follows.

1) For the 50~65 year old people in the study, all-cause mortality and mortality by cancer over the next 18 years occurred in 75%, and the rates were four-fold higher in the high protein group than in the low protein group.
2) This effect is lost or diminished if the proteins are derived from plants.
3) For the people older than 65, the results are reversed, that is, both mortality by cancer and all-cause mortality decrease in the high protein group.
4) Mortality by diabetes is five-fold higher in the high protein group than in the low protein group for all ages.
5) When all these results are combined, it is suggested that low protein intake (10% of the total calories) is best before 65 years old and high protein intake (more than 20% of the total calories) is best after 65 years old for health and longevity. Also, plant proteins are recommended especially for high protein intakes.

Another important study was published in 2016 (Song et al. 2016, 1453-1463). The subjects of this study were more than 120,000 females (nurses) who were 30~55 years old at the start in 1976 and more than 50,000 males (engaged in medical service) who were 40~75 years old in 1986. The study was maintained for very long periods of 32 or 26 years and carried out on a large scale. In this study, the diets included animal and plant proteins at 9~22% (median 14%) and 2~6% (median 4%), respectively, of the total calories. Both protein levels were divided into five classes, and mortalities were compared among the subjects corresponding to these protein classes.

The results were as follows.

1) The intakes of animal proteins do not correlate with the all-cause mortalities, but correlate positively with mortalities by cardiovascular diseases.
2) The intakes of plant proteins correlate negatively with both all-cause mortalities and mortalities by cardiovascular diseases (more protein intake, lower mortality) for people who have one or more unhealthy habit or characteristic, such as smoking, drinking alcohol, obesity or poor levels of physical activity. The correlation is not clear however for healthy people.
3) When various animal proteins are changed into plant proteins, the mortalities decrease.

The average protein intake is 18% of the total calories, and when plant protein intake is the highest (6%), animal protein intake is 9% at the lowest, and therefore the total protein intake is 15% or more and much higher than 10%. These results suggest that higher protein intakes (15~18%?) are good at least for Americans.

The third important study was done in Japan, and led to a paper on the relations between intakes of plant proteins and deaths by cardiovascular diseases (Kurihara et al. 2019, 198-206). This study was based on the results of research carried out over 15 years on 7,744 people who did not have a cardiovascular disease and were ≧30 years old at the start. The main conclusion of the study is that intakes of plant proteins are negatively correlated with mortality by a cardiovascular disease or by cerebral hemorrhage (more intake, lower mortality), and that this relation is stronger for people without a high blood pressure.

In the first paper described above (Levine et al. 2014, 407-417), the results for the people up to 65 years old may be more important, the group for whom lower protein intake (less than 10% of the total calories) is better. However, the reason for the difference from the results of the second paper (Song et al. 2016, 1453-1463) is not clear. The second paper is better in four ways: that there are nearly 30 times as many participants, that the research period is longer, that animal proteins and plant proteins are distinguished, and that protein intakes are divided into five and not three classes. But the second paper lacks research on lower protein intakes down to about 10%, which may be a problem. I think that the result indicating a lower protein intake (below 10%) is better for people up to 65 years old is the most important. However, it may be right that a general conclusion has not yet been found on protein intakes from an objective point of view. Also, since we Japanese differ from Americans in meal contents and in race or genes, it is not clear that the results obtained for Americans are also right for Japanese people, or indeed for others across the world. A comprehensive study on the relation between protein intakes and mortalities in Japan may be necessary. The inference that plant proteins are better for health than animal proteins seems really conclusive.

4-4 The relationship between sleep duration and mortality

Many people may feel that sleep is important for maintenance of good health. Related to this, many studies on the association between sleep duration and mortality have been published since around the year 2000 (Yin et al. 2017, 1-13). The countries and participants of these studies are varied, and their conclusions are not consistent. In the review cited above (Yin et al. 2017, 1-13), the results of a meta-analysis integrating many studies, which were published before December 1, 2016 and included in PubMed in the USA or EmBase in Europe, were reported. This analysis selected and meta-analyzed 141 reports which satisfied the criteria set by the authors. **Fig. 4-5** shows the main results.

In all four graphs, the abscissa indicates the subjects' average sleep durations per day. The ordinate shows the relative risk of mortality for all causes (A), for all causes related to cardiovascular disease (B), for coronary heart diseases (CHD, C) or for strokes (D). The solid curves in the graphs are cubic functions showing the average relative risks, and the dotted curves show 95% confidence intervals.

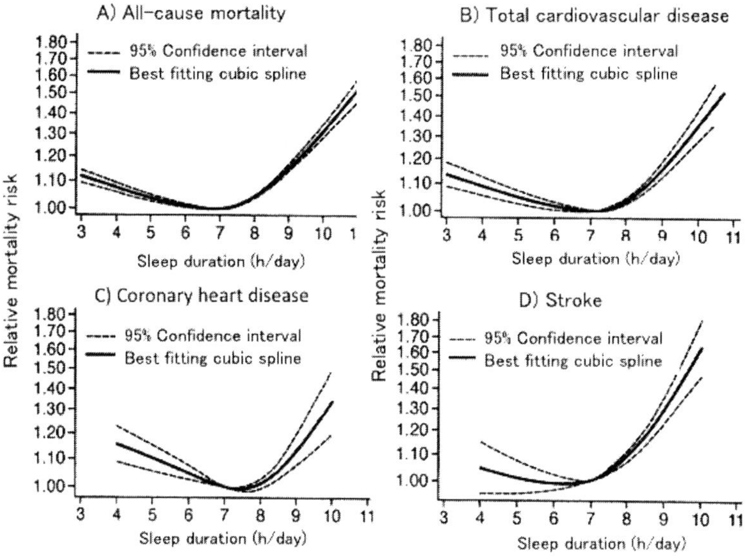

Fig. 4-5: Association between sleep duration and mortality (adapted from Fig. 2 of Yin et al. 2017, 6).

Based on these results, we can see that **the people with a sleep duration of about 7h have the lowest mortality, and the mortality is higher both for shorter and longer sleep durations in all cases**. As for all-cause mortality, the relative risk gets higher by a magnitude of 1.06 when the sleep duration gets shorter by 1hr for durations less than 7h, and it gets higher by a magnitude of 1.13 when the duration gets longer by 1hr for durations longer than 7h. The result that a sleep duration longer than 7h is more dangerous than a duration shorter than 7h was unexpected. It is written in the paper that it is not clear by what mechanism these results were achieved and that future studies will be necessary. However, such a study would be difficult. It is easy to understand that a shortage in sleep duration leads to a higher mortality and shortens a lifespan, but it is difficult to imagine why longer sleep duration is bad.

In the second paper introduced here on the association between sleep duration and mortality (Akerstedt et al. 2017, 881-891), analyses based on the ages of the subjects were added. The studies in this paper were done on 39,191 subjects 18 years or older among the participants of an event in Sweden in 1997. 64% of the subjects were female and it's likely most of the participants were Swedish. The studies were done during 13 years thereafter and based on the reports of the participants. First, the results on sleep durations on weekdays classified by age is shown in **Fig. 4-6**.

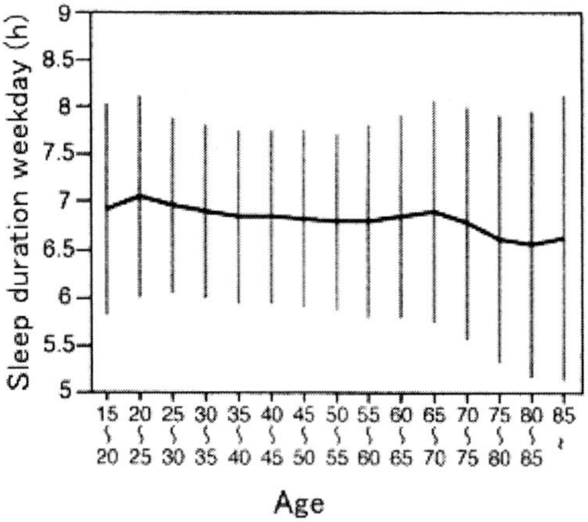

Fig. 4-6: Changes in weekday sleep durations by age in Sweden
(adapted from Fig. 1 of Akerstedt et al. 2017, 886).

There are no large changes in the average sleep durations among ages of 5-year intervals: the longest is 7.1h for 20~25 years old and the shortest is

6.6h for 80~85 years old. The standard deviations (σ) are around 1hr for all of the age intervals, and rough ranges of sleep durations (±2σ) are 3.5~5.6h and considerably large. I suppose that this result would not change greatly if similar research was done in Japan, and therefore the result should be informative to us.

In this study, the subjects were divided into four groups depending on sleep durations (≦5h, 6h, 7h = standard and ≧8h), and their mortalities were compared. The main results (**Fig. 4-7**) show changes of mortality hazard ratios organized by age, taking that of the standard group as 1. The short (≦5h) duration group is shown in (a) and the long (≧8h) duration group in (b).

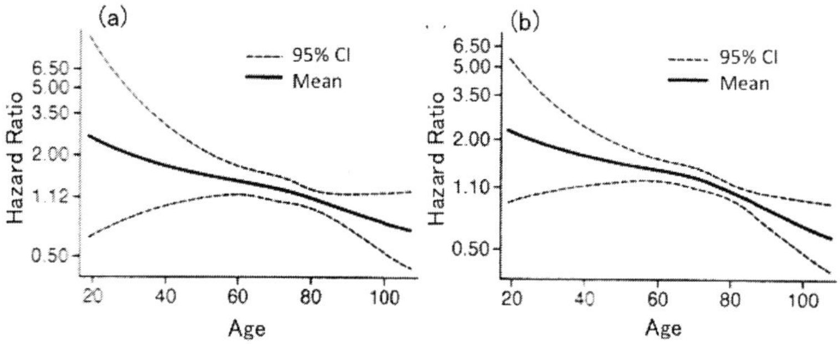

Fig. 4-7: Mortality expressed as age-varying hazard ratios for short (a) and long (b) sleepers. Solid lines and dotted lines show hazard ratios and 95% confidence intervals, respectively (adapted from Fig. 2 of Akerstedt et al. 2017, 887).

The solid and dotted lines represent average hazard ratios and 95% confidence intervals, respectively. Their distributions are very similar between the two groups: the hazard ratios are lower as the ages increase, and they are less than 1 for the ages of ≧80. The paper concludes that the hazard ratios for the subjects younger than 65 are significantly higher than 1 for both the short and long duration groups (1.37 and 1.27 on average), but that there is no statistically significant relation between sleep durations and hazard ratios for older people (≧65 years old). The result that the mortality rates of old people do not become significantly higher at least for the short durations (a) differs from many results such as those described above. It too was unexpected. The paper offers no good explanation for this outcome, but the reason may be related to the uniqueness of Sweden, to its very cold climate and many nights with a midnight sun. Also, the paper states that the relation between sleep duration and mortality changes depending on age, which I think is true at least to some extent.

The third paper on the relation between sleep durations and mortality which merits discussion is one which was recently published about a region in Japan by Kyushu University (Ohara et al. 2018, 1911-1918). The subject area is the town of Hisayama next to the city of Fukuoka where I live, and which is familiar to me. Hisayama is a town which the Medical School and Institute of Kyushu University has engaged in its various medical studies for a long time, and this paper is about one such study. This town has an area of 37 km^2 and a population of about 9,000 (4,270 males and 4,715 females). About half of the town area consists of a lower mountainous area, and agricultural fields and houses are scattered across its plains. The main reasons that this town has long been the subject area for medical studies by

Kyushu University are that its residents are fairly static, it is quite a small community, and the various health parameters of the residents are near the average values in the whole of Japan. The epidemiological studies in this town are said to be famous in the related fields. I could read only the abstract of the paper, and will describe here the conclusions given. The subjects in this study were the residents ≧60 years old; they were divided into five groups based on sleep durations (＜5h, 5.0~6.9h, 7.0~7.9h, 8.0~9.9h and ≧10h). The main result was that the people with a sleep duration less than 5hrs or ≧10hrs showed significantly higher hazard ratios for all-cause mortality and for dementia (2.64 and 2.23) compared to those with a 5.0~6.9h sleep duration. This result shows features similar to the results of the large-scale study on Americans and Europeans stated above (Yin et al. 2017), and differs from the results in Sweden (Akerstedt et al. 2017). Since Hisayama is said to represent Japan and its results are similar to those in Yin et al., a study in which there are a great many subjects, it stands to reason that the Hisayama results (the people ≧60 years old show higher mortalities both when sleep durations are too short and too long) can be applied to us Japanese. The result on the relation between sleep durations and the ratio at which people suffer from dementia is similar, and is novel and interesting.

4-5 Exercise is effective for lifespan extension

Meals, exercise and stress are known as the largest three factors related to lifespan. Exercise is also referred to as physical activity. When physical activity and mortality are used as key words for a literature search, we can understand that many studies have been done on the subject. Here, I will introduce representative studies and those in Japan.

The paper which is likely to be the most informative on the effects of exercise (Arem et al. 2015, 959-967) is introduced first. The studies in this paper were begun from 1992~2003 and were analyzed in 2014 by the National Cancer Institute in the USA. The subjects were about 661,000 men and women living in the USA or Europe, they were between 21 and 98 years old and the median age was 62 years old. About 117,000 subjects died during the total study period, and the average study period was 14.2 years. From the results and their analysis by Cox proportional hazards regression, mortality risks (hazard ratios) and their 95% confidence intervals were obtained. The main results are shown in **Fig. 4-8**.

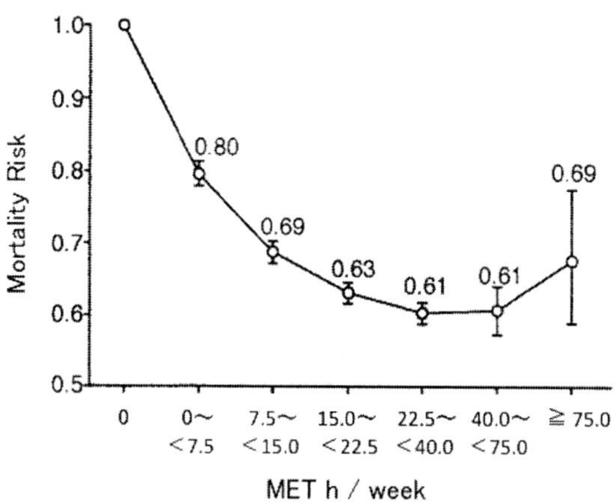

Fig. 4-8: Association between physical activity levels and relative mortality risks. The risk in the case of no physical activity is taken as the standard (1.00) (adapted from the figure of Arem et al. 2015, 962).

The abscissa represents physical activity levels of the subjects divided into seven classes, and their unit is the product of the metabolic equivalent and the exercise period during a week.

The **metabolic equivalent** is the relative value showing the metabolic activity during the exercise taking the value at resting (in kcal) as 1. The unit for the metabolic equivalent is written as MET or METs. For example, the metabolic equivalent of a slow walk (about 4km/h) is 3 MET, and if this is continued for an hour, the physical activity is 3 MET h. If it is continued for a week, the total physical activity is 21 MET h, and this value corresponds to the fourth point from left in Fig. 4-8 (mortality risk of 0.63). In this graph, the mortality risk of the subjects whose physical activities are 22.5~40 MET h is the lowest at 0.61. Even rather light physical activity of 7.5~22.5 MET h can reduce the mortality risk to 69% of that without any exercise.

Here, how much metabolic equivalents of various exercises or physical activities correspond is important. Detailed data for this was released in the USA in 2011 (Ainsworth et al. 2011, 1575-1581), and its Japanese translation was released on the web by the National Institute of Health and Nutrition (国立健康・栄養研究所、2012). This is a voluminous table of 50 pages, so I have condensed it to around 20 kinds of physical activities in which the readers may be interested (**Table 4-4**). We can understand that eating a meal and taking a bath (1.5 MET), which are not usually thought of as exercises, and various home tasks (about 2.5 MET) are classed as light physical activities. Riding a bicycle as a commute and rather a fast walk for exercise correspond to about 4 MET, and running and fast bicycle riding correspond to more than 8 MET.

Table 4-4: Metabolic equivalents (M. E.) of various physical activities

Physical activity	M. E. (MET)	Physical activity	M. E. (MET)
Watching TV (sitting)	1.3	Sitting-up	2.8
Talking (sitting)	1.5	Walking at 4km/h	3.0
Eating a meal (sitting)	1.5	Cleaning	3.5
Taking a bath	1.5	Fishing	3.5
Going to the toilet	1.8	Bicycle (< 16km/h)	4.0
Changing clothes or hair	1.5	Carpentry	4.3
(standing)		Walking (at 5.6km/h)	4.3
Light gymnastics	2.3	Simple muscle work	4.5~6.5
(stretching, yoga, balance)		Aerobics dance	5.0~7.5
Shopping	2.3	Jogging	7.0
Washing clothes or dishes	2.3~2.5	Cycling	8.0
Meal preparation	2.5	(at 19.3~22.4km/h)	
Driving a car	2.5	Running (at 8.0km/h)	8.3
		Running (at 16.1km/h)	14.5

Abstracted from 国立健康・栄養研究所、2012.

Table 4-5: Relations between physical activities and mortality

Physical activity (MET h/W)	Subjects (%)	Death by cancer		Death by CVD	
		Number (%)	Mortality risk (95% C.I.)	Number (%)	Mortality risk (95% C.I.)
0	52,848 (8.0%)	3,143 (10.7%)	1.00	3,238 (12.8%)	1.00
0.1~<7.5	172,203 (26.1%)	8,854 (29.3%)	0.87 (0.83~0.90)	7,592 (31.4%)	0.80 (0.77~0.84)
7.5~<15.0	170,563 (25.8%)	7,375 (25.2%)	0.79 (0.75~0.82)	6,316 (24.9%)	0.67 (0.65~0.70)
15.0~<22.5	118,169 (17.9%)	4,373 (14.9%)	0.75 (0.72~0.79)	3,293 (13.0%)	0.59 (0.57~0.63)
22.5~<40.0	124,446 (18.8%)	5,187 (17.7%)	0.74 (0.71~0.77)	4,044 (15.9%)	0.58 (0.56~0.61)
40.0~<75.0	18,831 (2.9%)	557 (1.9%)	0.72 (0.66~0.79)	457 (1.8%)	0.61 (0.55~0.67)
≧75.0	4,077 (0.6%)	75 (0.3%)	0.69 (0.55~0.87)	69 (0.3%)	0.71 (0.56~0.91)
Total (%)	661,137 (100%)	29,294 (100%)		25,639 (100%)	

Columns for total numbers at the bottom were added to Table 3 of Arem et al. 2015, 964.

In this paper, the relations between physical activities and the number of deaths by cancer or cardiovascular diseases and mortality risks are also reported (**Table 4-5**). Based on this table, mortality risks by cancer are below 0.8 for physical activities higher than or equal to the third rank from the lowest (7.5~15 MET h/week), and are lower for higher ranks. The lowest is 0.69. As for the risk of cardiovascular diseases, the fifth physical activity rank (22.5~40 MET h/week) shows the lowest risk of 0.58, and the risks are lower than ~0.7 for all the ranks higher than or equal to the third rank.

The deaths by cancer or cardiovascular diseases during the entire study period were 29,294 and 25,369, respectively, from a total of 116,686 deaths. They correspond to 25.1% and 21.7%, respectively, and the total is about 50% and very high.

Even a full-time housewife who does little specific exercise is likely to be in a good state with a mortality risk near 0.6 based on Fig. 4-8, since her physical activity is probably over 15 MET h/week from house-keeping activities. As for myself, I walk slowly (3 MET) for over 30 min, do light whole-body gymnastics in the morning and evening and a few kinds of exercises with my feet every day. Therefore, my physical activity is probably over 22.5 MET h/week and may be good. As for the people not participating in physical activity, it is desired that they correct this by walking or cycling in their commute, and by walking or participating in light exercise during their holidays. I think that this study is important in that it introduced an **objective evaluation of physical activities by giving numerical values to them** and that it made clear that even light physical activity is effective in reducing the risk of mortality.

For calculation of the real energy consumption in kcal from a metabolic equivalent, the body weight of the participant is needed as a part of the following equation: physical activity (MET) x time (h) x body weight (kg) x 1.05 (https: 105). For example, the energy consumption of a person of 60kg by walking at 3 MET for 1h is 3 x 1 x 60 x 1.05 = 189kcal.

Another recent paper (Stamatakis et al. 2019, 2062-2072) examined not only the effects of physical activities on all-cause mortality, but also the effects of sitting times. The subjects of this study were about 267,000 residents of 45 years old and above in the State of New South Wales, Australia, and the study was begun in 2006~2009. Thereafter, follow-up surveys were done for 8.9 years on average. During this period, 8,689 people (5.8%) died. **Fig. 4-9** shows the main result.

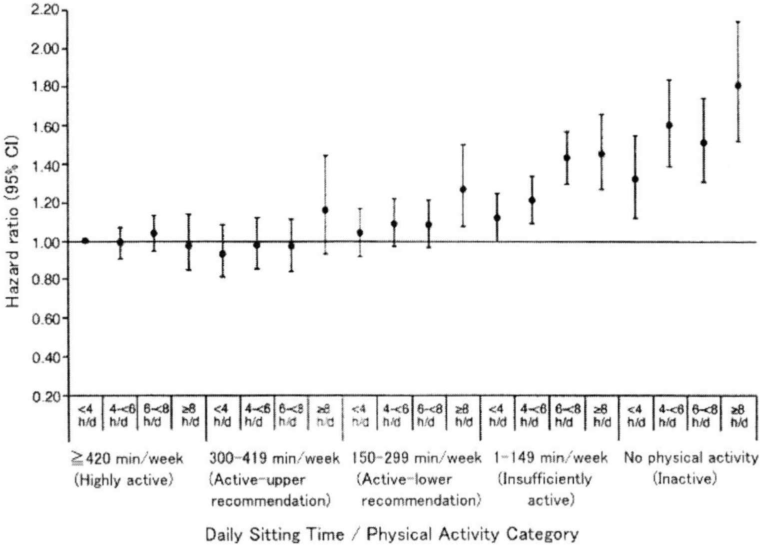

Fig. 4-9: Joint associations of sitting times and physical activity with all-cause mortalities (adapted from the central illustration of Stamatakis et al. 2019, 2066).

This graph shows hazard ratios or average values of relative mortalities and their 95% confidence intervals. These data are presented for four groups of physical activities, each of which is further divided into four groups depending on daily sitting times. For the people at the left whose physical activities are ≧420 min/week, the hazard ratios change little (around 1.0) by sitting times. As physical activities decrease, hazard ratios for the people sitting for a longer time increase up to 1.4~1.8. The graph shows that the people sitting for 8h/day or 4~8h/day need active exercises of ≧300 min/week or ≧150 min/week, respectively. The criteria for the strength of physical activities are based on those of Australia, and the details are not described. I would estimate that active-upper and active-lower physical activities correspond to 3~4 MET. These probably include normal walking. The people who belong to the class of the standard hazard ratio (1.00) in Fig. 4-9 should correspond to those of the lowest ratio (0.61) in the last paper. Therefore, the hazard ratios of 1.4 or 1.8 in this figure are thought to correspond to the ratios of 1.4 x 0.61 = 0.85 or 1.8 x 0.61 = 1.10 in Fig. 4-8. If so, the ratio 1.4 may be OK. This study is based on the situation that many people in the present world sit to work for a long time. The results showing that necessary physical activities change considerably depending on the sitting times are unique, and will be informative to many people.

The third paper to be introduced is a study done in Japan on Japanese people (https 107; Kikuchi et al. 2018, 715-721). The study reports the results of research on about 83,000 men and women who were 50~79 years old and who lived in one of the areas under the control of one of the ten Health

Centers in 1990 or 1993, or who joined in the research 10 years later (in 2000 or 2003). All of the subjects were followed until 2012. The main result is cited in **Fig. 4-10**. This result shows that hazard ratios of mortality in the

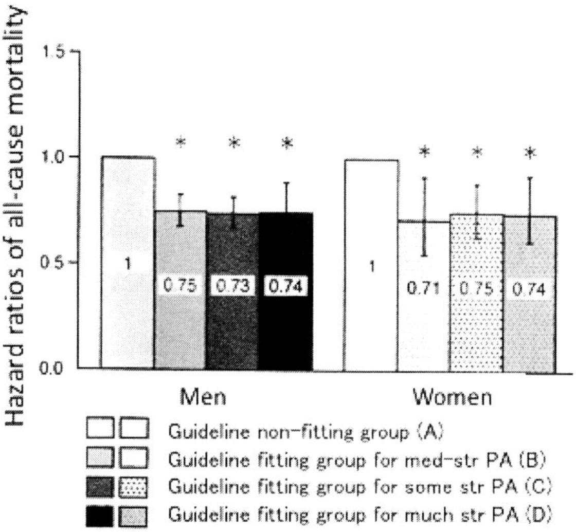

Fig. 4-10: Relations between physical activities and all-cause mortality hazard ratios (adapted from Kikuchi et al. 2018, 715-721).

three groups doing some exercise (B~D) decrease to about 0.7 in comparison to that of the no exercise group (A [1.0]). As for the criteria of the physical activities, 150 min or more/week of medium-strong activities (becoming lightly out of breath, such as walking and golf, 3~4 MET) was used for group B, 75 min or more/week of strong activities (becoming out of breath, such as jogging, cycling and soccer, ≧7 MET) was used for group C, and combinations of B and C's activities but of a total strength about equal to that of C was used for group D. This result is easy to understand, and indicates that results similar to those of the first and the second papers can be applied to Japanese people, and so is informative to us.

Besides these studies, in a paper published in Korea (Shin et al. 2018), relations between physical activities and hazard ratios were reported not only for healthy people but also for diabetes patients. The result for healthy people was largely similar to the results of other papers (decrease to 0.7~0.85 through exercise), and the hazard ratios were about 1.35 for no physical activity and 0.9 for 5~6 exercises/week in the case of the diabetes patients. This indicates that hazard ratios are considerably higher in diabetes patients than in healthy people and that stronger activities are required to reduce the ratio to below 1.0. In the national search by the Ministry of Health and Labor in Japan (https 110), the number of both diabetes patients and prospective patients in Japan is estimated to be around 10 million. Thus, diabetes is a big problem in Japan, and physical activities seem to be important also for these patients to reduce their mortality rates.

Why are exercises effective for longevity?

As indicated in the first paper introduced above, adequate exercises reduce not only all-cause mortalities but also mortalities due to cancer or cardiovascular diseases. Recently, an important paper was published which meta-analyzed studies on the effects of physical activities on various health parameters (Chastin et al. 2019, 370-376). Based on this paper, **doing light exercise sometimes through a day reduced levels of blood glucose and insulin after a meal much more than when sitting. Also, the lipid storage**

decreased, and blood pressure and hyperlipemia were improved, by a different light exercise program. These results are important for preventing cardiovascular diseases. Besides, exercises are clearly effective for prevention and improvement of obesity. All these reasons are answers to the question posed above. The reason for the decrease of mortality by cancer is not clear, but it may possibly be an increase of suppressive power on cancer, such as self-immunity by an improvement in general health situation.

4-6 Smoking greatly shortens the lifespan

The statistical result indicating that non-smoking is a factor for longevity was stated in Section 4-2. So, smoking is known to be a risk factor for lifespan. More than 1,000 papers on the relations between smoking and mortality are found, and I will introduce a few important ones.

The first of them is the valuable paper on the results of research in the USA published in 2013, which estimated how many years of the lifespan are reduced by smoking (Jha et al. 2013, 341-350). This study is based on the results of interviews with 113,752 women and 88,496 men 25 years or older from 1997~2004 and relates the causes of their deaths until December 31, 2006. 8,236 women and 7,479 men died during this period. For the 25~79 year old subjects, **hazard ratios of mortality of the smokers were about three-fold (3.0 for women and 2.8 for men) when never-smokers (those without any smoking experience) are taken as the standard.**

Fig. 4-11 compares the survival curves of current smokers and never smokers (A: women, B: men). The survival rates at 79 years old from 25 are

70% for never smokers and 38% for current smokers in women, and 61% and 26% in men, thus representing a survival rate around twice as high for the never smokers.

The graphs also show that the average age of 70% survival is shorter by 11 years in women and that of 60% survival is 12 years shorter in men. That the age for 50% survival shortens from 86 to 76 in women and from 83 to 72 in men is indicated by the figure. Namely, **average residual days become shorter by more than 10 years by smoking.**

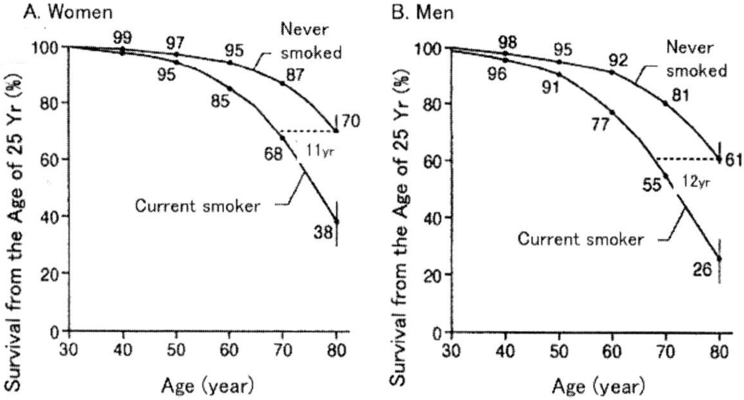

Fig. 4-11: Comparison of the survival curves of current smokers and never smokers (A: women, B: men) (Fig. 2 of Jha et al. 2013, 350).

As for the people who had quit smoking in the past, the risk of death correlated to the age of quitting (**Fig. 4-12**). For the people who quit smoking at the ages of 55~64 years old, the risk greatly decreases from 2.9 to 1.7 in spite of 30 years or longer smoking. We can understand that it is better for longevity for smokers to stop smoking as early as possible. As to the background for this study, the estimation that **smoking occupies 25% of the causes of death** for men and women of 35~69 years old in the USA is written in the abstract of the paper.

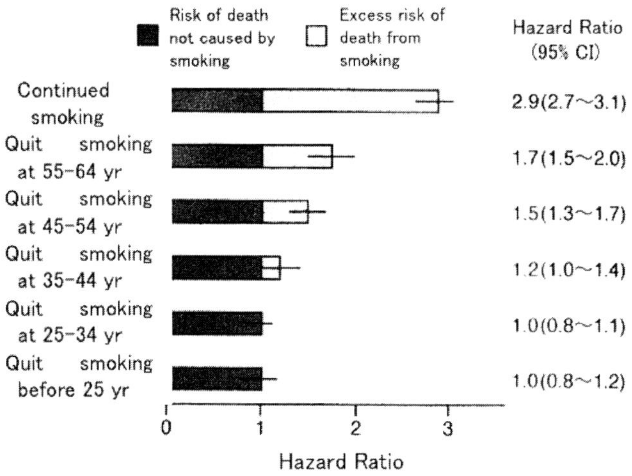

Fig. 4-12: Decreases of hazard ratios of mortality in the people who quit smoking (adapted from Fig. 4 of Jha et al. 2013, 350).

The reasons for the high mortality risk of a smoker are diseases which are thought to be induced by smoking such as cancer, ischemic heart diseases (angina, heart attack) and respiratory diseases. These are known as the three big diseases related to smoking. Cancers caused by smoking develop in the lungs, esophagus, pancreas, mouth, pharynx and so on. The reason for carcinogenesis is a mutation which is made by the actions of carcinogenic substances contained in cigarette smoke, such as benzo[a]pyrene, on intracellular DNA in the body.

It is known that cancers in general develop by 3~4 mutations in the genes related to cancer. It is believed that ischemic heart diseases are caused by arteriosclerosis in the coronary arteries of the heart induced by the actions of nicotine and carbon monoxide (CO) in cigarette smoke. Respiratory diseases include chronic bronchitis caused by stimulation of cigarette smoke, pulmonary emphysema caused by enhanced secretion of proteases in lung, and so on (http: 113).

The second paper on smoking to be introduced concerns a study in Japan and was published in 2012 (Sakata et al. 2012, 1-12). The study was performed mainly by the Radiation Research Foundation in Hiroshima. The subjects of this study were selected from atomic bomb survivors in Hiroshima and Nagasaki and people who were born before August 1945 and lived in Hiroshima or Nagasaki in 1950 but did not live in either city at the time of bombing (with this latter group acting as a control). These subjects may be special, but the study is on the effects of smoking, and so the effect of atomic bomb radiation on the results can be neglected. The smoking statuses of the subjects, 27,311 men and 40,662 women, were surveyed from 1963 till 1992, and the deaths were surveyed starting a year after the first survey until January 1, 2008.

Fig. 4-13 shows the survival curves of never smokers and current smokers who had started smoking before 20 years old, with the members of both groups being born from 1920~1945. Based on these results, the paper concludes that life expectancy decreases by 8 years in men and 10 years in women due to smoking. The average numbers of cigarettes used per day were 23 for men and 17 for women, and most male smokers began smoking around 20 years old. The average mortality risk of current smokers was 2.21 in men and 2.61 in women.

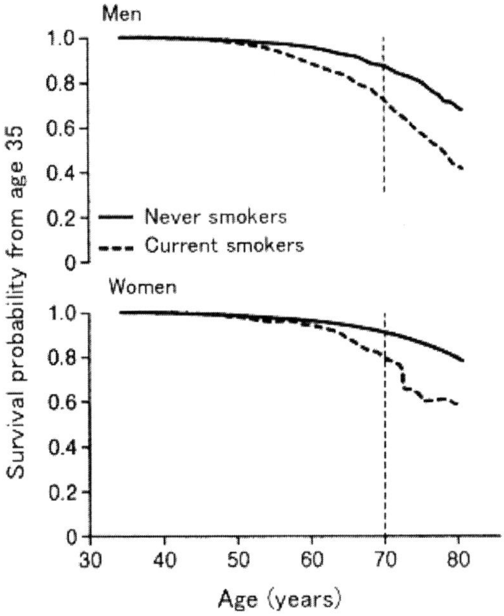

Fig. 4-13; Survival curves of Japanese men and women born between 1920 and 1945 who were never smokers or current smokers who started to smoke before age 20 (adapted from Fig. 2 of Sakata et al. 2012,12).

By the way, two papers on previous and similar topics in Japan (Ozasa et al. 2008, 111-8; Murakami et al. 2007, 31-7) are cited in the introduction of the paper, which states that reduction in life expectancy by smoking was reported to be 4 and 2 years, respectively, in these previous papers. The paper described above (Sakata et al. 2012, 1-12) claims that the results of this paper are right in contrast to the two previous papers, since the difference between them is due to the previous papers being based on older results and that the reduction in life expectancy had been increasing recently. Since its results are similar to those of an English paper (Doll et al. 2004, 1519-28) and of the American paper introduced earlier, I agree with this claim and suppose that life expectancy is likewise reduced by about 10 years due to smoking in Japan. However, I feel that research or studies on the lifespan are difficult since the results depend on various conditions.

Next, I introduce the summary of a very recent study in Japan (Zha et al. 2019, 11-17). This paper reports the results of the surveys on about 98,000 subjects over a period similar to that of the Sakata et al. paper. The surveys were started from 1990~93 and done again at every 5-year period for 15 years by cooperating researchers at Osaka University and the National Cancer Center.

The main results are shown in **Fig. 4-14**. These graphs show the mortality risks of not only current smokers but also former smokers, as well as the risks of lung cancer, which is the most important cause of death related to smoking, and so they are valuable for our purposes in this section. The relative risk of all-cause mortality of current smokers is 1.74 in men and 1.91 in women, taking that of never smokers as the standard (1.00). These figures are lower than those in the Sakata et al. paper (2.21 and 2.61).

This difference seems to be due to the fact that plural surveys were done in this report and so the results were based on more recent data. It is probable that the risks have been decreasing, perhaps due to medical developments and people becoming more cautious about health recently. The degree of lifespan reduction by smoking may also have decreased somewhat recently.

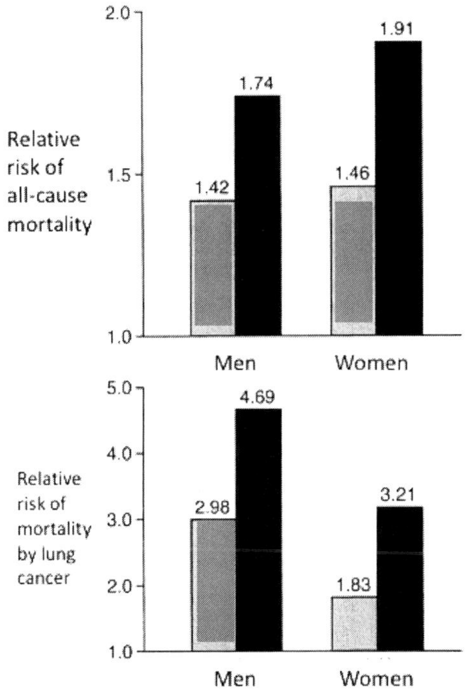

Fig. 4-14: Comparison of all-cause and lung cancer mortality risks by smoking status in Japan. The bars, in pairs, show the data for former smokers (left) and current smokers (right). The graphs were made from the data in Table 3 of Zha et al. 2019, 15.

Here, I show annual changes in the ratios of smokers for men and women in Japan from 1965 to 2018 (**Fig. 4-15**). The graph shows that the rate of male smokers greatly decreased from more than 80% to about 28% over the period of about 50 years. The rate of female smokers also decreased, from more than 15% to 8.7%. These data are hugely encouraging for our health.

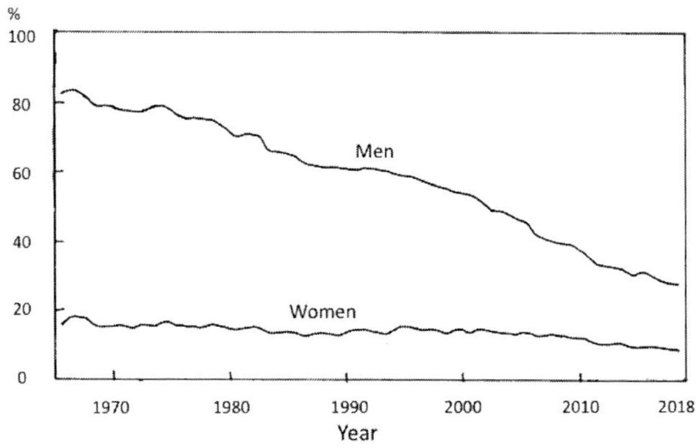

Fig. 4-15: Annual changes in the ratios of smokers among men and women in Japan from 1965 to 2018 (abstracted from the figure in http: 119).

The last paper to mention here on smoking was published in 2019, as the third paper was, and summarizes the enormous results of surveys not only in Japan but also in six other Asian countries such as China and India (Yang et al. 2019, 1-14). It is a pity that the results are rather old and thus they are omitted here. Instead, I want to introduce the 2017 report of the WHO (https 121) cited in the introduction of the paper, which states that **about 7 million people die from smoking per year in the world** and this number is expected to increase to 8.3 million by 2030. One paper published in 2017 in *Lancet* (GBD 2015 Tobacco Collaborators 2017, 1885-1906) stated that about half of the total smokers in the world are residents of three countries – China, India and Indonesia – and that Japan and Bangladesh are included in the top ten. Greater decrease in smokers is thus needed also in Japan.

4-7 Diabetes and its effects

As will be described later, the amount of people who suffer from diabetes in Japan, and indeed all over the world, is tremendous. Besides, the mortality risk of diabetes is as high as that of smoking, and so diabetes is clearly a big problem. Here, I cite the description of what diabetes is, translated from a big medical dictionary in Japan (伊藤 et al. 2003, 1758):

> "Diabetes is a continuous state of high blood sugar induced by insufficiency of insulin. The causes are genetic factors and environmental factors, and many candidate genetic factors are reported. Environmental factors are obesity, over eating, stress, drugs and so on. Type I diabetes induced by self-immunity and type II diabetes by the other reasons are known, and most of the patients are type II. Based on the criteria for diagnosis of the Japan Diabetes Association in 1999, if blood sugar level at any time is ≧ 200mg/dl, blood sugar level in hunger is ≧ 126mg/dl or 2h value in an oral load test using 75g glucose is ≧ 200mg/dl, the subject is estimated to be a prospective diabetes patient. If he or she is estimated to be a prospective patient again on a later day, he/she shows symptoms characteristic to diabetes, his/her HbA_{1c} level is ≧6.5% or he/she shows diabetic retinopathy, he/she is

> diagnosed as a diabetes patient. Diabetes sometimes induces complications such as diabetic retinopathy, diabetic nephropathy or diabetic neuropathy. Also, diabetes is a risk factor for arteriosclerosis and may cause heart attack and cerebral infarction, as well as hyperlipidemia, hypertension and obesity. Nutritional therapy and athletic therapy are the main medical therapies for diabetes, and various oral blood sugar-reducingdrugs and insulin are used."

The diagnostic criteria are complicated but are related to the following numbers of patients or prospective patients. The number of diabetes patients based on the related data in Japan are shown in detail online (https 123). Based on the survey on diabetes by the Ministry of Health, Labor and Welfare in 2016 (https 110), the number of probable patients was about 10 million, representing about 12.1% of adults, and was on the rise after 1997. Among them, the ratio of the people who were medically treated was 76.6% (about 7.7 million). Also, about 10 million other people were prospective patients. In contrast, another survey by the same ministry on diabetes patients in 2014 reported 3,160,000 as the number of diabetes patients, and so the two numbers differ hugely. The two surveys differ in time by two years (2016 and 2014) and since the former is an estimation, the data in 2014 may be more reliable. However, there were also other differences in the criteria between the two surveys. Based on the report in 2014, high blood pressure patients, hyperlipidemia patients, cardiovascular patients and cancer patients numbered 11.1, 2.06, 1.73 and 1.63 million, respectively. Based on these data, the number of diabetes patients was the second largest following that of high blood pressure patients. The number of deaths by diabetes was 13,669 (7,265 men and 6,404 women) in 2014 (data on the population provided by the Ministry of Health, Labor and Welfare, Japan).

As for the entire world, the number of diabetes patients was 415 million in 2015, having increased by 28.3 million from the previous year, and was – at the time of the study – expected to increase up to 642 million by 2040 (according to a report by the International Diabetes Association in November 2015). **The ratio of the diabetes patients among 70~79 year old people was reported to be 8.8% or 1 in 11**. Among the countries in the world, the largest number was in China (109.6 million), the second and third were in India (69.2 million) and the USA (29.3 million), respectively. The number in Japan (7.2 million) was the ninth in this estimation.

A great many papers, in total around 3,000, on the relations between diabetes and mortality or lifespan can be found online. Let me introduce a few recent papers here in brief. First is an important paper on mortalities in seven Asian countries including Japan, which was published in 2019 (Yang et al. 2019,1-14). This paper reports the summary of the results of 22 cohort studies done between 1963 and 2006 by Asia Cohort Consortium. The summary was obtained during January to August of 2018. The subjects were residents in one of seven countries (China, Japan, Korea, Singapore, Taiwan, India and Bangladesh), their total number was 1,002,551, and the median value of the research period was 12.6 years. 51.7% of the subjects were women, the ages of the total participants were 30~98 years old and their median age was 54 years old. The number of deaths during the research period was 148,868. The most important results of this study are the hazard ratios of all-cause mortality and the disease-specific mortalities related to diabetes, which are shown in **Fig. 4-16**. The all-cause mortality ratios were 1.74 for men and 2.09 for women, which are close to the values for smoking shown in Fig. 4-14 (1.74 and 1.91).

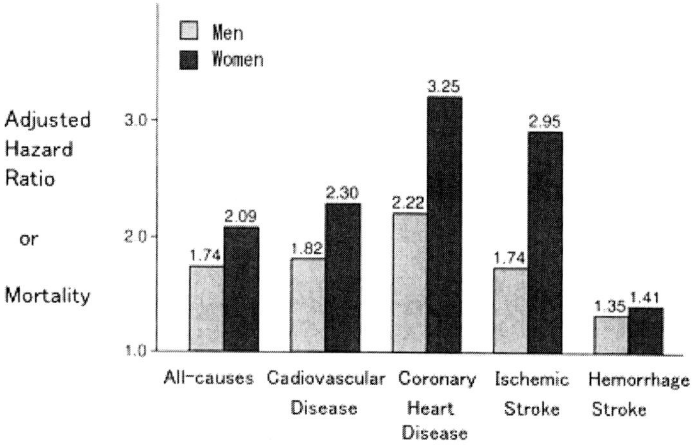

Fig. 4-16: Hazard ratios of all-cause mortality and disease-specific mortalities related to diabetes in 7 Asian countries (made from the data in Table 4 of Yang et al. 2019, 7/14).

The second paper introduced here is one from the USA (Preston et al. 2018, 139-151). In the survey reported in this paper, the subjects were selected from those of the National Health Interview Survey done from 1997~2009 and the data were based on the death records by December 31, 2011. The main conclusion is that the average life expectancy of 30 year old diabetes patients are 0.83 (men) and 0.89 (women), a year shorter than that of people without the disease.

Another significant paper was published in Japan in 2019 (Goto et al. 2019, 1-9). The survey in this paper was based on the death record of a diabetes-specific clinic. The study comprised 6,140 diabetes patients who came to this clinic, their average age was 58.1, 77% of them were men, the survey period was 1980~1999, and 261 people among them died during the period. The main conclusion is that the average life expectancy of 40-year-old patients was another 39.2 and 43.6 years for men and women, respectively (thus they would be estimated to live until 79.2 and 83.6 years old). Since the average lifespan was probably 80~81 years in men and 84~85 years in women, reduction of the lifespan by diabetes may be 1~2 years, a conclusion similar to the results in the above American paper. The reason for the fact that reduction of life expectancy by diabetes is much shorter than that by smoking (1~2 years vs. about 10 years), although the mortality hazard ratios are nearly the same, is not clear.

By the way, based on the report of surveys by the Committee on the Causes of Death by Diabetes of the Japan Diabetes Association in 2017, the average ages of diabetes patients during the 10 years from 2001 to 2010 in Japan were 71. 4 in men and 75.1 in women, and had extended by 3.4 or 3.5 years from the previous decade (https 123). These results are thought to be related to the fact that diabetes patients tend to be old people, that diabetes patients have become to live longer and that the average lifespan of the entire Japanese population has extended.

4-8 Blood pressure and pulse

A high blood pressure or hypertension may be a symptom rather than a disease. The number of Japanese people with this symptom is 11.1 million based on the data cited in the last section and thus is greater than that of prospective diabetes patients. Hypertension induces cardiovascular diseases which are important causes of death, and so it is thought probably to have a bad effect on lifespan. How significant, though, is the effect? How much blood pressure is taken as high is shown under **Fig. 4-17**. The paper from which this figure was derived is a report on the results of a survey in Japan published in 2019, and it is thought to be important to us (Yamagishi et al. 2019, 1366-1371). In this paper, blood pressure levels are divided into six cases, and systolic (maximal) blood pressures ≧ 140mmHg are defined as hypertension, which in turn is divided into three cases (grade 2 and 3 hypertensions are combined in Fig. 4-17). Quite recently, it was reported that classifying blood pressures ≧ 130mmHg as hypertension was proposed by the related associations, but here we follow the previous classification described in the paper.

The survey in this paper was based on the data by a national epidemiological study on cancer (JACC Study) begun in 1988. The subjects of the original data were 110,585 men and women who were 40~79 years old at the start. The survey on hypertension was done on 27,728 people (10,091 men and 17,637 women) who were selected from the JACC Study subjects and whose health information could be obtained from the local community. The subjects were not suffering from cerebral stroke, cardiovascular disease, cancer or kidney disease at the start. The follow-up survey of death was done until 2009 and for 21.6 years at the maximum (median period of 18.5 years). During this period, 5,239 people died. The causes of the death included cardiovascular diseases (1,477), strokes (682) and coronary artery diseases (304), and the sum of these three occupies 47% of the total.

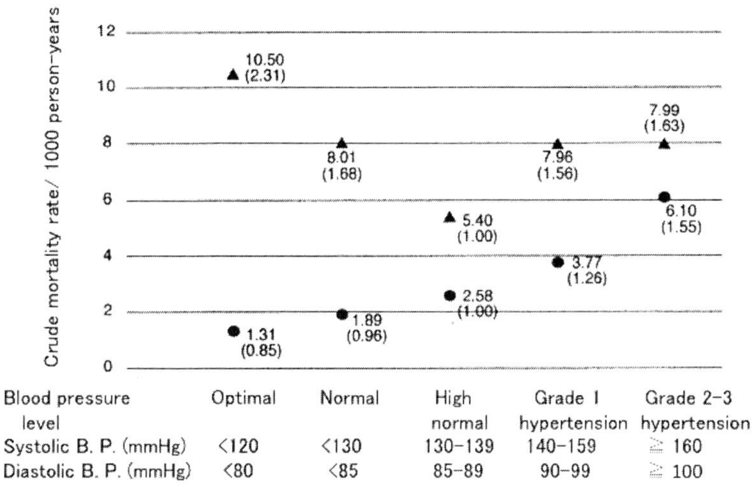

Fig. 4-17: Crude mortality rate (ordinate) and hazard ratios (in parentheses) by cardiovascular diseases in Japan classified by the level of blood pressure (made from Fig. 1 and the data in Table 2 of Yamagishi et al. 2019, 1368-69).

The main results of this survey are mortality rates for cardiovascular diseases classified by blood pressure levels, and they are shown in **Fig-4-17** for 23,153 people who had not been treated (-●-) and 3,164 people who had been treated (-▲-) for decreasing blood pressure by the start of the survey.

The numbers without parentheses are crude mortality rates/1000 person-years, and are 8 for treated people and 2 for non-treated people on average. The rate for the treated people is about four-fold as high as that for the non-treated people. The sum of the people who were not treated but were hypertension patients (systolic and diastolic blood pressures are ≧140 and 90mmHg, respectively) and those treated for hypertension occupied 39.1% of the total subjects. The numbers in parentheses are relative mortality hazard ratios which were calculated by the Cox proportional hazards model and adjusted for age and gender etc., and their standards are the data of the 'High normal' group (with a systolic blood pressure of 130-139mmHg) both for the untreated and treated groups. As for the untreated groups, the higher the blood pressure, the higher the hazard ratio (the average is 1.55 for grade 2-3 hypertension), as expected. However, as for the treated groups, the distribution of the hazard ratios is U-shaped. Namely, the lowest ratio was for the 'High normal' group (1.00), and the highest ratio was for the group with the lowest (optimal) blood pressure (2.31) unexpectedly. These results indicate that when decreasing blood pressure by a drug is tried, the systolic blood pressure should be in the range of 130~139mmHg (High normal) and that the hazard ratios tend to be higher for blood pressures lower than this range. These results seem to be important in the medical treatment of hypertension.

Next, two papers on hypertension survey results are summarized. The first (Wei et al. 2017,1-15) meta-analyzed the papers on differences in cardiovascular diseases by gender and mortality hazard ratios in the USA which were published in late 2015. One of the conclusions they arrive at is that the hazard ratios for suffering from a cardiovascular disease increase by 25% in women and by 15% in men (the increase rate is higher in women) due to an increase in the systolic blood pressure by 10mmHg, which was based on eight pertinent papers found on cardiovascular diseases. Also, the mortality hazard ratios by cardiovascular diseases increase 1.16-fold in women and 1.17-fold in men due to an increase of systolic blood pressure by 10mmHg (i.e., there is little difference between men and women).

The survey of the other paper (Yu et al. 2019, 1-10) was done to see the relations between two or a combination of the five indices for metabolic syndromes including hypertension and all-cause mortalities. The five indices and the criteria for what is considered a risk are shown in Table 4-6. If three or more criteria fit a risk, the subject is judged as a metabolic syndrome patient.

Table 4-6 Criteria for metabolic syndrome

Waist circumference	≧102cm in men or ≧88cm in women
Fasting serum triglyceride concentration	≧ 1.7mmol/L, or on dyslipidemia medication
Serum concentration of HDL cholesterol	＜1.03mmol/L in men, ＜1.3mmol/L in women, or under dyslipidemia medication
Blood pressure	Systolic ≧130, diastolic ≧85mmHg, or on antihypertensive medication
Fasting serum sugar concentration	≧ 5.6mmol/L, or on diabetes medication

The standard of National Cholesterol Education Program in the USA, updated in 2005.

The subjects of this survey were seven groups of American adults, the total number of whom came to 82,717. The rates of metabolic syndrome were 32% in men, 34% in women, 28% in the 18~65 year old people and 62% in the people older than 65. In the follow-up period 14,989 subjects died, and their median living period was 14.6 years. In the results of the survey on the correlations between one, two, three, four or all five risk factors and the all-cause mortalities, the mortalities were higher as the number of risks was higher in the 18~65 year old group, but only the people carrying all five risk factors had a significantly higher mortality. Also, **hypertension showed the highest correlation with mortality among the five risk factors irrespective of age or gender.** In the people without any other risk factor than hypertension, the mortality hazard ratio was 1.56 for men and 1.62 for women, which is considerably high. In contrast, anyone with a 'risky' waist circumference, serum sugar concentration or serum triglyceride concentration did not significantly correlate with the mortality hazard ratio.

Thus, hypertension is a mortality risk factor which cannot be ignored, and therefore it is important to prevent hypertension. The main points to consider in preventing hypertension are:

1) Be careful with meals by preventing blood pressure increase through reducing salt intake and preventing obesity due to excess calories.
2) Obese people should decrease their body weight.
3) Take pertinent exercise to improve blood flow, to suppress blood pressure and to prevent obesity (https 130). By the way, the criteria of hypertension at this site are a systolic blood pressure ≧140mmHg

and a diastolic blood pressure ≧ 90mmHg, as in Fig. 4-17.

Pulse

A pulse or a heart rate changes depending on the time of the day, body activity and the measuring method, as with blood pressure. Many papers have been published on the relation between the pulse and mortality or cardiovascular diseases, but the relation is more delicate than in the case of blood pressure and the conclusions seem to be various. In brief, the majority of the conclusions suggest that faster (more frequent) pulses are more dangerous, and it seems to be right. Here, two reports on pulse are briefly introduced. The first is a voluminous review published in 2017 (Aune et al. 2017, 504-517). This review integrated and meta-analyzed 87 survey reports published globally up to March 2017. The main conclusions were that the adjusted relative risk of the increase by 10 beats per minute in the resting heart rate is 1.17 for all-cause mortality, 1.15 for a cardiovascular disease, 1.09 for a sudden cardiac death, 1.18 for heart failures (heart attack) and 1.14 for total cancer. These conclusions, based on many results, seem to be valuable.

The second paper I'd like to mention is on a survey done several years earlier in Japan (Hozawa et al. 2004, 1005-1010). It was one of the epidemiological surveys on a local area done by Tohoku University Medical School since 1987 (Ohasama Study). The target area is likely to be the town of Ohasama as it used to be known, which is now a part of the present-day city Hanamaki in Iwate Prefecture. In this study, there were 1,780 Japanese subjects in this area who were ≧40 years old and had no significant arrhythmia. The main conclusion is the relation between the resting heart rates measured in the morning at home and the risk of cardiovascular mortality (adjusted for various factors based on the Cox proportional hazards model), which is cited in **Table 4-7**.

Table 4-7: Relationship between the home heart rate and the hazard ratios of the cardiovascular mortality

Morning heart rate /minute	Hazard ratio of cardiovascular mortality (95% confidence interval)
≦ 60	1.13 (0.54~2.33)
61~64	1.00
65~69	1.63 (0.81~3.29)
70~73	2.54 (1.16~5.58)
≧ 74	2.61 (1.29~5.31)

Abstracted from Table 2 of Hozawa et al. 2004, 1008.

In this result, the mortality of a person with a heart rate of 61-64 is the lowest, and if this is taken as the standard (1.00), that of a person with a heart rate of 70 or more is higher than 2, and the difference is significant. If the heart rate is assumed as a continuous variable, cardiovascular mortality increases by 17% every time the heart rate per minute is increased by 5. The relation between resting heart rates measured in the evening and the risk of cardiovascular mortality was similar, however that for morning data showed a clearer correlation.

A big characteristic of this study was using the heart rate measured at home in the morning. There seem to be three merits to this method: there is no nervous tension which occurs in a hospital, an average rate obtained by measurement over several days can be used, and morning is the best resting time. Also, the standard heart rate values are shown for reference and so the measured heart rate is easy to understand. Since the result was obtained in Japan, the probability by which it can be applied to us Japanese may be high, and so it is valuable for us to refer to.

4-9 Human genes related to lifespan

Studies on the human genes related to lifespan have been done actively. Here, I will introduce several representative ones (numbered 1~5) and the related genes in brief. Before that, let us remember that significant correlations between a specific mutation or genotype and the lifespan of his/her parent were found on the four genes in the statistical study of a great scale which was described in Section 4-2. The four genes are: 1) a gene for the human major histocompatibility antigen system (HLA-DQA1/DRB1), 2) the lipoprotein (a) gene (LPA), 3) the gene for neuronal nicotinic cholinergic receptorα(CHRNA3/5), and 4) the gene for apolipoprotein E (APOE). Among them, the APOE gene encodes a precursor of lipoprotein E. Since lipoproteins are risk factors for arteriosclerosis which is an important risk factor for cardiovascular diseases, it is easy to understand this gene's relation to lifespan.

(1) One paper examined correlations between a specific

genotype of a gene and longevity (Revelas et al. 2018, 24-34). This paper meta-analyzed 65 studies in the world which compared people 85 or above and a control group of young people. By this analysis, significant correlations were found between specific genotypes in one of the five genes and the lifespan of a person carrying one of those genotypes. The strongest correlation among them was found for the apolipoprotein E gene described in section 4-2, and the correlation coefficient (odds ratio) was 1.45 (leading to a longer lifespan) in a genotype and 0.42 (leading to a shorter lifespan) in another genotype. As for a FOXO3A (forkhead box O3 transcription factor) genotype, the correlation coefficient was 1.45 in men and 1.12 in total. As for the angiotensin converting enzyme (ACE) gene, a weak correlation of 1.11 was found for a genotype. The angiotensin converting enzyme is the enzyme that changes an angiotensin precursor to an active angiotensin, and therefore its action for increasing the blood pressure by contracting blood vessels is probably the reason for its relation to lifespan. A weak correlation was also found for the Klotho gene and the interleukin 6 (IL6) gene.

(2) A study which compared the genotypes of 1,089 people aged 90~99 and those of 736 people aged 46~55 was done by Dato et al. (2018, 1-12). A specific feature of this study is that since most single changes in genotype do not seem to have a large effect on lifespan, the effects of two simultaneous changes in a metabolic pathway, which can have a larger effect, were examined. In this strategy, the effects of combinations of two different genotypes in the insulin-IGF-1(insulin-like growth factor) action pathway, a DNA repair pathway and an antioxidant-precursor pathway were examined, and several combinations were found significantly to correlate with the lifespan.

(3) At the end of the last chapter on mouse lifespan it was shown that the drug rapamycin extended the lifespan of mice. The same drug showed similar effects in yeast, nematodes and fruit flies. Rapamycin and its derivatives act through the protein known as TOR (Target of Rapamycin, mTOR in mammals). TOR is a molecule that acts as a protein phosphorylating enzyme which phosphorylates serine or threonine in a protein. Also, TOR proteins constitute complexes called TORC1 or TORC2 with several kinds of other proteins, and perform physiological functions in lifespan extension and various related physiological actions in these forms. Therefore, all the genes of molecules related to rapamycin are related to lifespan. Rapamycin also affects the insulin-IGF-1 action pathway described in the previous study. By the way, it is said that development of a rapamycin derivative which has no side-effect and can extend the human lifespan is actively being sought (Johnson et al. 2013).

(4) It is known that there are seven longevity genes and their products called Sirtuins (SIRT1~SIRT7). Sir2 which is engaged in lifespan extension by caloric restriction was the first molecule found as a member of the Sirtuins. Deficiency of Sir2 leads to lifespan reduction and an over-expression of this gene leads to lifespan extension. Molecules related to Sir2 are found in various organisms. These Sirtuin molecules have NAD^+-dependent histone deacetylating activities, and are thought to suppress oxidative stress, ageing and ageing-related diseases through these activities and finally to extend the lifespan (大田 2010, 11-16). Among these Sirtuins, SIRT1 has the highest similarity with Sir2 in mammals, and its expression

was found to be considerably high in old people (**Fig. 4-18**, Killic et al. 2015, 1-19). The genes for these Sirtuins and several related molecules also belong to a kind of gene group related to lifespan. By the way, it was described previously that the drug resveratrol extended the lifespan of mice, and this drug acts through a Sirtuin similar to Sir2.

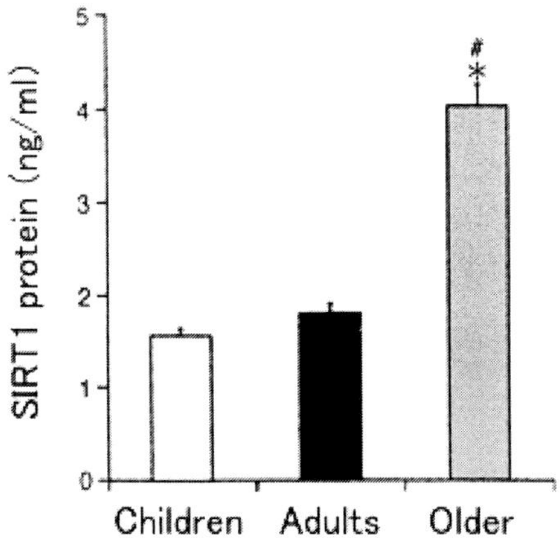

Fig. 4-18: Comparison of expression levels of SIRT1 protein among children (3~16 years old), adults (32~55) and older adults (56~92) (adapted from Fig. 2A of Killic et al. 2015, 6).

(5) There are many genes related to diabetes, hypertension,

a pulse and so on which have been described as important factors of the human lifespan. To put it more generally, since lifespan is the final result of the total life of an organism, there should be many genes indirectly related to the lifespan. For example, the first paper introduced above (Revelas et al. 2018, 24-34) cited a different paper which stated that the contribution of genes in the determination of the human lifespan is 20~30%. We may be able to say that about a quarter of all human genes are related to our lifespan.

Explanations for a hazard ratio for mortality or disease, a relative hazard ratio and Cox proportional hazard model etc.

In the main body of the text or in the titles of the figures or tables throughout this chapter, the words 'hazard ratio for mortality or disease' have been used many times (for example, Section 4-1, Tables 4-1 and 4-2). This "hazard" is the probability with which something occurs, and a hazard ratio is its relative probability taking that of the control status as 1.00 (Relative hazard regression model, http://www.amed.go.jp>content).

To obtain a specific hazard ratio, its simulation using a function of time is done. More generally, hazard ratios are said to be averages obtained by assuming that they are the same in a certain period. However, for example, when I read the studies from which Tables 4-1 and 4-2 are derived, references for specialists were included and I could not understand how to get the hazard ratios.

In the ordinates of Fig. 4-14, "Relative risk" is written. Since the paper states that a hazard ratio is taken as the risk, so a relative risk is the same as a hazard ratio. As for Fig. 4-7 for example, since the paper states that hazard ratios were calculated by assuming that they were the same at all points according to the "Cox proportional hazards regression", the used method seems to be the same. If a reader wishes to fully understand these methods, please refer to the books for specialists cited on Wikipedia or the paper on statistical methods cited in Yin et al. (2017, 1-13).

CHAPTER 5

THE SECRETS OF THE LONGEVITY OF CENTENARIANS

A centenarian usually means a person of 100 years old or older, and in some research means a person of ≧ 99 or 98 years old. A person ≧ 110 or 105 years old is often called a supercentenarian. In a report by the United Nations in 2015, the number of centenarians in the world was estimated to be 417,000 (https 138). Since the total population in the world was 6.9 billion according to another report by the United Nations in 2014, 6.0 people per 100,000 were centenarians on average. Supercentenarians ≧ 110 years old make up only about 1 person per 1,000 among centenarians (https 138), meaning a total of 400~500 people in the world. Also, people ≧ 115 years old are said to be very few, and the total number of them recorded in the whole of human history is estimated to be 62 (https 138).

5-1 An outline of centenarians

Fig. 5-1 shows recent numbers of **centenarians** (≧ 100 years old) per 100,000 population in many countries in the world. Japan is at the top with 48, last is India with 2, second last is China with 3, and the top number is nearly 20 times as many as the bottom. The difference in the ratios of centenarians among the countries is much larger than, or about 10 times as much as, that of the average lifespans.

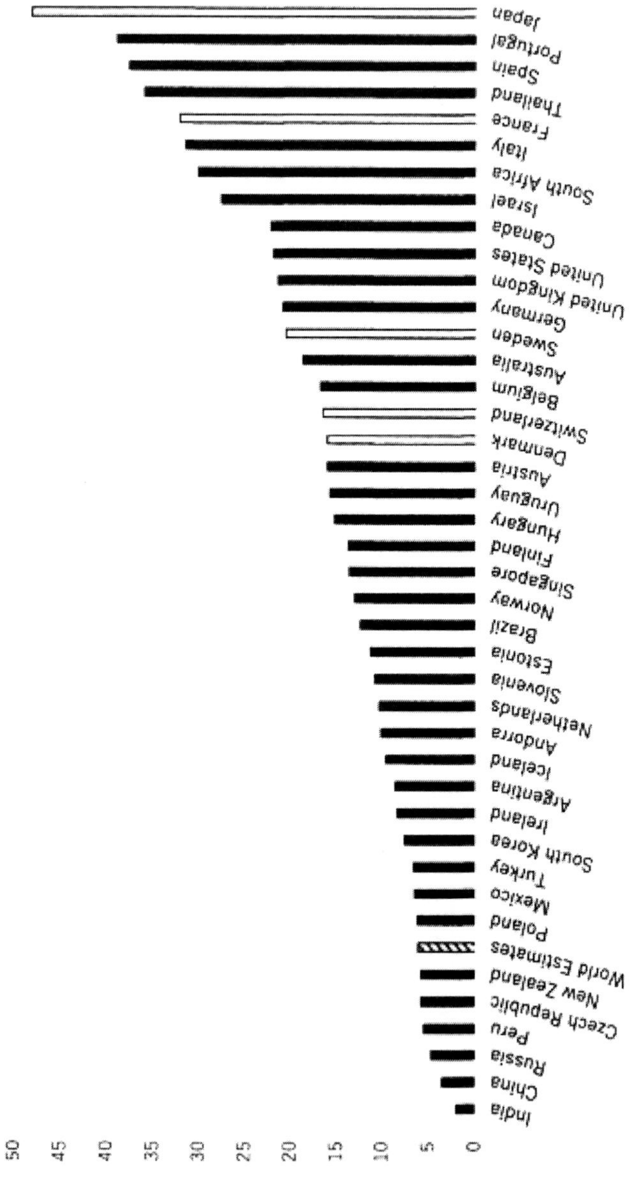

Fig. 5-1 The numbers of the centenarians per 100,000 population in major countries. White bars correspond to the members of 5-COOP, and the bar of slant lines shows the world average estimated by the United Nations (権藤 2018, 574).

The estimated average for all over the world is about 6 and is shown by the slanted bar. The five countries shown by white bars (Japan, France, Sweden, Switzerland, and Denmark) joined the cooperative study called 5-COOP (5 Country Oldest Old Project).

Fig. 5-2 shows the rates of the increase in the numbers of centenarians during the 10 years from 1996 to 2006 in these five countries. Comparing the rates, that in Japan is the highest among the five countries, and the average value for men and women together is close to 4. The total number of centenarians in the whole world was 23,000 in 1950, 110,000 in 1990, 209,000 in 2000 and 455,000 in 2009 according to estimations by the United Nations in 2010 (https 138). Since the estimated number in 2009 was 455,000 as stated above, the increase during the recent 60 years is about 20-fold, and that during the recent 9 year period is about 2-fold.

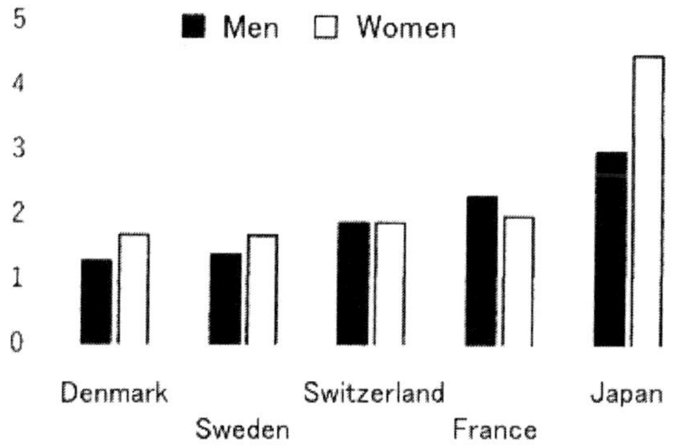

Fig. 5-2: The rates of increase in the number of centenarians in the 5-COOP countries between 1996~2006 (adapted from Fig. 3 of 権藤 2018, 574).

Next, let us see the numbers of centenarians etc. in Japan. **Fig. 5-3** shows such numbers and their ratios to the total population based on the national census in 2015.

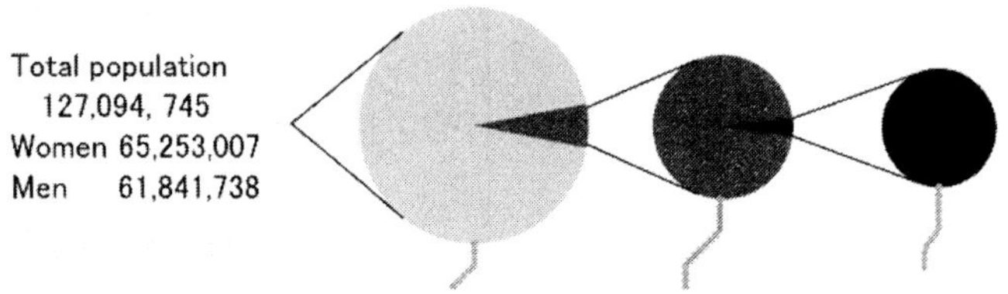

		Centenarian	Semi-super centenarian	Supercentenarian
	Total	61,763	3,916	146
	Women	53,380	3,524	137
	Men	8,383	392	9
Ratio in the population	Total	1/2,057	1/32,455	1/870,511
	Women	1/1,222	1/18,516	1/476,299
	Men	1/7,377	1/157,759	1/6,871,304

Fig. 5-3: The numbers and ratios of centenarians etc. based on the national census in 2015 (re-drawn from Fig. 1 of 新井・広瀬 2018, 579).

The numbers of centenarians, semi-supercentenarians (people ≧ 105 years old) and supercentenarians were about 62,000, about 4,000 and 146, respectively. In all of these, there were many more women than men. This is because the average lifespan in women is 6 years longer than in men. The number of supercentenarians was 0.23% (about 1/4,000) of that of centenarians, and their ratios to the total population (127 million) were about 1/870,000 and 1/2,000, respectively.

Fig. 5-4 shows the increase of supercentenarians since 1991, in which we see that the increase since 2010 is much.

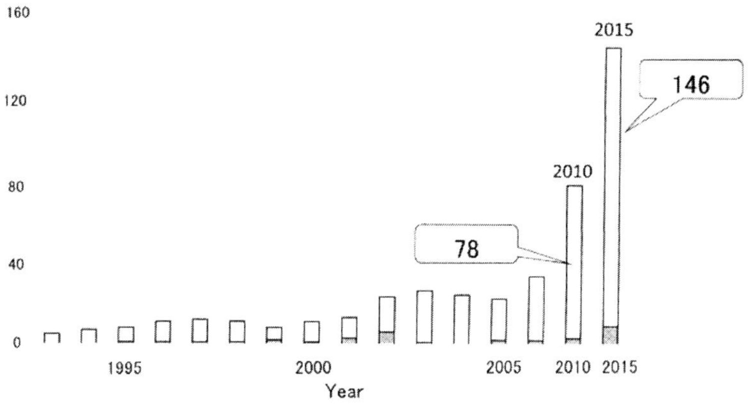

Fig. 5-4: The annual change in the numbers of supercentenarians (≧ 110 years old) in Japan. Shaded parts and white parts in the bars represent men and women, respectively (Fig. 2 of 新井・広瀬 2018, 579).

As for very old people such as centenarians, , their health statuses, independence of life, levels of dementia and so on are important. A worldwide analysis on these indices is not found, but let me describe such analyses on several countries or regions. In these analyses, The Barthel Index and MMSE (Mini-Mental State Examination) are often used. The **Barthel Index** (**Fig. 5-5**) is a test to survey to what extent one can do the basic activities required for a normal daily life（Activities of Daily Living, ADL)independently. Its full score is 100 points, but we can understand by looking at the sheet that even a full score does not necessarily ensure that

THE BARTHEL INDEX

Patient Name: ______________

Rater Name: ______________

Date: ______________

Activity	Score
FEEDING 0 = unable 5 = needs help cutting, spreading butter, etc., or requires modified diet 10 = independent	____
BATHING 0 = dependent 5 = independent (or in shower)	____
GROOMING 0 = needs to help with personal care 5 = independent face/hair/teeth/shaving (implements provided)	____
DRESSING 0 = dependent 5 = needs help but can do about half unaided 10 = independent (including buttons, zips, laces, etc.)	____
BOWELS 0 = incontinent (or needs to be given enemas) 5 = occasional accident 10 = continent	____
BLADDER 0 = incontinent, or catheterized and unable to manage alone 5 = occasional accident 10 = continent	____
TOILET USE 0 = dependent 5 = needs some help, but can do something alone 10 = independent (on and off, dressing, wiping)	____
TRANSFERS (BED TO CHAIR AND BACK) 0 = unable, no sitting balance 5 = major help (one or two people, physical), can sit 10 = minor help (verbal or physical) 15 = independent	____
MOBILITY (ON LEVEL SURFACES) 0 = immobile or < 50 yards 5 = wheelchair independent, including corners, > 50 yards 10 = walks with help of one person (verbal or physical) > 50 yards 15 = independent (but may use any aid; for example, stick) > 50 yards	____
STAIRS 0 = unable 5 = needs help (verbal, physical, carrying aid) 10 = independent	____
TOTAL (0–100):	____

Fig. 5-5: Barthel Index test sheet (from Fig. 2 of Armenteros-Yeguas et al. 2017, 4270).

the participant can live by themself. Most old people without any disability in their bodies should get the full score of 100 points. Also, since the Barthel Index lacks a mental activity test, its full score cannot assure normal mental activity, which needs a test like MMSE. **MMSE** evaluates mental memory, ability to understand words, calculation ability and ability to write or draw sentences or simple figures. Its full score is 30 points, and ≧ 24 points, less than 10 points and 10~19 points are judged as normal, serious or medium decline of intelligence (伊藤 et al. 2003, 2364).

5-2 Centenarian studies in Japan

General trends

First, we shall examine a paper surveying centenarians in Japan (excluding Okinawa) (Arai et al. 2017, 80-85). The introduction of the paper notes that Japan is adequate for a centenarian study because the data on birthdays of old people are certain due to the family registers since 1872. The first centenarian survey in Japan was the nationwide one in 1973 done by the Tokyo Metropolitan Institute of Gerontology. Based on its results, about 97% of centenarians were suffering from chronic diseases including hypertension and gastro-intestinal diseases, but only a few were at risk of cardiovascular diseases. Also, it was characteristic of centenarians that diabetes and arteriosclerosis in the carotid artery were rare.

More recently, a study on the centenarians of Tokyo (Tokyo Centenarian Study: TCS) was done from 2000~2002. It was published in 2006 and introduced in the above paper (Arai et al. 2017, 80-85). This study was done on 1,194 centenarians by mail; answers were obtained from 514 people, and 304 people among them were surveyed by visiting. Their ages were 100~108 years, the average was 101 years, and there were 65 men and 239 women. **Fig. 5-6** shows the Barthel indices and MMSE results during the period of 100~104 years old, which are classified by the ages at the point of the survey. As for the people who were 100~104 years old at the point of the survey (YC in the figure), Barthel indices and MMSE results were about 40 and 12 on average, respectively, and both were considerably bad. As for the supercentenarians (110 years or older at the point of the survey, SC), both scores were much higher than those of the 100~104 year olds. We can understand that very rare supercentenarians were especially excellent in body and mentality in the ages of 100~104 years.

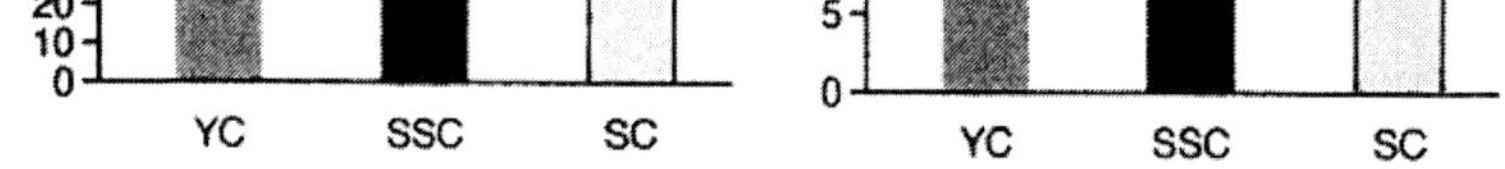

Fig. 5-6: Barthel indices (A) and MMSE results (B) of the centenarians in the period of 100~104 years old. YC, SSC and SC are the people who died at 100~104, 105~109 or ≧ 110 years old (adapted from Fig. 2 of Arai et al. 2017, 83).

Among all the centenarians, 18.5% of men and 5.9% of women got a full score (100 points) in the Barthel indices, and 24.6% of men and 13.4% of women got 80~99 points and were highly independent. The average Barthel Index result was 54.3 in men and 34.3 in women, with that of men being considerably higher. The ratio of the people without trouble in either sight or hearing was 33.3% in men and 22.0% in women, and so most of the people had trouble with either one or in both.

The average MMSE score was 16.1 in men and 11.5 in women, and that in men was higher, too. Based on Clinical Dementia Rating (CDR), 43.1% of male centenarians and 19.2% of female centenarians had no dementia, whereas 41.6% of men and 67.1% of women suffered from dementia in some degree.

To live up to 100 years old may be celebrated. However, the status of a centenarian is in fact considerably hard or severe based on the above data. Especially, female centenarians, who comprise most centenarians, cannot live by themselves and so their states are severe. Extension of a **healthy lifespan** is important, and not of simple longevity.

Centenarians in Okinawa

The subjects of the studies described above were residents in Japan excluding Okinawa (Honshu). Here, a study on the residents of Okinawa Island, where most of the residents in Okinawa prefecture live, is introduced (Wilcox et al. 2017, 75-79). Okinawa prefecture had been the best longevity prefecture in Japan until some time ago. However, the average lifespan of men in Okinawa has dropped below the average in Japan in recent years (30th in 2013) because of the changes in foods and lifestyles (westernization). The average lifespan of women of Okinawa is still long and ranks third in the Japanese prefectures. Also, the average life expectancy for people ≧75 years old is longer than the average in Japan in both men and women. This is likely to be due to the fact that those old people are continuing the lifestyles of their youth, and their diet is probably most important. Another paper (Robine et al. 2012, 660-71) states that the major reasons for the longevity of Okinawans are, on the one hand, that people do not eat rice because of its poor production on the island, and on the other hand the warm climate in which a winter season is almost non-existent.

The Okinawan Centenarian Study (OCS) was begun in 1975 and studied centenarians and old people in Okinawa (Wilcox et al. 2017, 75-79). There were fewer than 30 centenarians on Okinawa Island in 1975, but the number reached about 1,200 in 2014. Their number per 100,000 population is not certain, but probably about 100 and much more than the average in the whole of Japan, 48. This result may be partly because Okinawan centenarians are defined as ≧ 99 years old people, but the ratio of those ≧100 years old is probably more than the average in Japan too. These results are thought to reflect the fact that Okinawans have been the most long-living people in Japan.

As for the health statuses of Okinawans, their good cardiovascular state is said to be the most important factor. In more detail, hypertension, diabetes, obesity, high blood cholesterol and smoking, which are the risk factors for cardiovascular diseases, tend to be less frequent in Okinawans than in other groups. In the autopsies of centenarians after death, cardiovascular diseases are not found. **Table 5-1** shows valuable data on the mortalities of ≧85 year old people in a comparison of Okinawa and Honshu (Japan except Okinawa), and classifies them by death due to major diseases.

The all-cause mortality in Okinawa is considerably lower than that in Honshu: 84% in men and 83% in women. All of the disease-specific mortalities are also lower in Okinawa, especially in those by cancer, cardiovascular disease or hypertension. Old people in Okinawa are said to have a higher bone density and to have lower rates of dementia. The ratios of the people in Okinawa who can live independently are 80% at 92, 63% at 97, 40% at 99 and 25% at 102 years old, and so they are considerably fine until their mid- nineties.

Table 5-1: Comparison of the number of deaths of the people ≧ 85 years old between Okinawa and Honshu per 100,000 population (made from the data of Table 1 of Wilcox et al. 2017, 78).

Cause	All causes		Cancer		Heart disease	
M/W	Men	Women	Men	Women	Men	Women
Honshu	15,651	10,883	2,971	1,458	2,579	2,259
Okinawa	13,137	9,016	2,156	1,116	1,879	1,629
Cause	Cardiovascular disease		Hypertension		Diabetes	
M/W	Men	Women	Men	Women	Men	Women
Honshu	2,454	2,055	136	161	121	109
Okinawa	1,552	1,213	49	91	81	108

In this paper by Wilcox et al. (2017, 75-79), studies on genes were also done. The authors found that the FOXO3 (Fox O3) gene, which was shown to relate to longevity in several studies, is related to the longevity of Okinawans and residents in Hawaii of Japanese descent. In humans, there are about 50 kinds of FOX (Fork-head box) proteins and they are members of a group of transcription factors carrying a common structure. Among them, the O subclass is conserved from nematodes to mammals and involved in the lifespan and stress resistance. Four kinds of them are known in mammals (FOXO1, 3, 4, 6). Also, nonagenarians and centenarians in Okinawa were found to have a higher prevalence of anti-inflammatory type 2 HLA (human major histocompatibility antigen system 2) alleles, and a lower prevalence of a pro-inflammatory alleles of the same gene.

Based on the survey of family histories in Okinawan Centenarian Studies, male and female siblings of centenarians had a 5.43-fold and 2.58-fold likelihood of reaching 90 years old, respectively. Also, the genes of Okinawans in general have a close relation with those of East Asians, and Okinawans are distinct from the people of China and Honshu in Japan although somewhat related to them based on anthropological studies.

5-3 Studies on centenarians across the world

Centenarians in Portugal and their trends in meals

Portugal is a European country with an area about 1/4 of that of Japan and its population in 2013 was about 10.61 million or less than 1/10 of that in Japan. Therefore, it is a relatively small country. The average lifespan of the people in this country was 78.3 years for men, 84.5 years for women and 81.5 years on average in 2016. The rankings of their average lifespans in the world were 28th, 11th and 18th, respectively (WHO World Average Lifespan Ranking, 2018). Portugal is situated at 37~42°N, and the recent average temperature in the capital Lisbon was 17.2℃, which is close to that of Tokyo in Japan.

As for the centenarians in Portugal, survey results which mainly compared the contents of their meals with those of control people were published in 2018 (Pereira da Silva et al. 2018, 1-10). The surveys were done during 2012~2015. The subjects were 253 centenarians (ages 100.26±1.98 years old, 197 women and 56 men), and the control group comprised 268 people (67.51±3.25 years old, 164 women and 104 men). The control people were classified into low and high cardiovascular disease groups (LCR and HCR) based on certain criteria, and both were compared with the centenarians. Many of the centenarians lived in Lisbon or its suburbs, but the rest were scattered all over Portugal.

The main survey results relate to comparisons of meal contents and meal habits among the centenarians, LCR and HCR groups. There were 12 survey items: number of meals per day, amount per day and intake frequency of each of the 10 kinds of food (red meat, fish, eggs, sweets, dairy products, vegetables, legumes, fruits, oilseeds, and canned food).

Fig 5-7 shows the most important result, that is the difference in the frequency of red meat intake. The ratio of the people who ate red meat once or more per week was only 18% in centenarians, but 78% in the HCR group and 76% in the LCR group and so there was a big difference. 54% of the centenarians ate red meat scarcely, less than once per month. Meat containing much fat is probably worse for our bodies than red meat, however nothing about this is written in the paper. Probably, Portuguese people don't eat such meats.

As for the amount of meals, 60% of the centenarians ate a small amount, but 91% of the LCR and 89% of the HCR groups ate medium or large amounts. The frequency of the intake of fish or sweets is considerably lower in the centenarians than in the LCR and HCR groups.

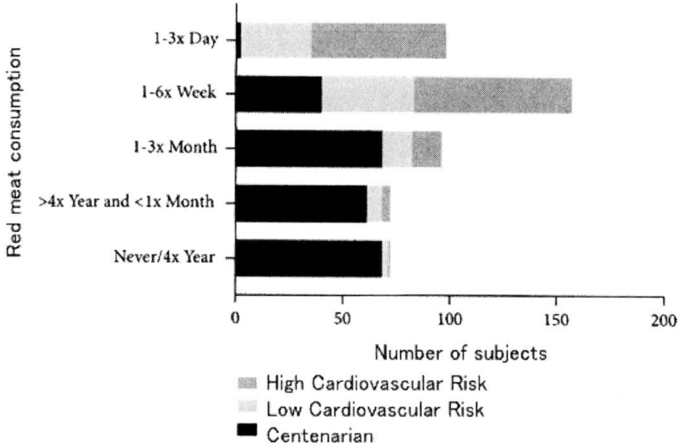

Fig. 5-7: Comparison of the numbers of subjects among centenarians, HCR and LCR groups classified by the frequency of red meat intake (adapted from Fig. 2 of Pereira da Silva et al. 2018, 6).

In contrast, the frequency of vegetable intake is much higher in the centenarians than in either control group, and most centenarians ate them once to three times a day. **The characteristics in the meals of the centenarians are that the meal amounts and the frequencies of consumption of red meat, fish or sweets are low, and that they eat much vegetables.**

Because of these differences, the average BMI index is 21.1 in centenarians, 28.5 in the LCR and 29.6 in the HCR group. The centenarians had a normal body weight, but people in both the LCR and HCR group were obese. This paper concludes that meals which contain small amounts of red meat or heme-iron may be the key for longevity. However, it also says that this kind of meal induces a decrease in the amount of muscles, or sarcopenia.

Surprising facts about the centenarians in China

As for the centenarians in China, the results of a survey of the largest scale in the world were published in 2017 (Zeng et al. 2017, 86-97). The survey began in 1998 and is called the Chinese Longitudinal Healthy Longevity Study or CLHLS. For this study, from the counties and cities in the 22 districts among the 31 provinces or 4 municipalities (Beijing, Tianjin, Shanghai and Chongqing), half of them were randomly selected, and ≧80 year old people including many centenarians and control people in these regions were the subjects. The population of all the target regions was about 1.15 billion, which comprised 85% of the total population in China, and therefore the study was done on a very big scale.

Table 5-2: Numbers of the people who participated in the seven interviews in China (modified from Table 1 of Zeng et al. 2017, 88).

Age	Number of living subjects			Number of dead subjects		
	Men	Women	Total	Men	Women	Total
35~64	7,023	4,183	11,206	4	2	6
65~79	10,610	9,525	20,135	828	610	1,438
80~89	12,860	12,853	25,713	2,954	2 ,325	5,279
90~99	9,806	13,401	23,207	4,383	5,283	9,666
≧100	3,401	13,181	**16,582**	2,159	7,694	**9,853**
Total	43,700	53,143	96,843	10,328	15,914	26,242

For the right columns, the ages are those at death (lifespans).

First, the subjects of the seven interviews for the study are shown in **Table 5-2**. These interviews were done not only with living people but also with the families of the people who had died earlier at an old age, and such results are shown on the right of the table.

The subjects included 16,582 living centenarians and the families of 9,853 people who had died at ≧100 years old. There are about four times more women than men both in the living and deceased centenarians columns (≧100 years old). As for the living people, those in their eighties and nonagenarians numbered 25,713 and 23, 207, respectively.

The ages of the living centenarians are shown in Table 5-3. For the ages 100~104 years old, the numbers of living people decrease as the age increases. The numbers of people 100~104, 105~109 or ≧110 years old are 11,257, 712 and 78, respectively.

Table 5-3: Age distribution of the centenarian subjects in the seven interviews (modified from Table 2 of Zeng et al. 2017, 88).

Age	Men	Women	Total
100	1,023	3,410	4,433
101	705	2,559	3,264
102	386	1,579	1,965
103	175	840	1,015
104	108	472	580
100~104	2,397	8,860	11,257
105~109	132	580	712
≧110	4	74	78
Total	2,533	9,514	12,047

The total number of the centenarians in this table is 12,047 and less than that of the living centenarians in Table 5-2 (16,582), for which the reason is not clear. The times of the surveys might be different, or the people with an unknown precise age might have been omitted from Table 5-3. If the total number of the living centenarians in the target regions was 16,582, the number per 100,000 population should have been 1.4 (for 1998~2014).

Table 5-4 shows the demographic and socioeconomic characteristics of the 3,413 centenarian subjects in 2008. Most of them had lost their spouses and were living with their families. The age of their first marriage was about 20 years old on average, and the average number of children was 3~6 for about 60% of them. It is surprising that the schooling years were zero for 86% of them. However, schooling days for these centenarians were between 1910~

Table 5-4: Demographic and socioeconomic characteristics of the centenarian subjects in 2008 (abstracted from Table 3 of Zeng et al. 2017, 89).

Items and classes		Ratio (%)	Items and classes		Ratio (%)
Marital status	Married	3.52	Number of schooling years	0	86.11
	Divorced	0.09		1~2	3.65
	Widowed	95.56		3~4	4.12
	Never	0.44		5~6	3.99
Living status	With family	88.98		7~9	1.41
	Alone	7.88		10~12	0.71
	In an institution	3.14		≧13	0.62
Age at their first marriage	≦14	4.53		Average	0.68
	15~19	45.71		Total	100.0
	20~24	38.25	Occupation before age 60	Professionals	1.76
	25~29	7.34		Admin. managers	0.59
	≧30	4.18		Clerks	6.36
	Average	20.04		Self-employed	1.44
Number of children	0	2.53		Agriculture, fishery	70.71
	1~2	19.24		Houseworkers	15.89
	3~4	30.89		Military	0.47
	5~6	28.16		Never worked	1.38
	7~9	15.71		Others	1.41
	≧10	3.47		Total	100.0

1930, and therefore schooling systems were probably not yet established. The overwhelming majority of occupations before age 60 were related to agriculture or fishery.

Table 5-5 shows health indicators of centenarians based on their reports. Life satisfaction was good in 2/3 of the subjects, but severe or mild disability in activities of daily living (ADL) were reported by about half of the subjects.

Table 5-5: Percentage distributions of self-reported indicators of health and life satisfaction in the Chinese centenarians in 2008

(abstracted from Table 4 of Zeng et al. 2017, 90).

Items	Health satisfaction			Life satisfaction		
	Good	Moderate	Bad	Good	Moderate	Bad
%	51.8	35.1	13.0	64.6	30.1	5.3
Item	Activities of daily living (ADL)					
	Active		Mild disability		Severe disability	
%	47.3		24.8		27.9	

The most important survey result in this paper may be the objective health indicators of the centenarians shown in **Table 5-6.** The Mini Mental State Examination (MMSE) results indicated that more than half of the subjects had a severe impairment. As for the ability to stand up from a chair or to pick up a book from the floor, the results were similar. About half of the subjects had little visual function, and about 1/3 of the subjects had satisfactory vision.

The most surprising result was the number of residual teeth: zero in 60% and ≦9 in 90% of subjects. The presence or number of false or artificial teeth was not reported, but most of the centenarians should likely face some difficulties in eating meals. Such kinds of detailed survey results are not found elsewhere. Although the status in other countries may be different, the above information should be valuable.

Table 5-6: Percentage distributions of the objective health indicators of the Chinese centenarians in 2008 (abstracted from Table 5 of Zeng et al. 2017).

Indicators and classes		%	Indicators and classes		%
MMSE	Maximum	11.6	Visual function	Can see and distinguish	31.4
	Normal	17.7		Can see	23.8
	Mild impairment	16.7		Can't see	41.0
	Severe impairment	54.0		Blind	3.8
Activity: standing up	Yes, without hands	33.9	Number of residual teeth	0	60.3
	Yes, using hands	44.7		1-3	17.2
	Unable	21.4		4-6	11.0
Activity: picking up a book	Yes, standing	29.9		7-9	4.0
	Yes, sitting	36.8		10-12	3.5
	Unable	33.4		13-15	1.2
Activity: turning around	Yes,≦10 steps	34.5		16-18	1.0
	Yes,＞10 steps	2.4		≧19	1.9
	Unable	63.0			

The author proposes similar surveys in Japan, and wishes to know the results. Also, the status of centenarians will be improved step by step both in China and Japan by the development of living states and medical treatments.

CHAPTER 6

STUDIES ON THE LIFESPANS OF VARIOUS PLANTS

In Chapter 2, several examples of the plants with extreme longevity were introduced. Here, the lifespans of various plants and individual studies of plant lifespans will be described. Many studies have been done also on plant lifespans and their life histories, and thereby we now understand the actual figures of plants and the factors determining plant lifespans to some extent. It is difficult to find extremely long-living plants (such as those shown in Table 2-1) and to estimate their lifespans. Also, for example, while the average lifespan of a tree is important, its examination is very laborious.

6-1 The lifespans of perennial grass

(1) An orchid has an average lifespan of several years: The first study to be stated (Hutchings et al. 2010, 867-878) is **a great model study to examine the ecology of a plant including its lifespan**. The material of this study is an orchid. There are many kinds of orchids, and they belong to the class Monocotyledonopsida, subclass Liliidae and order orchidales. This subclass Liliidae alaso includes plants of the order Liliales including lilies, irises and narcissuses, and orchids are perennial plants in general. In this study, *Ophrys sphegodes* or the spider orchid as a common name (**Fig. 6-1**), was the subject. This orchid is a plant on grassland over a limestone area, short-lived and rare. The plant grows from an underground tuber. It develops leaves in an arrangement like a rose flower in September-October, and blooms in April-May. It has a special feature that some of its plants are dormant, namely plant bodies over the ground do not appear. Some plants multiply asexually from tubers. An inflorescence of this plant rarely grows over 15cm. Its flowers can self-pollinate. In many of the years surveyed, only 6~18% of the fruits had seeds. The plants which do not bloom and therefore do not produce seeds die early, but those which produce seeds do not die until the end of August after spreading their seeds.

Fig. 6-1: A flower of spider orchid (*Ophrys sphegodes*) (from https 150).

In the wild, this orchid grows in the Central and Southern Europe, and this study was done using a 47ha piece of land within a national park. Also, since this orchid is a rare species, the study was done during a very long period of 32 years from 1975 to 2006 and so is quite precious. During this period, cattle and sheep were grazed in the area from 1975~79 and 1980~2006, respectively. Both dormant plants and plants which appeared over the ground were surveyed. The number of plants over the ground changed little during 1975~89, increased logarithmically thereafter, and increased 10 times during the total study period of 32 years. The ratio of dormant plants among the total plants was 28.7±2.7% during the total period, but this increased during 1997~2003. In 2003 the ratio was 67.7% and more than that of plants over the ground. Thus, the ratio of dormant plants varied greatly.

The rate of flowering among the over ground plants also varied: it was low and then 20~30% in the period of total plant number increase in the early 1990s, and became 71% at the time of the second increase in the last survey period. The relationships between the ratio of the flowering plants, average inflorescence length or the average number of leaves per plant and rainfall in March-April, and average temperature of each season or average daylight time were examined. The results were complex, and positive or negative relationships with some of the climate indicators were found.

Fig. 6-2 shows changes in the numbers of new born or dead plants during a year (a) and the differences between them (b), which are related to their lifespan. We see that the number of plants greatly increased after 10 years from 1980 when sheep grazing started, and that a decrease occurred frequently in the year next to an increase. Throughout the whole period, 52.0±13.1% of the newly born plants died within a year, and therefore it is thought that an increase and a decrease of the plant number occurred in turn. Based on these results, the living durations (lifespans) were exactly surveyed for the plants with accurate records of the first year of emergence and the last year spent above-ground, and plotted as shown in **Fig. 6-3**. By this result, the longest lifespan among those of the examined plants was 26 years, the half-life (to be explained later) was 2.25 years, and therefore the average lifespan is estimated to be around 4 years.

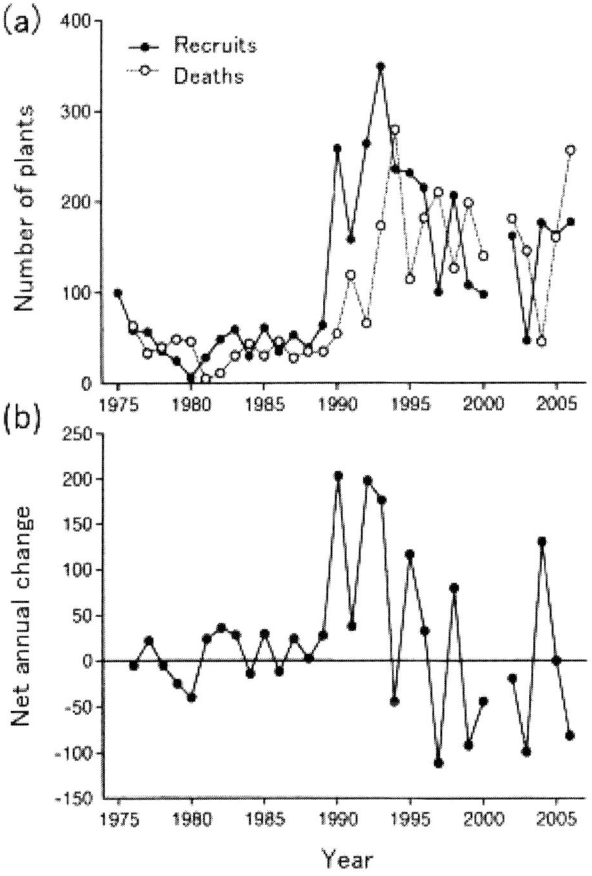

Fig. 6-2: Changes in the numbers of new born or dead plants during a year (a) and the differences between them (b) (adapted from Fig. 5(a), (b) of Hutchings 2010, 873).

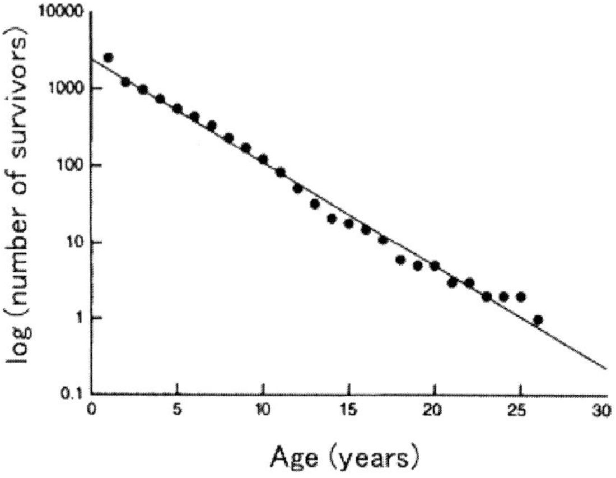

Fig. 6-3: Age-specific numbers of spider orchid (adapted from Fig.4(b) of Hutchings 2010, 873).

(2) *Plantago lanceolata*: The second paper described here concerns *Plantago lanceolata* (Shefferson and Roach 2013, 577-584). This is the plant seen in **Fig.6-4**; its origin is European and it is seen also in Japan as a naturalized plant. It is a member of plantains genus which are representative weeds, and belongs to the class Dicotyledonopsida, order Plantaginales and family Plantaginaceae (八杉龍一 et al. 1996, 1557). Six species of this family are shown in an illustrated book on grass (佐竹義輔 et al. 1985, PL.III-115, 116). In Japan, this plantain is larger than *Plantago asiatica* (the most common plantain), is 20~70cm high, and blooms dark brown flowers in April-August. Their color is different from that of *P. asiatica*.

Fig. 6-4: ***Plantago lanceolata*** (https 152).

In this study, a total of more than 8,000 plants located in four areas in the State of Virginia (USA) were included. They were followed for more than 10 years, and therefore the study is valuable. The average number of leaves per plant was around 20. One of the special features of this study was that the prehistory of a dead plant was followed. Since the detailed results are somewhat difficult to understand, only the conclusions are described here. They are that the numbers of leaves and inflorescences decrease in the three years before dying, irrespective of the ages of the plants. These signs demonstrate that physiological ageing including such decreases takes place, and these are thought to be the causes of death. The authors state that these conclusions are inconsistent with the general hypothesis that plants including trees continue to grow and become larger with age. Therefore, they claim that it is necessary to decide whether their case is special or there are many kinds of cases. By the way, the causes leading to the death of plants were not studied. The average lifespan of *P. lanceolata* is likely to be several years.

(3) Grass living for more than 300 years: The third study introduced here on grass is on a small mountain herb with a very long lifespan (Garcia et al. 2011, 1424-1430). This plant (*Borderea pyrenaica*) belongs to the class Monocotyledonopsida, order Liliales and family Dioscoreaceae, and is believed to grow only on the heights higher than 1,800m in the Pyrenees bordering France and Spain. This species probably does not grow in Japan. There are three reasons for which this herb was selected as the subject: its very long lifespan, that it is not a colony plant, and that the age of an individual plant can be estimated exactly since a distinct scar of the annual stem is left on the tuber every year after the stem dies in September. The last characteristic is quite unique and probably rare. Also, there are males and females in this species, or it is dioecious in other words, and the authors distinguished males and females in this study. This also seems to be rather a unique feature. **Fig. 6-5** shows male plants growing among stones, and some have plural inflorescences. A 305 year old plant of this species had been found by a previous study, and this is likely to have one of the longest lifespans among herbs (Garcia and Antor 1995, 59-67).

As for this herb, the growth above the ground and flowering begin almost at the same time in June, fruits ripe in July and seeds are spread in September. Since it is dioecious, it has male and female flowers, and pollination is carried out by flies, ants, ladybugs and so on.

Fig. 6-5: Male plants of *Borderea pyrenaica* (http 155).

Actual studies were done on the plant populations in two valleys, Pineta and Ordesa. Pineta is a steep slope with a thick layer of stones at an altitude of 2,000m, and several hundreds of the subject plants grow per m^2. Ordesa is a flatter area with fewer stones at an altitude of 2,100m, and less than a hundred subjects grow per m^2. Based on the data of total area of leaves on a plant in the Ordesa area, *B. pyrenaica* plants grow until about 50 years old, thereafter the total area changes little and the longest lifespan of a live plant was 260 years. **Fig. 6-6** shows the relationship between the ages and the survival probabilities of the plants in Ordesa (the method to obtain these data is described in the paper quite concisely and the author was unsure of its exact nature).

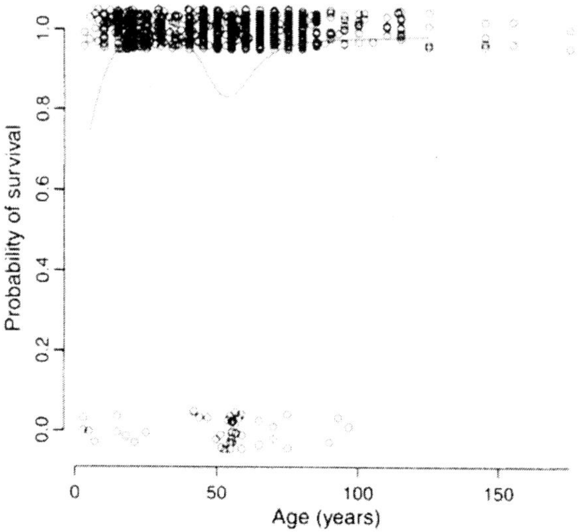

Fig. 6-6: Survival probabilities of *B. pyrenaica* over age in the Ordesa population plotted by small circles and the line representing the averages (Fig. 3 of Garcia et al. 2011, 1428).

Based on this result, the survival rate decreased to around 0.9 after 50 years old, but later it was close to 1.0, i.e., the rate did not decrease. Furthermore, flowering probability increased with age until 250 years old both in male and female plants. Therefore, the paper concluded that ageing was not detected in this very long-lived plant. Also, the paper guesses that little ageing will occur in long-lived plants in general. These results are quite interesting. However, since this plant is not immortal, why and when it dies remain unsolved. Anyway, the most important point related to *B. pyrenaica* is that **a non-colony herb can live for more than 300 years**. This is quite surprising to us.

6-2 The lifespan of a tree

The lifespans of various trees on Yakushima Island

As for the trees in Japan, valuable studies on the lifespans and related measures of 14 kinds of trees on Yakushima Island were reported (Aiba and Kohyama 1996, 207-218). Yakushima Island is an island which is situated to the south of Kyushu and at 30°N. It is warm and rains much there, and the island is covered with forests with features of a southern temperate zone. The studies reported in the paper are based on surveys in 1983 and 1993 of the trees which were located in either of the two areas of 2,000~2,500m^2 and at altitudes of 500~700m.

Table 6-1 was made by abstracting two tables from the paper, and it shows the names, families, half-lives etc. of the trees in one of the survey areas (Koyouji district). Most people probably do not know the names of these trees. Three of the species names are "japonica", and those of two others (sasanqua and tashiroi) are derived from the Japanese language, which is related to the fact that this island is located in Japan.

As for classification, only *Podocarpus nagi* is a gymnosperm, and all the others belong to phylum Anthophyta and class Dicotylenodopsida. All the trees are broad-leaved, only *Eurya japonica* is deciduous and all the others are evergreen. All the trees are classified by their heights over the ground into three groups (canopy, subcanopy and understory).

Table 6-1 The names and the indicators of the 14 kinds of trees examined in Yakushima Island.

Size category		Family	Maximum height	Mortality per year	Half life (year)
Canopy (high)	*Distylium racemosum*	Hamamelidaceae	20m	0.00762	131
	Listea acuminata	Lauraceae	15m	0.0201	49.8
	Podocarpus nagi	Podocarpaceae	20m	0.0221	45.2
	Neolitcea aciculata	Lauraceae	10m	0.0189	52.9
	Symplocos prunifolia	Symplocaceae	10m	0.0511	19.6
Subcanopy (medium)	*Camellia sasanqua*	Theaceae	2~6m	0.00499	200
	Symplocos tanakae	Symploaceae	3m	0.0327	30.6
	Camellia japonica	Theaceae	5~6m	0.00539	185.5
	Illicium anisatum	Illiciaceae	2~5m	0.0175	57.1
	Cleyera japonica	Theaceae	10m	0.0112	89.3
	Myrsine seguinii	Myrcinaceae	Shrub	0.00797	125
	Symplocos glauca	Symplocaceae	Medium	0.0430	23.3
Understorey (low)	*Eurya japonica*	Theaceae	Shrub	0.0198	50.5
	Rhododendron tashiroi	Eriaceae	Shrub	0.0300	33.3

Abstracted and combined from Table 1 and 4 of Aiba and Kohyama 1996, 207-218.

The mortality in the table was calculated from the ratio of trees which died during the ten years among all the surveyed trees of the same species, and is accurate. From this mortality per year, the half-life can be calculated as the reciprocal number. Half-life is defined as described here, and it means that 1/2 of the plants, which existed at the start, die in about 70% (exactly ln (2) = 0.693) of the time indicated by the half-life if the population is assumed to die randomly (Marba et al. 2007, 207-218). Based on my examination of the assumed examples, **the half-life is also the period in which about 1/3 (35%) of the members remain or about 2/3 (65%) of the members die**. The relationship between the half-life and the average lifespan is not simple. If the average age of the starting population is zero, the half-life and the average lifespan are close, and therefore the half-life is thought to be the minimal value of the estimated average lifespan. In general, half-life < average lifespan < half-life x 2, and **in most cases the average lifespan is estimated to be around 1.5 times the half-life**. To exactly measure the average lifespan of a kind of tree, the only method available may be to examine the ages of all the dead trees (lifespans) of the kind in the area and to obtain an average for them. This is thought to be probably difficult in general for various reasons, for example since it takes a long time. Therefore, data on average tree lifespans are rarely found. Even half-life data are precious.

As for the half-lives in the table, the shortest (about 20 years) and the longest (200 years) vary 10-fold. The simple average of the 14 half-lives is 66 years. The total number of the trees surveyed in 1993 was 1,287, and the average number per species was 91. It is possible that the height and the trunk size are related to the lifespan in the trees as a whole as will be stated later, however such a relation is not found for the 14 trees described here.

In **Fig. 6-7**, the plots show the trunk diameters at breast height or at 1.3m from the ground (d. b. h.) and the maximum heights of the 14 kinds of trees surveyed in Koyouji district in 1993.

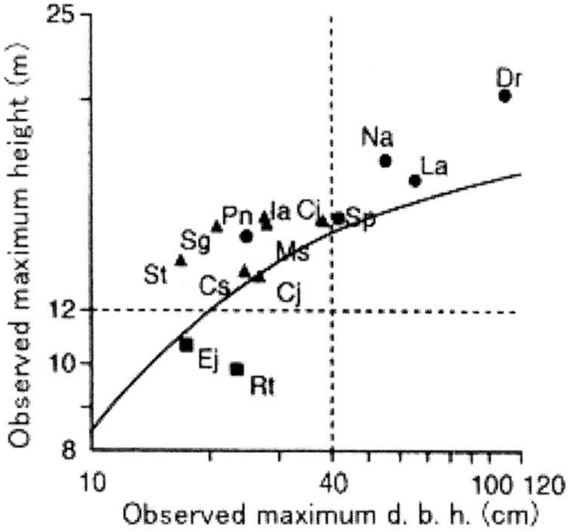

Fig. 6-7: The relationship between the maximum trunk diameters (d. b. h.) and the maximum heights of the 14 kinds of trees on Yakushima Island. The initialisms such as Dr, La etc. represent the tree names shown in Table 6-1 (adapted from Fig. 1(a) of Aiba and Kohyama 1996, 209).

The maximum value of the trunk diameters was about 120cm and the maximum height of the trees was about 22m, with both of these attributes belonging to *D. racemosum* at the top of the table. We can see that the maximum trunk diameter and the maximum height are related to each other in the 14 kinds of trees as a whole. These are likely to be the general features related to the lifespan or tree size for typical Japanese forests. The rate at which new trees of a particular kind appear, the data for the other district, and the relationship between the trunk diameter and the growth rate (amongst other things) are also described in the paper, but they are not introduced here. In this paper, the Japanese cedar which is typical in Japan was not described, and the reason is not clear. Perhaps no Japanese cedar trees can be found in the surveyed districts.

Thuja in Canada

The life history of *Thuja occidentalis* (**Fig. 6-8**), a gymnosperm conifer belonging to the order Taxodiales and family Cupressaceae, was studied by Kelly and Larson (1997, 467-478).

Fig. 6-8: ***Thuja occidentalis*** (https 159).

It is a tall evergreen tree, usually grows to 15m high (reaching up to 38m high at its maximum) and a trunk diameter of 0.9m. Also, it has the longest lifespan record of 1,650 years. It originally grew in areas around the Great Lakes in the northeast USA, New England and neighboring Canada, and it was introduced into Europe as the first tree of American origin. In Japan, there are botanical gardens where this tree can be seen (https 159; https 162).

This study was done in the forests located on steep slopes at the edge of the water near Niagara Falls, a famous tourist spot. The density of the subject trees in this area was 1,003/ha (10,000 m^2), namely about 1/10 m^2 on average. The materials used to measure its age were collected from the trunks of *T. occidentalis* near the root, and the ages were estimated based on the annual rings. The birth periods of the trees were calculated from their ages, and the numbers of trees living at each period were estimated and plotted as shown in **Fig. 6-9**.

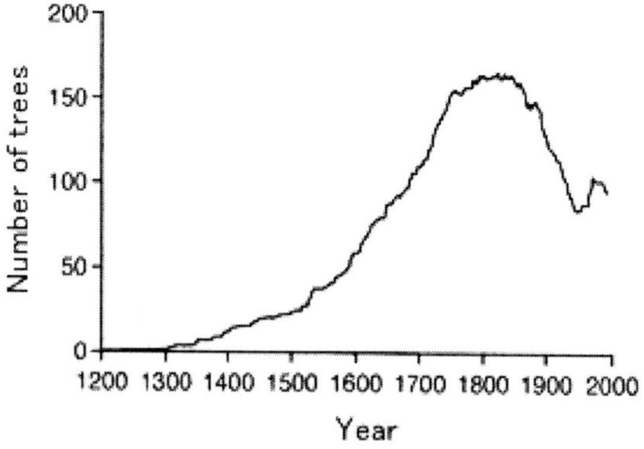

Fig. 6-9: The estimated numbers of *T. occidentalis* trees living at each period (adapted from Fig. 3 of Kelly and Larson 1997, 472).

We can see that the oldest tree among the examined trees is about 700 years old. The average age of these trees may be around 200 years.

The average lifespans of various trees

Table 6-2: The average lifespans or the half-lives of various trees.

Species	Order/Family	Survey area
Aralia elata	Apiales/Araliaceae	Japan
Camelia japonica	Theales/Theaceae	Yakushima, Japan
Daphne odora	Myrtales/Thymelaeaceae	Japan
Diospyros kaki	Ebenales/Ebenaceae	Japan
Amygdalus persica	Rosales/Rosaceae	Japan
Castanea crenata	Fagales/Fagaceae	Japan
Parashorea macrophyla	Theales/Dipterocarpaceae	Sarawak in Malaysia
Neolistea aciculata	Laurales/Lauraceae	Yakushima, Japan
Betula platyphylla	Fagales/Betulaceae	Japan
Cornus controversa	Cornales/Cornaceae	Japan
Populus tremuloides	Salicales/Salicaceae	Japan
Dryobalanops lanceolata	Theales/Dipterocarpaceae	Sarawak in Malaysia
Distylium racemosum	Hamamelidales/Hamamelidaceae	Yakushima, Japan
Aesculus turbinata	Sapindales/Hipocastanaceae	Japan
Camellia sasanqua	Theales/Theaceae	Yakushima, Japan
Thuja occidentalis	Taxodiales/Cupressaceae	Canada
Fagus crenata	Fasales/Fagaceae	Europe
Quercus crispula	Fasales/Fagaceae	Europe
Castanopsis sieboldii	Fasales/Fagaceae	Japan
Picea sp.	Taxodiales/Pinaceae	Europe
Abies sp.	Taxodiales/Pinaceae	Europe

All the exact numbers represent the half-lives and the others for the average lifespans, and those with* are approximate data without solid evidence.

Leaf	Height	Av. lifespan or half-life (years)	Ref.
Broad, deciduous	Low (2~4m)	~10*	2)
Broad, evergreen	High (5~6m)	186	1)
Broad, evergreen	Shrub	20~30*	2)
Broad, deciduous	High	~50*	2)
Broad, deciduous	Med-high	~50*	2)
Broad, deciduous	High	~50*	2)
Broad, evergreen	High	50	3)
Broad, evergreen	High (10m)	52.9	1)
Broad, deciduous	High	~70*	2)
Broad, deciduous	High	~80*	2)
Broad, deciduous	High	70~100*	2)
Broad, evergreen	High	105	3)
Broad, evergreen	High (20m)	131	1)
Broad, deciduous	High	150~200*	2)
Broad, evergreen	2~6m	200	1)
Conifer, evergreen	High (15m)	~200	5)
Broad, deciduous	High	230~260	4)
Broad, deciduous	High	270~300	2)
Broad, evergreen	High	~300*	2)
Conifer, evergreen	High	300~350	4)
Conifer, evergreen	High	359~460	4)

1)Table 6-1; 2) http162; 3) Ashton and Hall 1992, 459-481; 4) https 164; 5) Kelly and Larson 1997, 467-478.

Table 6-2 shows average lifespans or half-lives of various trees. I have not found an exactly measured average lifespan of a tree, and although the average lifespans shown in the table are approximate figures without solid evidence, they may be informative to some extent. The half-lives of the 14 kinds of trees were exactly measured on Yakushima Island as shown in Table 6-1, and four of them are listed again in Table 6-2. A half-life is an estimated minimum average lifespan as described earlier, and the latter is likely to be near 1.5 times the half-life in many cases. An average lifespan is the most desirable value, but the situation of a tree's lifespan is different from that of a human lifespan for which accurate records are available, and the measurement of the lifespan of a long-lived tree is especially difficult.

In Table 6-2, the lifespans of 21 kinds of trees are shown: there are 3 **conifers** (all evergreen), 8 **evergreen broad-leaved trees** and 10 **deciduous broad-leaved trees**. The estimated shortest average lifespan is about 10 years for *Aralia elata* (fatsia) and the longest is over 400 years for *Abies* (white fir). The surveyed areas range from a tropical zone to a northern part of the temperate zone and include Japan, North America and Malaysia. Most trees are taller than 10m, and four are marked as low or medium in terms of height. **All the long-lived trees are tall** (marked 'high') and we see that all three conifers listed here are long-lived.

Reliable data of the average lifespan or half-life of the Japanese cedar, which is abundant in Japan and can live for more than 2,000 years, is not available. Most of the Japanese cedar trees in Japan are artificially grown and their lifespans may be mostly below 100 years, and the average lifespan of natural trees may be 300~500 years. The mean of the average lifespans of the trees listed in Table 6-2 is likely to be 100~200 years. Since the average lifespan of a tree can vary greatly depending on the environmental conditions such as the temperature, the geological features and so on, measurement of an average lifespan across the whole world would be quite difficult.

Fig. 6-10: A beech tree (https 165).

Fig. 6-10 shows a beech tree (*Fagus crenata*), a representative broad-leaved, deciduous tree in Japan.

As for the relationship between the average lifespan and the longest lifespan of a tree, 200 years vs 1,653 years (about 1/8) in *Thuja occidentalis* and 300 years vs 9,550 years in spruce or *Picea* (Table 6-2 and 2-1, about 1/30) are good examples.

6-3 Why are trees long-lived?

The answer to the question why trees can live for up to several thousand years and differ from other organisms is not simple. The answer will be given in the following several sections.

1) First, a basic factor for tree longevity is that most parts of a tree are made of the physically strong **xylem** and therefore a tree can support the large body resulting from long growth. In fact, in a large tree that is several hundred years old, most cells inside the tree are dead and it becomes hollow in many cases, but it can still live as a tree. The reasons for this feature are that the structure of a plant is much simpler than that of an animal and that it does not require integration of the whole body nor movement.

2) Even a very old tree needs enough photosynthesis to continue living as a tree, and so it needs many leaves and a **vascular bundle system** such as a root and a vessel, which sucks and provides nutrients. The lifespan of a leaf is around a year in most cases and therefore a tree needs to make leaves every year. **To maintain and regenerate such leaves, vascular bundles, roots, active cell divisions and growth are required, and that this is possible is an important factor for tree longevity.** As for a plant in general, a **meristem** at a stem top, a leaf axil meristem at the root of a leaf and a meristem at a root end exist, and they are maintained through the growth period (**Fig. 6-11**). A meristem at a root end develops a root, a meristem at

a stem top develops a leaf axil meristem and a leaf axil meristem develops stems, branches, flowers and new leaf axil meristems. In trees, leaf axil meristems develop up to several thousand branches step by step (Burian et a l. 2016, 1385-1398; 八杉 et al. 1996, 1263).

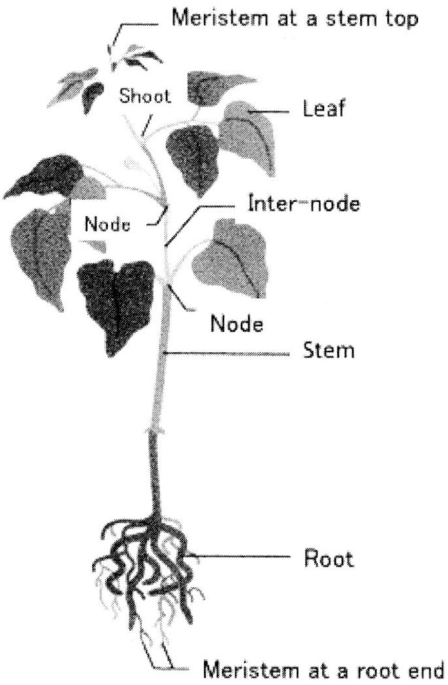

Fig. 6-11: A model structure of a plant. A leaf axil meristem exists at the root of each leaf, and is not indicated in the figure (adapted from the figure in Alberts et al. 2010, 1404).

3) A **leaf axil meristem** can develop flowers and fruits even in trees that are several hundred or thousand years old, and this maintenance of reproductive activity is a large difference from the situation in animals. In most animals,

reproductive activity is lost as the animals become old to some extent, and this is thought to be the reason that an animal lifespan seems to be genetically determined or programmed. In contrast, even old trees can help maintenance and development of the species, which is thought to be the evolutionary reason that the lifespan of a tree is not so limited.

4) As stated above, various meristems participate in important functions. Therefore, if division numbers of the meristems increase logarithmically with the age of a tree, many mutations will occur in the genes, they will lose their normal functions, and thus development of tissues and flowers and meristem functions will be lost (genetic ageing). The paper cited above (Burian et al. 2016, 1385-1394) is important for its analysis of this issue. The study in the paper was done by eliminating the stem cells in the meristem and analyzing the cell lineages in *Arabidopsis thaliana* and tomatoes. Based on the result, the precursor cells of a leaf axil meristem in an early stage of growth remain in a state without cell division. Also, while the other cells divide many times and multiply logarithmically, the precursor cells of a leaf axil meristem divide only 7~9 times until they become a new leaf axil meristem; in other words the division numbers increase only linearly. This result was obtained with the herbs *A. thaliana* and tomato, however it was thought to be applicable also to trees. Therefore, even if formation of new branches occurs 10 times uniformly and the branches multiply to 2^{10} or about 1,000, a leaf axil meristem is expected to divide only several ten times and the accumulation of mutations is expected to be at a low level. **This study probably represents the most fundamental**

reason for the longevity of a tree.

5) The reasons for the death of these trees are thought to be external factors such as strong winds, accumulated snow, infection of a pathogen and so on. Then, what are the reasons for the death of an annual herb within a year, and for the death of the aboveground part of a perennial herb in winter and the death of its entire body in several years? The differences among an annual herb, a biennial herb and a perennial herb may be genetically determined or programmed. Is the longest lifespan of a tree programmed in the gene, too, then? This is a very difficult question to answer; there are many hypotheses and the real answer is thought to be completely unknown. The mechanisms for the determination of the lifespans of herbs are mostly unknown, too. Although it is said that there are no fundamental differences between herbs and trees, important differences have been found in their genes (as described in a later section).

6) If the lifespan of a tree is greatly influenced by external factors such as falling down due to a strong wind, the density or specific gravity of a tree, which is a factor to determine the strength of a tree, may possibly be an important factor for its lifespan. Therefore, the specific gravities of various trees were surveyed. In the results, the specific gravities varied from about 0.2 to over 1.0: those of Japanese cedar, American cedar and spruce which are long-lived conifers are relatively low, and that of a chestnut tree (with a lifespan of about 50 years) is high. Thus, it is likely that there is no significant relationship between the lifespan and specific gravity of a tree. By the way, it is interesting that rosewood and ebony which are materials

for high-class furnitures have very high specific gravities (around 1.0), and in contrast paulownia which is used for the material of high-class drawers is very low, measuring at about 0.2 (https 168).

The secrets of the longevity of a conifer

As shown in Table 2-1, many **conifers** such as the spruce, bristlecone pine, Japanese cedar and cypress are especially long-lived. It is thought that there are two reasons for this. The first reason is related to the difference in the **lignin**, a component included in the timber. Timbers are made by increasing the physical strength of fibrous cell walls by the binding of lignin. Lignins are complex molecules with a high molecular weight, and are formed by polymerization of many C_6-C_3 (hydroxyl-phenyl propane) units (今堀・山川 2007, 1429). There are several molecular species of lignin which differ in their structures, and the lignin molecular species are different among conifers in Gymnosperms, Dicotyledonopsida and Monocotylenodopsida in Angiosperms. These lignins can be degraded by various decaying fungi, and only a few of them degrade conifer lignin and therefore conifers rich in lignins don't easily decay.

The second reason is thought to be that conifers are resistant to tree-biting worms because they secrete resins like pine resin. In contrast, there are few broad-leaved trees which secrete a resin (鈴木 2002, 161).

The average lifespan and the longest lifespan of a tree

If there is a tree with an average lifespan of 1,000 years, how long can its longest lifespan be? As described before, when the time of about 70%

(0.693) of a half-life has past, the survival rate should be about 50%. Therefore, if the average lifespan is 1.5 times a half-life, the half–life of the tree is about 700 years, the survival rate will be 1/2 after 700 years x 70% or about 500 years. Therefore, the survival rate after 500 x 10 or 5,000 years will be $(1/2)^{10}$ =0.00098 (about 1/1,000). This means that 1/1,000 of trees will remain alive after 5,000 years. Based on these results, the longest lifespan of a bristlecone pine of 5,000 years should be quite possible if its average lifespan is 1,000 years. This discussion is based on the assumption that the lifespan of a long-lived tree is not genetically programmed and it dies randomly by an external factor, which is probably true. This discussion cannot be applicable to animals whose lifespans are considered to be genetically programmed.

6-4 The lifespans of leaves and seeds

Both leaf lifespans and seed lifespans are different from those of whole plant bodies. To what extent are these lifespans understood? To my surprise, both have been studied considerably well. Leaf lifespans, for instance, are easy to study since they are much shorter than the lifespans of whole trees. In general, the study of a leaf lifespan seems to be extensive since it is deeply related to the physiological functions of a plant such as photosynthetic activity. As for a seed lifespan, one of the motivations for its study may be that the seed storage is important in agriculture.

Leaf lifespans

How long are leaf lifespans? Based on a review (及川 et al. 2013, 11-17), the shortest is 4 days, attributed to the marine plant *Halophia ovalis*; the second longest is 15 years, that of the red pine (*Pinus aristate*); and the longest is 45 years for *Pinus longaeva*. The ratio of the longest lifespan compared to the shortest is more than 1,000 times, and therefore the difference among the species is huge. As for the difference among the plant groups, a valuable graph is shown in the same review (**Fig. 6-12**). The thick lines in the boxes represent the median values close to the averages. The under and upper sides of a box represent the values larger by a quarter from the lowest value or smaller by a quarter from the highest value, and a half of all the data is within a box. The horizontal lines over or below a box represent values 1% lower from the highest or higher from the lowest, and 98% of all the data should be included between them.

Based on this graph, the shortest of the median leaf lifespans is about 2 months in water plants. The following order from short to long is **deciduous grass** (~2.5 months), deciduous shrubs (~3 months), **deciduous trees** (~6 months), **evergreen shrubs** (~1.5 years), and **evergreen trees** (~2 years). Although the median or average leaf lifespan of evergreen trees is about 2 years as above, leaf lifespans of specific species include 4~6 years for spruce, 5~7 years for fir and 6~8 years for yew (Flindt, 2007, 135).

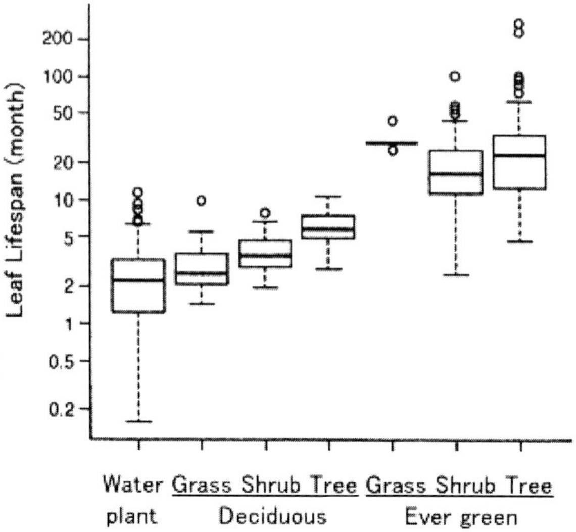

Fig. 6-12 Differences in leaf lifespans among the plant groups (Fig. 2 of 及川 et al. 2013, 12).

As shown above, the ratio of the longest average / the shortest average for a group differs more than 10-fold. In deciduous plants, a leaf lifespan should be less than a year even at its longest, and it is likely to be about 2 years in evergreen trees. Among evergreen trees, the leaf lifespan of Gymnosperms (conifers) is longer than that of Angiosperms, and the leaf lifespan in some evergreen trees is said to be less than a year. In this particular study, the number of plants surveyed included 203 evergreen trees (highest) and just five types of evergreen grass (least). Evergreen grass is rare, and the only one I can remember is strawberry geranium. Fig. 6-12 was made by the authors of the review (及川 et al. 2013, 11-17) and was based on the database used for a comprehensive study by about 40 authors (Wright et al. 2004, 821-827).

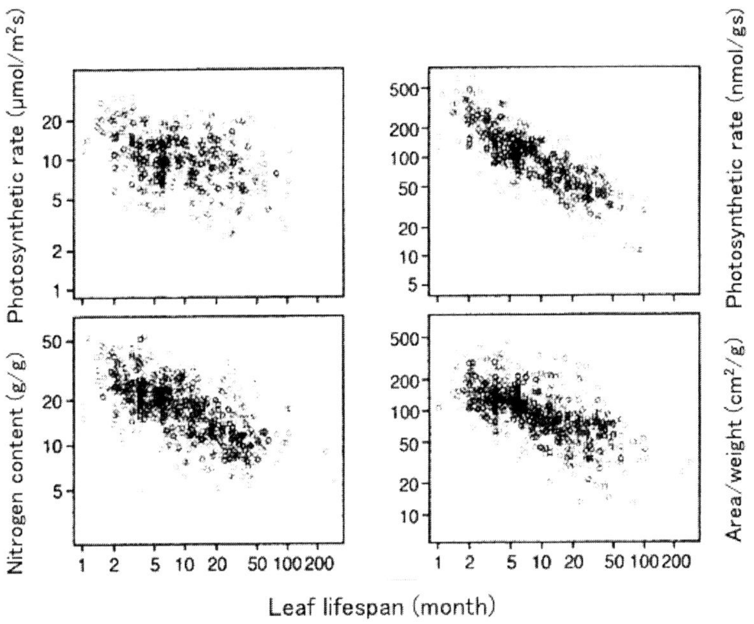

Fig. 6-13: Bilogarithmic relationships between leaf lifespan and each of the four kinds of values on the ordinates (adapted from Fig. 3 of 及川 et al. 2013, 14).

Related to the comparison of leaf lifespans, factors other than whether the plant was evergreen, deciduous, grass or a tree, which are all highly related to the leaf lifespan, were also examined. The main result of this examination is **Fig. 6-13**, which was shown in the same Japanese review (及川 et al. 2013, 11-17). The graphs in the figure are bi-logarithmic plots of the leaf lifespan on the abscissa and each of the four kinds of values on the ordinate (SLA=area/g of leaves). Based on the graphs, we can see that the species with a smaller value for the nitrogen content, the photosynthetic rate or the leaf area per weight have a tendency to live longer. It is likely that if the nitrogen content is low, the photosynthetic activity will also be low, and the plant stops dying of its leaves until the total photosynthetic products increase to a certain limit. A hypothesis is known which proposes that a leaf lifespan is set so as to maximize the acquisition of carbon in the whole plant.

Then, **why and how are there evergreen trees and deciduous trees?** For example, in the temperate zone where Japan is located, the photosynthetic activity of a plant is generally low in winter because sunlight is weak and the temperature is low. When the ages of leaves advance, the photosynthetic activity further decreases. As for the trees in which consumption of energies for leaf maintenance becomes of little value, to shed leaves in autumn and to make new leaves in spring are more economical than to maintain leaves over winter. It is thought that these are the reasons why trees shed leaves. Namely, the choice by a tree between evergreen leaves and shedding leaves is determined mainly based on its photosynthetic activity, resistance to the cold, and the climate.

There may be some relationship between the lifespan of a whole plant and those of its leaves, but the details of such a relationship is not clear. This might be due to the difficulty of studying plant lifespans.

Differences in leaf lifespan depending on the environment

As for the question 'How do leaf lifespans vary depending on their environment?', many studies have been done. The summarized results from many studies are described in detail in a review by 長田 et al. (2013, 19-

36). In this review, the results are classified into those for deciduous herbs, evergreen herbs, deciduous trees and evergreen trees. The results are also summarized separately for experimental results and outside survey results, and the whole contents of the review are enormous. I will describe here only the summaries.

1) The effects of light: a strong tendency was observed in which the stronger the light was, the shorter the leaf lifespan in most cases.
2) The effects of nutrient concentrations: poor nutrient concentrations led to a longer leaf lifespan in many experiments, but such a tendency was not observed in outside surveys.
3) Humidity of the soil: due to the CO_2 concentration in the atmosphere and the altitude or latitude of the examples, there was no tendency common to all four plant groups. However, soil drying led to a longer leaf lifespan in evergreen trees. Also, the higher the altitude or latitude was, the longer was the leaf lifespan in evergreen trees but the shorter in deciduous trees.
4) In evergreen trees, the longer the leaf lifespan was, the larger the difference in lifespan was depending on the strength of light in evergreen trees, but no such tendency was observed in deciduous herbs or trees.

With regard to (3), there is another report on the difference in leaf lifespan depending on altitude which surveyed artificial cypress woods on Shikoku Island in Japan (https 172). Based on this report, the average leaf lifespan was about 4 years in a lower altitude (320~370m) area and about 6 years in a higher altitude (850~970m) area. This is an actual result in line with the above review (the cypress is an evergreen tree). The main reason for the difference in the leaf lifespan depending on the altitude should be the difference in the temperature, and so this result probably shows that the lower is the temperature, the longer is the leaf lifespan of cypress trees.

Ranking of seed lifespans

As for **seed lifespans**, the longest lifespan records of seeds from various plants is shown in **Table 6-3**. In this table, four of the records are longer than 100 years, and one of them is over 1,000 years old. As for the longer records, their lifespans are based on the fact that they were found near the bases of the buildings such as churches whose built ages were reliable. As for the seed whose lifespan is marked with*, the budding activity was not known. Also, an approximate lifespan such as 600 years is clearly not accurate.

The lifespans of seeds vary depending on the states of the seeds and the conditions of their storage, as will be described later. While the conditions may be troublesome, we can understand that a seed's lifespan varies also depending on the species. The shortest is less than a year for chestnut, and the longest is 1,700 years for big clover, a difference of above 1,000 times. Most of the plants in the table are herbs, and trees only account for 4 entries (chestnut, beech, poplar and walnut). It is interesting that the lifespans of the seeds of all these trees are short – that is, less than 10 years. As for important agricultural plants such as wheat, corn and potato, the seed lifespans are 32, 37 and 200 years, respectively. **It seems that there is no relationship between the seed lifespan and the plant lifespan.** Rather, short-lived herbs may have selected the evolutionary strategy of making the seed lifespan long enough in order to maintain and prosper the species.

Table 6-3: The longest lifespans of various plant seeds

Species	Longest lifespan of seeds	Species	Longest lifespan of seeds
Chestnut	9 m	Corn	37 y
Horse chestnut	15 m	Tobacco	39 y
Beech	2 y	Mustard	50 y
Poplar	2 y	Dandelion	68 y
Walnut	5 y	Red clover	100 y
Pumpkin	10 y	Potato	200 y
Cabbage	19 y	Lotus	250 y
Onion	22 y	White clover*	600 y
Carrot	31 y	Big clover*	1,700 y
Wheat	32 y		

m=month; y=year. Abstracted from Table 2.4.1.5 of Flindt, 2007, 173.

Table 6-3 was made by abstracting a table in Flindt 2007, 173. As for the lifespan of a lotus seed, there is other information indicating a much longer lifespan. One such piece of information refers to the seed of a lotus called the **Oga lotus**. It is said to be over 2,000 years old, but it is known that it produces flowers (**Fig. 6-14**).

Fig. 6-14: Oga lotus (https 173).

Based on information online (https 173), the seed was one of the three particles found in the peat layer 6m under the ground at the Ochiai Ruins within the Kemigawa Farm of the University of Tokyo, located in the town of Asahigaoka, Hanamigawa-ku, Chiba city. The botanical scholar Ichiro Oga tried to grow these three particles. While two of them did not germinate, one did; it grew and produced a big flower in the following year 1952. As for the age when this seed was buried, it was estimated to be more than 2,000 years ago based on the measurement of the carbon radioactivity of a wood ship found above the seed. The details related to this discovery are described on this same website. Also, the Oga lotus is today grown at about 20 points in various areas in Japan (https 173).

As for the longevity record of a lotus seed, there is a report describing that a seed of 1,288+/-271 years old found in China had germinated and was growing. This was the oldest of the 6 seeds found. The youngest was 95 years old and the average was 595+/-380 years old (Shen-Miller et al. 1995, 1367-1380). The lotus (*Nelumbo nucifera*) is a deciduous water plant, belonging to Dicotylenodopsida, the order Nymphaeales and the family Nelumbonaceae. There are only two other plants in this family, and so it is rather unique (鈴木・横井、1998, 304). The lotus is a perennial plant, though I do not know its lifespan. It may form a colony and live for a long time. Examples of the Nymphaeaceae family of the order Nymphaeales include the *Victoria* and *Brasenia* water lilies (八杉 et al. 1996, 1553).

Changes in seed lifespan depending on the storage condition

The average value for seed lifespans is much shorter than the longest record, which is the same as the relation between the longest and the average lifespans of a plant. The following information is found online for seed lifespans (http 176), but without any information on their storage conditions.

Short (1 year): sweet corn, onion, scallion
Comparably short (2 years): cabbage, perilla, parsley, carrot, burdock, kidney beans, pea
About 3 years: eggplant, tomato, green pepper, cauliflower, Chinese cabbage, lettuce, daikon (radish), pumpkin, spinach
Comparably long (4~5 years): crown daisy, cucumber, water melon, broad bean.

Based on Table 6-3, the **longest lifespans** of seeds are 22, 19, 31 and 10 years in onion, cabbage, carrot and pumpkin, respectively, and their **average plant lifespans** are around 1/10 of these. The members in the above list are all agricultural plants, and the storage of their seeds is important in agriculture.

It is known that the average lifespan of a seed varies significantly depending on its storage condition. Therefore, studies on seed storage conditions are common. Examples described here are about the seeds of *Populus davidiana* and *P. koreana* (poplars) which are widely cultivated in Korea mainly as fuel (Kim et al. 2018, 1-16). It is possible to store the seeds of *P. davidiana* for 4 weeks at a room temperature if the water content of them is less than 6%. However, it was found to be impossible to store the seeds of *P. koreana* at a room temperature. As for the seeds of *P. davidiana* containing 3% water, the survival rate after storage at 4°C for 3 years was 74%, and the survival rate at 9-18% water content and after 4 years at -80°C was over 89%. The best storage temperature of *P. davidiana* seeds was -80°C, and at this temperature and 3-24% water content, 91-98% of the seeds germinated after 4 years of storage. In contrast, in the *P. koreana* seeds, the germination rate after storage at 3-24% water content and at -18 or -80°C for 3 years was less than 20%. These results indicate that a low water content and a lower temperature are good for seed storage in general, but to what extent the germination rate is maintained after storage varies significantly depending on the species, even for closely related plants.

Factors for the longevity of seeds

What are the factors which determine seed lifespan (the period while the germination activity is maintained)? The first is the process of ripening of the seed. Let me first introduce a study on soy beans (Lima et al. 2017, 1-25). The soy bean is a quite important crop for foods and feeds, and 240 million tons of it were produced worldwide in 2012 (⊠ ⊠ ⊠ ⊠ ⊠ ⊠ ⊠ , 2014, 211). The soy bean itself is a seed, and since its lifespan is brief, to lengthen its lifespan is important. Soy bean ripen, as shown in **Fig. 6-15**.

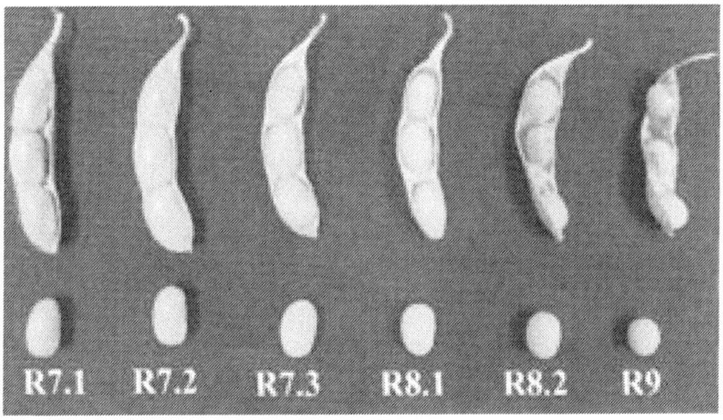

Fig. 6-15: The ripening stages of a soy bean (Fig. 1A of Lima et al. 2017, 4).

The numbers written at the bottom represent the steps of the ripening of the soy bean: the youngest step (R7.1) corresponds to 57 days after flowering, and the last, most dried step (R9) corresponds to 76 days after flowering. When soy beans of each step were stored in air of 75% humidity at 35°C, the period during which the germination rate diminished to 50% elongated from 25 days to 49 days as the ripening stage proceeded.

Also, changes in the gene expression during the seed ripening period were examined in detail in this paper. Based on the results, the expressions of the genes for heat-shock proteins, of nuclear and chloroplast genes for photosynthesis, and of genes related to the metabolism of oligosaccharides such as raffinose were found to be related to the proceeding of the ripening process. Besides, the expressions of the genes for 27 kinds of transcription factors related closely to the seed ripening.

The other paper related to the seed lifespan and to be introduced here is on *Arabidopsis thaliana* (Nguyen et al. 2015, 6399-6413). In this study, the germination activities of ripened seeds and those of the seeds stored in air of 50% humidity and at 21°C were examined. In the wild-type seeds, the storage under this condition for 4 years decreased the germination activity to 60%. Such changes were compared among various mutants, and their whole protein expression patterns were examined. The data indicated that the anti-oxidation systems (such as vitamin E) and the maintenance of protein translation and energy production systems are important for the seed lifespan. Also, the role of seed storage proteins such as cruciferins was identified. The paper proposed that the results re-confirmed that oxidation leads to the shortening of the seed lifespan and that the seed storage proteins suppress it.

6-5 Factors determining the lifespan of a plant

6-5-1 Allometric scaling

A precious paper which collected a vast amount of data on the weights (masses), mortalities and birth rates of all the known plant species – from very small plant planktons to trees – and which extracted numerical relations among them was published (Marba et al. 2007, 15777-15780). Such a study employs a method called “allometric scaling”, and since it is important for the factors determining the lifespan of a plant, I will introduce the paper here. **Table 6-4 (**transfered from Table 1 of the paper) shows the number of species studied, the averages of mass, the mortality and the half-life etc. of the plants in each plant group. The total number of species examined is 728, and that of trees is the largest and 230. As for a mangrove, it is defined in a Japanese biological encyclopedia as “evergreen lower or high trees or all the plants which grow in some parts of a sea coast or a river mouth located in a tropical or subtropical zone” (八杉 et al. 1996, 1355). However, the weight of a mangrove in the table is around 30g and is very small, so it should include only herbs if the data is correct. The data might be incorrect, however, and the unit should be kg for example.

As for the mass of an individual plant, that of a phytoplankton is the lightest and its average is in the order of 10^{-9}g or nanogram. The heaviest is a tree, and the average of the weights of all the trees is 770kg, and the largest value is 11,000kg (11 tons). It is not clear whether 11,000kg is the average or the largest value for a kind of tree, but anyway the tree is gigantic. The difference in the average mass between the largest and the smallest is about 10^{21} times.

Table 6-4 Mean, standard error and range of individual mass, mortality rate, life span (half-life) and birth rate across plant types (Marba et al. 2007).

Plant type	*n*	Individual mass, grams dry weight	Mortality rate, d^{-1}	Life span, d	Birth rate, d^{-1}
Phytoplankton	48	$3.5 \pm 2.4 \times 10^{-9}$	$39 \pm 7.0 \times 10^{-2}$	$2.3 \pm 1.2 \times 10^{1}$	$15 \pm 2.5 \times 10^{-1}$
		$(3.4 \times 10^{-15}$–$8.3 \times 10^{-8})$	$(1.2 \times 10^{-3}$–$2.5)$	$(2.8 \times 10^{-1}$–$5.8 \times 10^{2})$	$(4.0 \times 10^{-2}$–$3.7)$
Macroalgae	37	$7.2 \pm 4.6 \times 10^{1}$	$7.6 \pm 1.8 \times 10^{-3}$	$4.0 \pm 1.2 \times 10^{2}$	$1.4 \pm 0.63 \times 10^{-2}$
		$(7.3 \times 10^{-4}$–$1.5 \times 10^{3})$	$(2.2 \times 10^{-4}$–$5.8 \times 10^{-2})$	$(1.2 \times 10^{-1}$–$3.1 \times 10^{3})$	$(2.6 \times 10^{-4}$–$3.8 \times 10^{-2})$
Mosses	7	$2.1 \pm 0.26 \times 10^{-2}$	$1.8 \pm 0.27 \times 10^{-3}$	$4.8 \pm 1.0 \times 10^{2}$	
		$(1.6 \times 10^{-2}$–$3.3 \times 10^{-2})$	$(6.7 \times 10^{-4}$–$2.8 \times 10^{-3})$	$(2.5 \times 10^{2}$–$1.0 \times 10^{3})$	
Ferns	3		$2.6 \pm 1.0 \times 10^{-4}$	$3.4 \pm 1.1 \times 10^{3}$	$2.0 \pm 0.32 \times 10^{-4}$
			$(1.3 \times 10^{-4}$–$4.6 \times 10^{-4})$	$(1.5 \times 10^{3}$–$5.2 \times 10^{3})$	$(1.2 \times 10^{-4}$–$2.8 \times 10^{-4})$
Seagrasses	151	$3.1 \pm 0.37 \times 10^{-1}$	$2.5 \pm 0 - 35 \times 10^{-3}$	$13 \pm 1.4 \times 10^{2}$	$1.9 \pm 0.20 \times 10^{-3}$
		$(7.0 \times 10^{-3}$–$2.5)$	$(5.6 \times 10^{-5}$–$4.1 \times 10^{-2})$	$(1.7 \times 10^{1}$–$1.2 \times 10^{4})$	$(3.9 \times 10^{-5}$–$1.2 \times 10^{-2})$
Land and salt marsh herbs	190	4.9 ± 2.4	$5.8 \pm 1.5 \times 10^{-3}$	$16 \pm 3.0 \times 10^{2}$	$2.1 \pm 0.44 \times 10^{-3}$
		$(1.8 \times 10^{-2}$–$1.2 \times 10^{2})$	$(1.4 \times 10^{-5}$–$2.2 \times 10^{-1})$	$(3.2$–$5.0 \times 10^{4})$	$(1.1 \times 10^{-5}$–$2.0 \times 10^{-2})$
Succulent plants	12	$2.9 \pm 1.4 \times 10^{3}$	$8.9 \pm 2.2 \times 10^{-3}$	$7.6 \pm 3.3 \times 10^{3}$	$2.1 \pm 0.8 \times 10^{-5}$
		$(4.4 \times 10^{2}$–$6.1 \times 10^{3})$	$(2.6 \times 10^{-5}$–$2.0 \times 10^{-2})$	$(3.5 \times 10^{1}$–$2.7 \times 10^{4})$	$(6.7 \times 10^{-6}$–$3.6 \times 10^{-5})$
Shrubs and lianas	20	$5.9 \pm 3.2 \times 10^{1}$	$1.1 \pm 0.6 \times 10^{-2}$	$14 \pm 4.1 \times 10^{2}$	
		$(4.5$–$1.8 \times 10^{2})$	$(1.1 \times 10^{-4}$–$1.2 \times 10^{-1})$	$(6.0$–$6.5 \times 10^{3})$	
Mangroves	30	$2.8 \pm 1.3 \times 10^{1}$	$3.5 \pm 0.94 \times 10^{-3}$	$1.8 \pm 0.94 \times 10^{3}$	
		$(6.4 \times 10^{-1}$–$3.2 \times 10^{2})$	$(2.4 \times 10^{-5}$–$2.3 \times 10^{-2})$	$(3.0 \times 10^{1}$–$2.8 \times 10^{4})$	
Trees	230	$7.7 \pm 1.2 \times 10^{5}$	$2.9 \pm 0.53 \times 10^{-4}$	$1.1 \pm 0.2 \times 10^{5}$	$4.1 \pm 0.65 \times 10^{-5}$
		$(11$–$11 \times 10^{6})$	$(2.8 \times 10^{-7}$–$5.2 \times 10^{-3})$	$(1.3 \times 10^{2}$–$2.5 \times 10^{6})$	$(3.0 \times 10^{-6}$–$3.1 \times 10^{-4})$
Overall	728	$23 \pm 4.2 \times 10^{4}$	$2.9 \pm 0.58 \times 10^{-2}$	$37 \pm 6.7 \times 10^{3}$	$1.3 \pm 0.32 \times 10^{-1}$
		$(3.4 \times 10^{-15}$–$11 \times 10^{6})$	$(2.8 \times 10^{-7}$–$2.5)$	$(2.8 \times 10^{-1}$–$2.5 \times 10^{6})$	$(3.0 \times 10^{-6}$–$3.7)$

n indicates the number of plant mortality estimates, the variable with the largest number of observations in the data set.

As for the half-life obtained as the reciprocal of the mortality rate, in which about 2/3 of the members die statistically, the shortest average is 2.6 days for phytoplankton and the longest average is 10.5 years for ferns. It was unexpected to me that the latter was longer than 9.4 years for trees. The longest half-life of a specific kind of tree is 9,900 years, and it is by far the longest. This value of 9,900 years is not the average value of a kind of tree, but is likely the longest record, that of the oldest spruce. Also, the shortest average half-life of a tree is 190 days, which is close to that of an annual herb. It is interesting that there is such a tree.

In contrast, the longest record of average half-lives of land or salt marsh herbs is 5.0 x 10^4 days or 190 years and is much longer. This herb might be the species with the longest lifespan of about 300 years (*B. pyrenaica*) described before. Thus, Table 6-4 tells us many facts.

Fig. 6-16 shows bi-logarithmic plots of masses on the abscissa and mortality rates and half-lives on the left and right ordinates, respectively, for the 392 plant species for which the required data exist. From this graph, it was concluded that **shorter half-lives are correlated with smaller masses and longer half-lives with larger masses**. More accurately, half-lives are about the fourth powers of masses (the 95% confidence limit of the slope of the line representing this relationship is -0.21~-0.23, and the square of the correlation coefficient r^2 = 0.77). This is an important conclusion of this paper.

However, as for trees (◇) in the mass range of 10^5~10^6 g, where many data are concentrated, their half-lives vary greatly from 10 years to several thousand years, and therefore the rule stated above does not seem to be well applicable to trees.

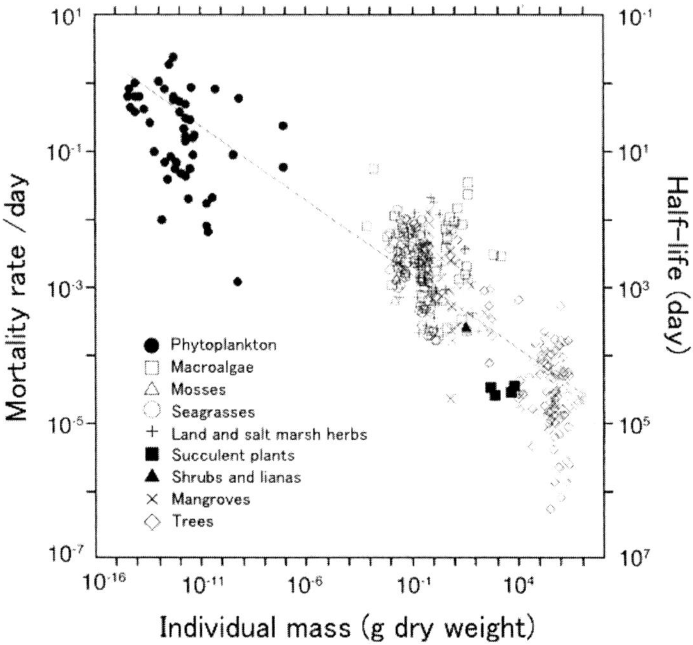

Fig. 6-16: Bi-logarithmic plots of masses, mortality rates per day and half-lives of 392 plants (adapted from Fig. 1 of Marba et al. 2007, 15778).

Next, **Fig. 6-17** shows bi-logarithmic plots of the birth rates and the mortality rates of 89 plants. We can see that both kinds of values are in a good positive relationship (95% confidence limits are 0.78 and 0.87, and $r^2 = 0.84$). Except for mono-cellular, photosynthetic plants (phytoplankton), the slope is 0.88~1.01 and is closer to 1.00. Therefore, the results show that the mortality rate is a little less than the birth rate, or that the individual number of each species is set to increase gradually, in multicellular plants.

I examined the references of this paper as much as possible and tried to find the actual data of the plants, but it was almost impossible since only a few of the references were available. Therefore, I am not sure to what extent the data used for this paper are accurate, but the main results in this paper are probably right.

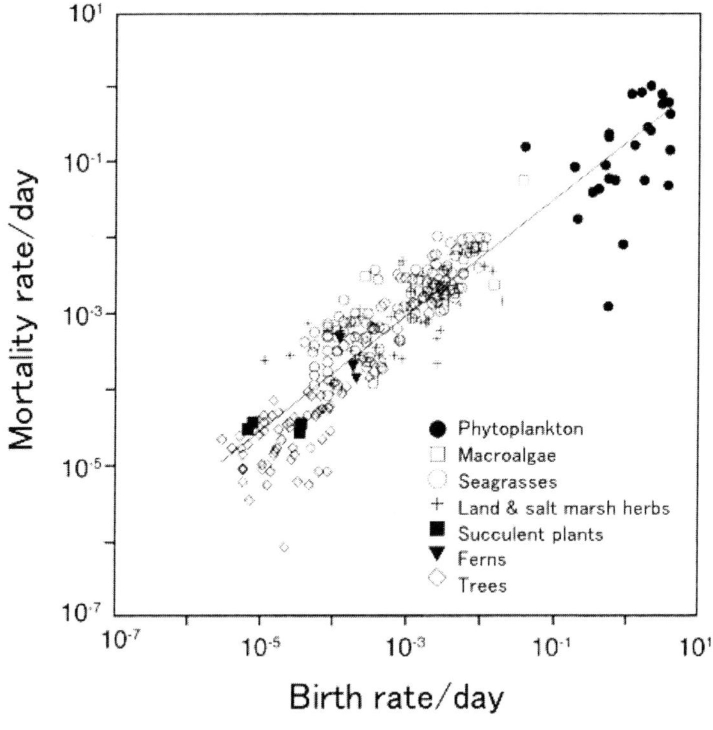

Fig. 6-17: Bi-logarithmic plots of the birth rates and the mortality rates of 89 plants (adapted from Fig. 3 of Marba et al. 2007, 15779).

6-5-2 Studies on the genes and the molecules regulating the lifespan of *Arabidopsis thaliana*

Arabidopsis thaliana is an annual herb which was introduced in Chapter 1. It is also the most often used plant for molecular biological studies. Therefore, studies on the genes and molecules related to the plant's lifespan are also actively done in this plant although such studies are not active in the whole plant world. I will introduce here two of the recent studies on the topic.

The first is a study indicating that overexpression of a gene leads to a lifespan extension in the leaves and plant body (Sharabi-Schwager et al. 2010, 261-273). This gene is called CBF-2, and is well known to increase the resistance of the plant to frost. In this paper, a genetic line overexpressing CBF-2 was made by introducing a second CBF-2 gene into a wild type plant carrying the original CBF-2 gene. In this overexpressing line, growth of the plant body was delayed: for example, the period from the sowing to the first flowering was delayed by 7 days on average from that of the wild type, i.e., from 29+/-2 days to 36+/-3 days. The rosette leaves, which spread over the ground at the initial growth, were a little smaller but greater in number than in the wild type. The lifespan of these rosette leaves became considerably longer, changing from 33 days on average in the wild type to 47 days in the modified plant. Also, as shown in **Fig. 6-18**, the lifespan of the whole plant (from sowing to the death in half of the plants) was elongated from 34 days to 45 days (more than 30%).

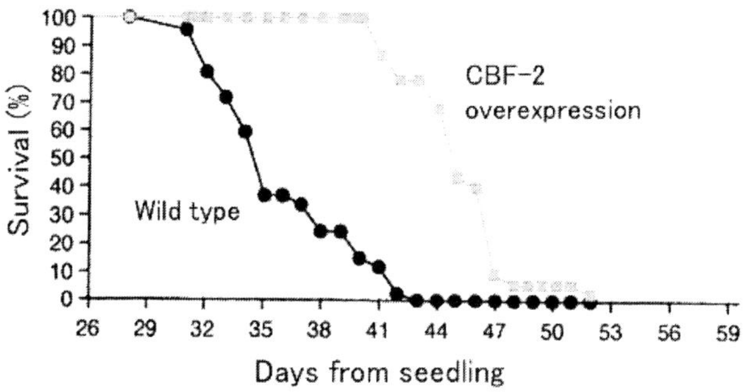

Fig. 6-18: Survival curves of the wild type and the CBF-2 overexpression line of *A. thaliana* (adapted from Fig. 4 of Sharabi-Schwager et al. 2010, 265).

The CBF-2 gene had been found to serve as a transcription factor regulating the expression of various other genes before the present study. To examine the effects of overexpression of this gene in detail, RNA was extracted from the leaves of the overexpression line and the wild type. Hybridization between each of them and the DNA of 24,000 *A. thaliana* genes was done, and the expression of each gene was compared by quantitation of the mRNAs. Based on the results, the expression of 286 genes in the leaves changed between the two lines. These genes included 30 kinds of stress-related genes and 20 kinds of genes for metabolism, degradation or modification of proteins. These results are thought to indicate that the CBF-2 gene affects developmental processes by regulating expression of the genes for other transcription factors and protein modification factors, in addition to encoding the frost-resistance protein. Thus, the lifespan extending effect of this gene is a result of its various functions. Also, the lifespan extension may be related to the delayed growth as shown in other cases.

The second study introduced here shows that decrease of intensity of light, which is important for plants, leads to the extension of the plant's lifespan (Minina et al. 2013, 327-329). It is known that caloric restriction extends the lifespan in various animals as described in this book, and this study was done to examine if there is a similar phenomenon in plants, too. It seems to be the unique point of this study that it utilized a decrease in the intensity of light, which is required for photosynthesis. **Fig. 6-19** is the most important result, which shows the change in the survival by decreasing the light intensity to 2/3 of the usual level (150→100 $\mu E/m^2 sec$). In the numerical values, the lifespan after the beginning of root development was elongated by 25% from 59.7 to 74.8 days.

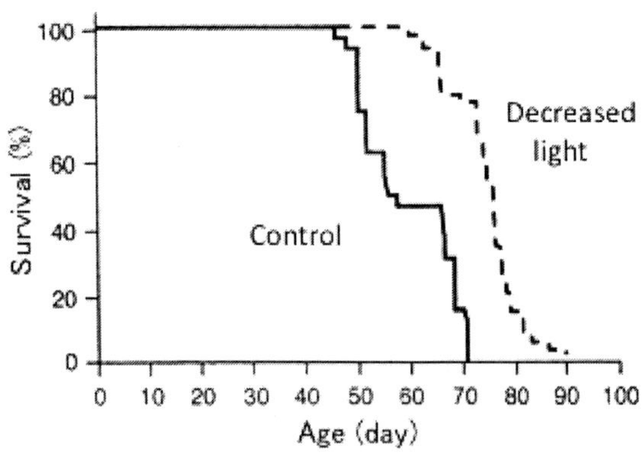

Fig. 6-19: The extension of the lifespan of the wild type *A. thaliana*

(abstracted from Fig. 1B of Minina et al. 2013, 328).

In this study, the relationship between lifespan extension and autophagy was also examined. **Autophagy** is defined as the process in which "a cell forms a vacuole which encloses a part of the cytoplasm such as a mitochondrion or an endoplasmic reticulum and digests it with hydrolytic enzymes provided by a lysosome, and it is induced by hunger etc." (八杉 et al. 1996, 567). Since it has recently been reported that activation of this autophagy is involved in lifespan extension in animals and yeasts, autophagy was examined also in *A. thaliana*. In the end, it was activated by decreasing the light intensity in *A. thaliana*, too. Furthermore, experiments by decreasing the light intensity were also done in the mutants of *atg 5* or *atg 6* genes, and little lifespan extension was observed. It is likely that autophagy is activated also in plants under conditions similar to caloric restrictions and that the lifespan is extended as one of the results.

6-5-3 Factors determining plant lifespan

Here, the factors which determine plant lifespan will be listed and summarized. The factors can be classified into environmental factors and those inherent to the plant, and they are related to each other.

Factors inherent to the plant

1) **The plant groups**: I think that the distinctions between **grass or herbs and trees**, those between **annual plants and perennial plants** and those between **gymnosperms (conifers) and angiosperms (broad-leaf trees)** are the most important. As stated before, the reasons for the longevity of trees are complex, and the factors to be described below reflect this. The specific

reasons for the long life of a conifer are the kinds and quantities of the lignin and secretion of resins. The difference in the lifespan among the large plant groups (as written above) and those among the species within a group are thought to depend basically on the genes or the evolution.

2) **Size**: The second important factor for longevity is likely to be the size or mass of the plant. This is described in the previous section on allometric scaling. The rule is that the lifespan of a plant correlates with the size of the whole plant body. However, the relationship is not accurate enough, especially for trees. As will be described later, a similar rule exists in animals. The reason for this rule in animals is likely to be that the larger their size, the smaller the ratio of body area/body weight is and so the energy loss is smaller. Is the same reason applicable to plants?

3) **Growth rate**: The growth rate of a plant is the possible third factor for plant longevity. This possibility is related to the fact that many conifers (gymnosperms) are long-lived and they are abundant in colder areas than broad-leaf trees are (mostly angiosperms). This may be because the lower the growth temperature is, the slower the plant's growth. Also, some examples indicate this in the relationship between the growth rate and the lifespan of an individual tree of a specific species. One is the paper on the mountain pine (*Pinus montana*) (Bigler 2016, 1-18). In this paper, annual rings of 200 dead mountain pine trees on a high mountain in the Swiss National Park were examined, and thereby the relationship between the lifespans at death and the annual growth rates of the trunk diameters were deduced. Based on the results, it was shown that the slower the growth rate

in the initial 50 years, the longer the lifespan was (**Fig. 6-20**). However, if the growth rate in the initial 50 years is slow, it is possible that the tree may die during its youth.

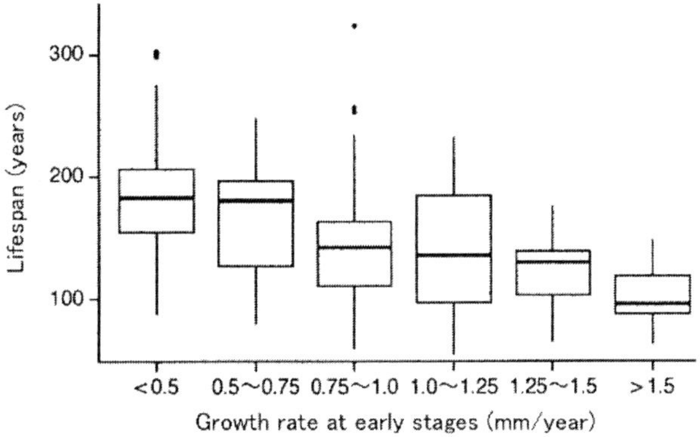

Fig. 6-20: Relationship between the early growth rate and lifespan in the mountain pine. The thick lines in the rectangles represent the medians and the under and upper sides for 1/4 and 3/4 from the minimal values, respectively (adapted from Fig. 2(b) of Bigler 2016, 8).

A different study by Ireland et al. had poplars (*Populus tremuloides*) in the USA as its focus (Ireland et al. 2014, 847-859). In this paper, since the standing death of poplar trees had spread in north-western America in the years prior to the study, the relationship between the growth pattern and the mortality of poplar trees was assessed in a northern area of Arizona in order to make the reason for the poplar deaths clear. Based on the result, the average growth rate of live trees is always faster than that of dead trees, at least in the past 100 years. This is a reverse result of the above case, and so we understand that both cases exist. When we think of the facts that many conifers live long and that slow growing species show more long-lived cases also in animals, it is supposed that longer lifespans are more abundant in slower growth species in general.

4) Organ lifespan: It is possible that the lifespan of a certain organ is an important determinant of the overall plant lifespan. The lifespans of leaves in annual herbs and that of the root in perennial plants were reported to be closely related to the lifespan of the whole plant (Li et al. 2014, 1-7).

5) Dormancy: In Section 6-1 in this chapter, it was described that there were dormant years in the spider orchid which is a rather short-lived herb. This dormancy phenomenon is sometimes observed in plants in general, and it may possibly lead to the extension of the plant's lifespan. Although different from this, plant seeds can live for a very long time maybe due to a kind of dormancy.

6) Genetic and molecular factors: It was described above that transcription factor CBF-2 is involved in the regulation of the lifespan in *A. thaliana*. There are many factors related to the functions of CBF-2 and probably some of them are related to lifespan.

The differences between herbs and trees are very important for the lifespan, and many tree-specific genes have been discerned by comparison of the two genomes. In a poplar (*Populus trichocarpa*), the genome was analyzed at first in trees (Tuscan et al. 2006, 1596-1604), and the comparison was made with the genome of *A. thaliana* which was analyzed first in plants (Arabidopsis Genome Initiative 2000, 796-815). The results are summarized in the following four paragraphs.

① Existence of the cambium and the formation of the xylem by the cambium are the basic characteristics which distinguish trees from herbs. The poplar has 93 genes involved in the synthesis of cellulose related to the xylem formation, and this number is higher than 78 in *A. thaliana.* Three of these poplar genes were simultaneously expressed in the period of xylem formation and another gene was unique and did not exist in *A. thaliana.*

② There are many genes involved in the synthesis of secondary metabolites in the poplar such as phenyl glycosides, tannins, flavonoids and terpenoids. The former two are very abundant in leaves, barks and roots, and many of their secondary metabolites are thought to help growth and interaction with harmful insects and microbes in the trees.

③ In plants, there are many genes to resist various diseases in general. The largest group of such genes is that of the NBS-R family proteins which have a nucleotide-binding site and repeated amino acid sequences rich in leucine. A poplar tree has as many as 399 such genes, and this number is about twice that of the genes in *A. thaliana.* These disease-resistance genes are thought to be important in order for a tree to live for a long time.

④ Since trees are so large, the supply of nutrients containing carbon and nitrogen from the root to leaves and branches is important. Also, the movement of metabolites in the plant body every year and every season is important. A poplar tree has as many as 1,722 transport protein genes for the above requirement, about twice those present in *A. thaliana*.

Therefore, **a tree has many tree-specific genes and molecules, a fact which is thought to be significantly related to its long lifespan**. When the genome of a perennial herb with a comparably long lifespan is analyzed in the future, the reasons for the difference in the lifespan between annual and perennial herbs may be estimated. Also, although molecular level studies in plant lifespan are not yet advanced, they will be much more refined in the future.

Environmental factors

Environmental conditions, i.e., the conditions of the place where plants grow, are very important factors as a whole. The environment greatly affects not only the lifespan of an individual plant, but also what kinds of plants grow there and how long they live there. Environmental conditions in a wide sense include various factors such as the nutrient status, the humidity in the soil, the temperature, the strength and amount of light reaching the plant, the wind levels, the humidity in the atmosphere, the plant groups growing in the surrounding area, possible harmful insects and animals, the kinds and densities of the pathogens there, and so on. The **nutrients and the humidity in the soil, the temperature** and **the light intensity** may be especially important. Each of these three factors strongly affects the growth rate, the size and the strength of a plant, and thereby the lifespan. The case in which a decrease of light intensity leads to a lifespan extension has been described above.

CHAPTER 7

MECHANISMS FOR THE DETERMINATION OF THE LIFESPAN OF AN ORGANISM

7-1 Overview of life from the patterns of birth and death

A unique and large-scale study that compares survival curves of many and various organisms was published in 2014. It is interesting also from the standpoint of the lifespan and is thus introduced here. In the paper (Jones et al. 2014, 169-173), **survivorships or survival curves of 46 organisms** in total are presented: 11 mammals (including humans), 12 other vertebrates, 10 invertebrates and 13 plants. As for the human, curves for three groups are included, and 48 survival curves in total are shown. Thirteen of themare selected and shown here in **Figs. 7-1 (a) and (b)**. As seen in the figure, not only the survival curve (thick line), but the **mortality** curve (dotted line), which is the important factor for survival, and **fertility** curve (thin line) are shown together, and thereby their relationships can be seen. The abscissa of each graph represents the age of the organism in years, months or days. The left and right ends of the abscissa correspond to the point of maturity and the point of 5% survival (95% dead), respectively. The organisms' mortality and fertility are both represented as the standardized or relative values which are calculated by taking the average value for the adult as 1.00 (shown by the horizontal dotted line), and their scales (0.0~25.0 or 0.0~5.0) are shown on the left-side ordinate. The survival curves (thick lines) are always right-side down, and their log scales are shown on the right-side ordinate.

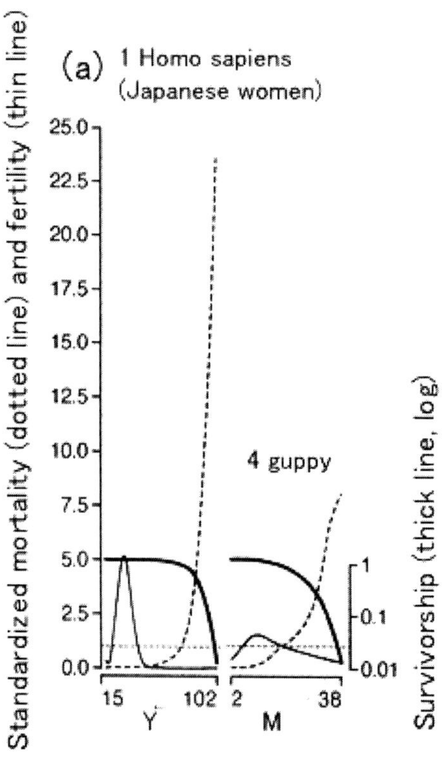

Fig. 7-1 (a): Changes in the survival (thick line), the mortality (dotted line) and the fertility (thin line) by age in women and guppy. Y: year, M: month (redrawn from a part of figure 1 in Jones et al. 2014, 170).

In the original figure for Figs. 7-1 (a) and (b), graphs were arranged in the order of the shape of the survival curve, namely from the most convex (human) to the most concave (mangrove).

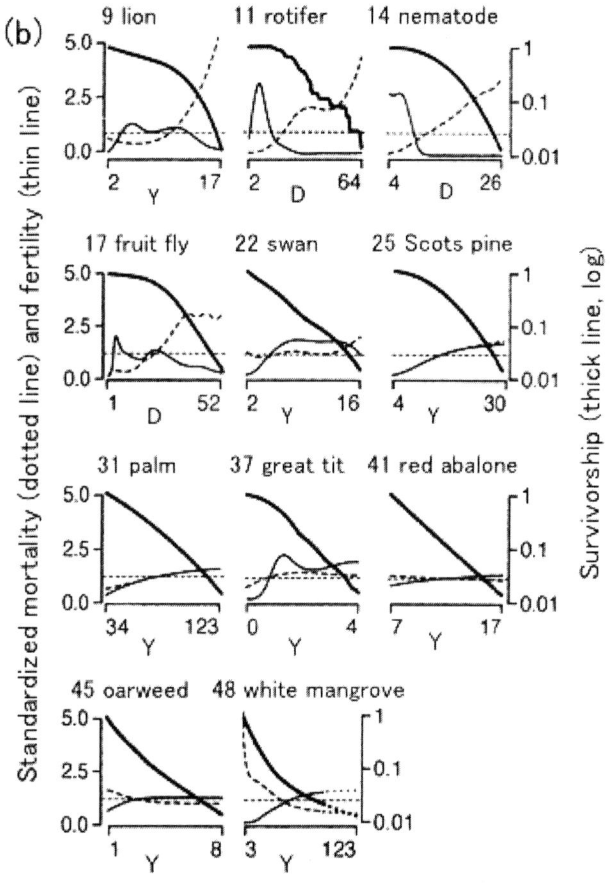

Fig. 7-1 (b): Changes in the survival (thick line), the mortality (dotted line) and the fertility (thin line) by age in 11 kinds of organisms. Y: year, D: day (redrawn from a part of figure 1 in Jones et al. 2014, 170).

In Figs. 7-1 (a) and (b), this order is also followed and numbered based on the original order such as #1 for a human and #48 for a mangrove. The original figure in the paper was made by selecting as many varied types of organisms as possible.

In the figures, I also tried to select various types and those which the readers may be interested in. The name of the organism shown in each graph and its classification is as follows: #1 human (mammal), #4 guppy (fish), #9 lion (mammal), #11 rotifer (Rotifera), #14 nematode (*C. elegans*, Nematoda), #22 swan (bird), #25 Scots pine (gymnosperm), #31 palm (monocotyledon), #37 great tit (bird), #41 red abalone (mollusk), #45 oarweed (green algae), and #48 mangrove (dicotyledon).

The figures are interesting to look at from various perspectives, and the main results can be summarized as follows.

1) For over half of the organisms (27/46), the mortality curves are right-side up and the mortality increases with age. In about 1/4 (11/46) of the organisms, such as the swan and red abalone in Fig. 7-1 (b), the mortality curves are nearly horizontal or the mortality is nearly constant. In 7 organisms, for instance oarweed and white mangrove in Fig. 7-1 (b), the mortality curves are right-side down and so the mortality decreases with the age. The fact that **there are organisms in which mortality decreases with the age or is nearly constant for the entire lifespan** is likely to have been unexpected and represents one of the most important findings.

As for the actual value of the human mortality, 2/3 of the average lifespan over the world (48 years) should be the half-lifespan, and therefore its reciprocal number of 0.02/year should be the average mortality for a whole life. The mortality value at a young age is probably below 0.01/year; it rapidly increases in old age and becomes about 0.5/year at 100 years old.

2) The type of a survival curve is basically determined by the mortality curve. This is reasonable since the reciprocal of the mortality is the lifespan as stated in the chapter on plant lifespan (Chapter 6). **The survival curves are classified into three types**: type I for a convex curve, type II for a nearly horizontal curve and type III for a concave curve. Among them type I curves are most abundant.

3) The relationships between the large-scale classification of the organisms and the types of mortality or survivorship are complex, but some tendency can be seen for each group of organisms. **For the mammals and most of the vertebrates, the mortality curve is right-side up and the survivorship is type 1. In plants, all three types of survival curves are seen.** Even for the plants in which mortality increases with age, the increase is gentle. In about half of the plants studied the mortality decreases with age (those of type III survivorship), which is characteristic for plants.

4) As for the age at which 5% survival is reached (shown at the right hand side of the graphs), the shortest is 26 days for the nematode and the longest is 123 years for the palm and mangrove. The longest is more than 1,700 times as long as the shortest. In the original figure in the paper, the shortest is the same and the longest is 1,400 years for a hydra, and the

longest/shortest ratio is over 20,000. **The lifespan of an organism is determined by the absolute value of mortality and is not related to the pattern of the relative mortality values shown in the graphs.**

5) **Reproduction or fertility** is an essential biological activity in order to maintain and develop a species. If much energy is dispensed for reproduction, the energy for the maintenance of the individual is decreased, and therefore it may be possible that the mortality is increased and the lifespan is shortened. But that possibility is through a change in the mortality and such an age-dependent mortality change should be included in the mortality curve. When I surveyed all the graphs in the original figure, a tendency toward mortality increase during a period of high fertility was scarcely seen. Therefore, **the effect of fertility on mortality is thought to be small**.

Also, as for fertility change by age, there are various patterns, which is interesting. In the human being, it is shown that fertility is high only in a younger period partly because the lifespan has become longer. Many mammals and vertebrates show patterns in which fertility is maintained during a long period in their life, as in the lion, swan and great tit in Fig. 7-1 (b). As for plants, fertility increases with age in Scots pine and palm, is nearly constant in oarweed, and **no example of fertility decrease with age is shown in plants**. This may be characteristic to plants.

6) As for the women whose data is shown in the graph above, the mortality increase in old age is the most extensive among the organisms shown here (and indeed in the original figure), but their lifespan is very long. This is

thought to be related to the low level of absolute mortality till middle age due to social developments such as in sanitation and to an extension of the average lifespan. By the way, the paper states that the human data in Fig. 7-1 (a) is that of Japanese women in 2009. This may be due to the fact that Japan had the longest average lifespan data then in the world. However, 102 years old at the 5% survival seems to me an error.

This paper appears to be the first trial to survey such an extensive array of the biological world based on the patterns of birth and death, and therefore it is interesting and valuable. The title of the paper is "The diversity of ageing across the tree of life". However, only the mortality is shown and discussed as an index of ageing in the paper, and the meaning or nature of "ageing" is not at all described. That would of course be another interesting theme.

7-2 The lifespan determinants common to animals and plants: genes and body size

Genes

The general and likely lifespan determinants common to animals and plants are genes and environments. Environments have large effects on the average lifespan of a species and on the individual organism itself, but are thought to be less related to the longest lifespan of a species. Therefore, genes likely remain the sole general determinant. The fact that the gene is an important lifespan determinant was first understood through the discovery of a lifespan gene in the nematode (*C. elegans*), and has been confirmed and developed by the studies on the lifespan-related genes in the fruit fly, mouse and so on. Human beings also have genes similar to those animal genes, and it is certain that the human lifespan is governed by genes.

The examples by which easy understanding the role of genes in human lifespan determination is possible may be the genetic diseases known as **genetic premature ageing syndromes**. These are genetic diseases due to natural mutations, which show various symptoms characteristic to ageing in young ages and lead to a short lifespan. Two of them are familiar. One of them is called "**Werner syndrome**" and is an autosome-recessive genetic disease. In the case of such a disease, usually both the parents of the patient do not show the disease, but they both have a mutation in the disease gene. If so, on average 1 in 4 of their children have a mutation in both the disease genes and become patients. It is said that a patient of the syndrome shows symptoms such as white hairs, vascular sclerosis, osteoporosis and diabetes at a young age. It is also associated with a high frequency for cancer, and most Werner syndrome patients die before the age of 50. This disease was first reported around 100 years ago, and it was found in 1994 that the causative gene *WRN* expresses the enzyme called a DNA helicase that unwinds usually double-stranded gene DNA into single stranded DNA. Therefore, a patient of Werner syndrome is supposed to show various premature-ageing symptoms and to die early because he/she cannot maintain normal functions or replicate the gene DNA. However, the actual mechanisms of the syndrome's expression are said to be unclear. Also, the estimated number of patients with this disease is about 2,000 globally, though more than 60% of them are said to be Japanese (伊藤 et al. 2003, 181; https 189).

Another example of a genetic premature ageing syndrome is **Hutchinson-Gilford syndrome** (or progeria). A patient of this syndrome stops growing in the childhood and so grows only up to 110cm tall and 15kg in weight. This syndrome is a surprising and miserable disease also because he/she develops vascular sclerosis and the average lifespan is about 13 years. **Fig. 7-2** shows an example of a patient. This syndrome is also an autosome-recessive genetic disease like Werner syndrome, and the causative gene was identified as the lamin A gene on the 1st chromosome in 2003. Lamin A is a component of a nuclear membrane, and it is supposed that its abnormal gene leads to an abnormal nuclear membrane, which makes the membrane function abnormal and the ageing much earlier. The probability of the syndrome's occurrence is 1 per 80 million infants, is very low and the total number of living patients is said to be about 40 (伊藤 et al. 2003, 1980; https 190).

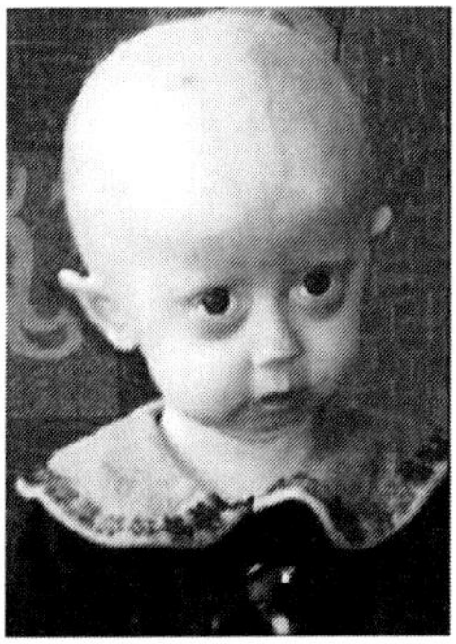

Fig. 7-2: A Hutchinson-Gilford syndrome patient (https 190).

In these two cases, the causative genes encode proteins essential for basic cellular functions, DNA helicase or lamin A, and therefore ageing occurs early and the lifespan is shortened due to the abnormality or deletion of the gene function. Namely, we see that neither of the genes directly govern the lifespan. It is thought that involvement of a gene in the lifespan determination is indirect in almost all cases, as it is in the two cases stated above.

The sirtuin gene family described as "**long lifespan genes**" in the Section 4-9 are examples of such genes. The discovery of sirtuin originated in the Sir2 gene in yeast, and genes very similar to Sir2 are found also in the nematode, fruit fly and various mammals. In the nematode and fruit fly, a deletion of sirtuin 2 leads to a shorter lifespan and its overexpression leads to a longer lifespan. All of these sirtuin genes encode an NAD^+ (nicotinamide adenine dinucleotide)–dependent histone deacetylase and express their functions such as lifespan control through the activity of the enzyme. In mammals including human beings, there are 7 sirtuins named SIRT 1~SIRT7, and SIRT1, which is the closest to Sir2 in yeast, is said to be the most relevant to the control of the lifespan (大田　2010, 11-16; Kenyon 2010, 504-512).

Body size

For whole plants, it was shown that body size or weight is a general factor which roughly determines mortality or lifespan (Section 6-5, Fig. 6-16). A similar relationship may be true also in animals when we think about various examples. Because I couldn't find any existing graphs on this subject I decided to create one. Although there are few reliable data on animal lifespan or body size in general, I was able to make a graph showing the weight-lifespan relationship in mammals (**Fig. 7-3**).

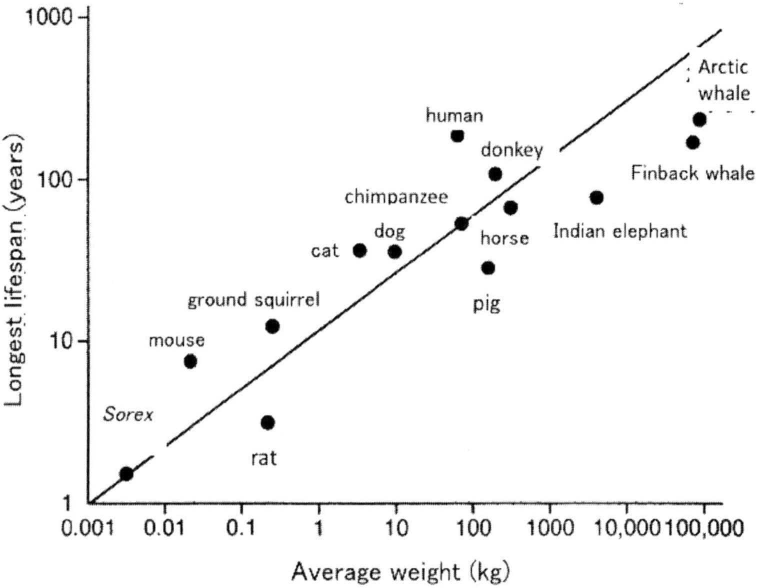

Fig. 7-3: Relation between average weight and longest lifespan of mammals in a bi-logarithmic plot. Values of average weight and longest lifespan used for the graph are as follows. Sorex 3g, 1.5y; mouse 20g, 4y; rat 200g, 3y; ground squirrel 160g, 12y; cat 3.5kg, 35y; dog 10kg, 34y; human 60kg, 122y; chimpanzee 70kg, 50y; pig 150kg, 27y; donkey 200kg, 100y; horse 300kg, 61y; Indian elephant 4t, 70y; Finback whale 76t, 116y; Arctic whale 90t, 211y. (Animal Encyclopedia for average weight data; Table 1-1 and Flindt, 2007, 7-9 for longest lifespan data).

For 12 of the 14 species in total, the longest lifespan data had already been shown in Table 1-1 in Chapter 1. Longest lifespan data for these 12 species were obtained from Animal Encyclopedia and other relevant sources. Their values are distributed in a very wide range of 10^7 order from the 3g of the Sorex to the 90 tons of the Finback whale. In the earlier table there were no animals weighing between 100g~1 kg, and I added rat and ground squirrel, and made the graph for the 14 species. We can clearly see a positive relationship between the average weight and the longest lifespan in mammals. Though the slant line in the graph was arbitrarily drawn by me, it shows that the longest lifespan is almost proportional to the third power of the average weight. Since the weight of an animal is proportional to the volume, and the volume is proportional to the cube or third power of one dimensional size such as body length, **the longest lifespan of a mammal is nearly proportional to the body length**.

It was unexpected to me that such a simple and easy-to-understand result was obtained. By the way, the farthest point up from the line representing weight$^{1/3}$ seems to be that of the human, which is probably an effect of the large extension of the human lifespan due to civilization.

Animals lose body heat from their body's surface, the surface area is proportional to the second power of the body length, and the body volume is proportional to the third power of the body length. Therefore, in mammals which are homoiotherms, the energy per unit of weight required to maintain the body temperature is higher the smaller the body size. It may be possible that this is the reason for the above relationship in mammals.

To test this possibility, it must be examined whether or not such a relationship is also true for poikilotherm animals. I found relatively more data on the average body length and the longest lifespan in fish which are poikilothrerm animals. So, I made bi-logarithmic plots for fish similar to Fig. 7-3. The result is **Fig. 7-4** and it shows a positive relationship between them also in fish. In this case, the longest lifespan is proportional to about 0.6^{th} power of the average body length, and not simply proportional.

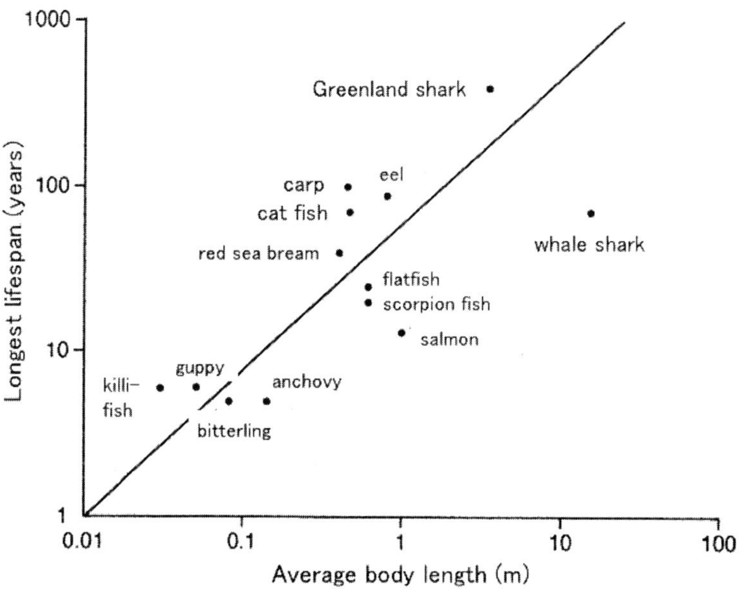

Fig. 7-4: Relationship between the average body length and the longest lifespan in fish. Values of the average body length and the longest lifespan used for the graph are as follows: killifish 3cm, 5y; guppy 5cm, 5y; bitterling 8cm, 4y; anchovy 14cm, 4y; red sea bream 40cm, 40y; carp 45cm, 100y; cat fish 47cm, 70y; scorpion fish 61cm, 20y, flat fish 61cm, 25y; eel

80cm, 88y; salmon 1m, 13y; Greenland shark 3.5m, 392y; whale shark 15m, 70y (Animal Encyclopedia, Flindt, 2007,7-9 and https 193).

In consideration of this result, the possibility of explaining the relationship in mammals by need of keeping a constant body temperature as stated above may not be true.

I could not find any reports which showed the actual relationship between the body size and the lifespan in mammals or fish, and therefore the data obtained by myself and shown above may be the first. Similar studies in other vertebrates and invertebrates are also desired, but seem to be difficult at present. It is supposed that similar relationships probably exist in the whole animal world.

7-3 Molecular mechanisms for the determination of an animal lifespan

Although studies on the mechanisms for the determination of an animal lifespan have been actively done also at the molecular level, an entire image of the mechanisms is not clear. The reason is that many factors are involved in the mechanisms and therefore the mechanisms are complex. Here, two examples of the mechanisms which are evident to some extent are described.

The first is the mechanism for the extension of the lifespan by caloric or diet restriction. Caloric restriction is the only common condition that has been demonstrated to be effective for lifespan extension in the nematode, fruit fly, mouse and an anthropoid ape (Lopez-Otin et al. 2016, 802-821). Also, as was stated in Section 4-3, caloric restriction was shown to have good effects on several human health indicators which are important factors for the lifespan. An outline of the mechanisms for lifespan extension by caloric restriction in the nematode, fruit fly and mouse is shown in **Fig. 7-5**. Historically, studies on the nematode lifespan were the earliest and done around 1990, and the studies extended to the fruit fly and mouse in reference to the nematode studies.

In the figure, a long vertical arrow indicates a signal transducing pathway, and upward or downward arrows beside a specific factor or function indicate activation or suppression of the function, respectively. When the pathways in the three animals are compared, a few common points are observed. The **TOR** (Target of Rapamycin, described in Section 3-7) and the **S6 kinase** (protein phosphorylating enzyme) are shown as the factors common to all three animals. The pathway including diet restriction→↓TOR→↓S6 kinase (→↓protein synthesis) →long lifespan is shown as a pathway including the two factors. This common pathway means that diet restriction suppresses TOR activity, which suppresses S6 kinase activity and this leads to a longer lifespan.

The mechanisms involved in this pathway are as follows.

1) The TOR itself is a protein kinase, which phosphorylates and thereby regulates the activities of many proteins including S6 kinase itself. The phosphorylating activity of the TOR is suppressed by diet restriction and thereby the S6 kinase activity decreases.
2) The S6 kinase activates translation (protein synthesis) by phosphorylation of a protein of a ribosome required in translation.

Diet restriction suppresses this translation through the decreased phosphorylation of S6 kinase. The phosphorylating activity of the TOR is suppressed by binding to rapamycin, which is the first step of the lifespan extension and is also shown in the figure.

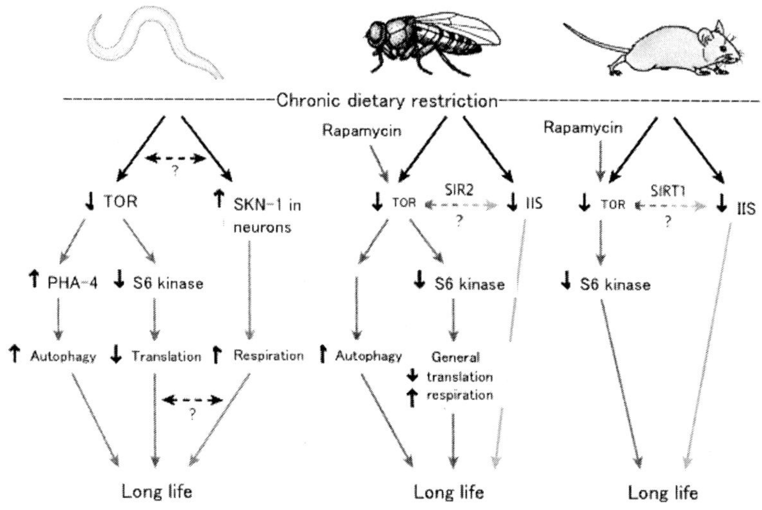

Fig. 7-5: An outline of the molecular mechanisms of lifespan extension by diet restriction in the nematode, fruit fly and mouse. TOR: target of rapamycin, Sir2 and SIRT1: proteins made from long lifespan genes sirtuin 2 and 1 (redrawn from Fig. 3 of Kenyon 2010, 507).

The autophagy in the pathways of the nematode and the fruit fly indicates the mechanism which degrades and re-utilizes cellular components during caloric restriction. It is shown in the figure that the longevity genes **Sir2** (sirtuin 2) and **SIRT1** (sirtuin 1) also control the lifespan in the fruit fly and mouse. However, the mechanisms for their functions are not well understood. In the fruit fly and mouse, the pathway starting from insulin or IGF-1 (Insulin-like Growth Factor 1) is also involved. This pathway is indicated by **IIS** in the figure. As explained here, the signal transduction pathways in the figure mean that binding to a factor such as a protein or chemical modification such as phosphorylation and that functional changes due to either of them take place continuously.

With this figure, we can understand that caloric restriction has an effect on lifespan extension via the regulation of protein synthesis, autophagy and the activation of respiration. Also, we can see that there are common mechanisms in lifespan extension by caloric restriction, which is a phenomenon important and common to animals. As for the other factors shown in the figure, PHA-4 indicates the protein made from the *pha-4* gene involved in the formation of the nematode pharynx, and SKN-1 is the transcription factor made from the gene *skn-1* involved in the formation of epidermal cells in the nematode. Also, the insulin/IGF-1 signal transduction pathway (IIS) has various functions except for caloric restriction and is one of the most important signal transduction pathways. In the IIS pathway and its downstream pathways, probably more than 100 factors are involved. The related contents are specialized and thus are not described here.

The second mechanism to be described here is an example of the **mechanism in ageing**. Ageing also occurs by various factors and mechanisms. **Fig. 7-6** shows an outline of the mechanism in which **injury in the gene DNA** and **mitochondrial dysfunction** interact with each other

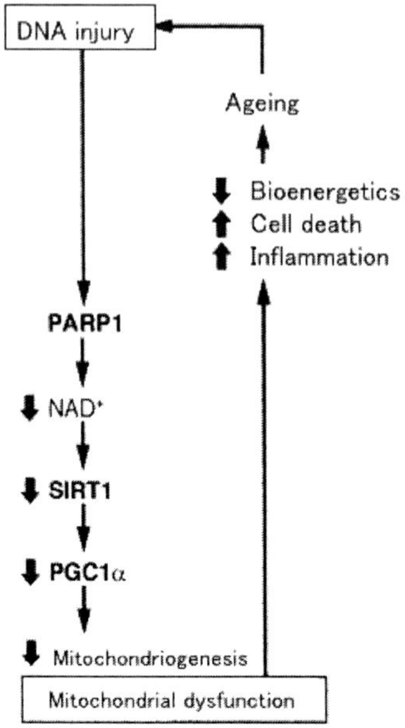

Fig. 7-6: An outline of the molecular mechanisms in ageing by DNA injury and mitochondrial dysfunction (adapted from a part of Fig. 1 in Lopez-Otin et al. 2016, 804).

and their interaction becomes a cause for cellular ageing. The genetic premature ageing syndromes introduced in the previous section were examples in which obstruction of functions or replication of gene DNA lead to premature ageing or a short lifespan. The longevity gene SIRT1 is involved in this figure, too. Although ageing as a whole cannot be avoided, it is possible that the lifespan can be extended to some extent by preventing one of the mechanisms for ageing. When Fig. 7-6 is observed, we think it possible in principle to prevent a decrease in mitochondrial functions and ageing if intracellular concentration of NAD^+ is increased in some way. By the way, PARP1 in the figure indicates poly-ADP ribose polymerase and PGC1α indicates co-activating factorα (PPARGC1A) of the receptor α which is activated by a peroxisome growth factor.

Fig. 7-5 was cited from the review on ageing (Kenyon, 2010, 504-512). In this review, the important pathways or factors related to ageing and the lifespan such as the insulin/IGF-1 signal pathway, TOR signal pathway, AMP-kinase and sirtuins are described. The original publication from which Fig. 7-6 was cited is a comprehensive and recent review with the title "Metabolic Control of Longevity" (Lopes-Otin et al. 2016, 802-821).

7-4 Characteristics in plant lifespans and their determination mechanisms

An important characteristic of plant lifespans may be that there are many more species with a long lifespan than species of animals. As described in Chapters 1 and 2, formation of a colony is the factor for a very long lifespan in both animals and plants. The longest lifespan record is over 40,000 years in plants and about 4,000 years in animals, with the former being about 10 times as long. As for the longest lifespan recorded among non-colony-forming organisms, the top among animals is 507 years (the ocean quahog, *A. islandica*, Table 1-3) and among plants is 5,062 years (the bristlecone pine, Table 2-1). Therefore, that of plants is much longer by an order.

The **determinants for plant lifespan** were already described in Section 6-5. As for these factors, genes and body sizes are also common to animals. The **distinctions among annual plants, perennial plants and trees**, the growth speed and the lifespan of an organ are the factors characteristic to plants. In perennial plants, the lifespan of over 300 years of *Bordea* described in Section 6-1 seems to be the longest, and this is much shorter than that of trees, many of which live longer than 1,000 years.

As described in Section 6-3, the **reasons for the long lifespan of trees** are as follows.

1) They are physically strong and can support their large body sizes.
2) Since their body structure is simple and they do not have to move unlike animals, they can live even if most of their body parts are dead due to ageing.
3) The vascular systems which transport materials and the cell division systems necessary for reproductive functions are maintained.
4) The reproductive functions do not decline in older ages as a general feature in plants.

As for the mechanisms for lifespan determination at the molecular level, a few examples were introduced in Section 6-5. Such studies have not advanced as much as those in animals and most molecular mechanisms seem to be unclear, and so they are not described here.

CHAPTER 8

MAIN POINTS TO MAKE OUR LIFESPANS AS LONG AS POSSIBLE

Meals, physical activity, purpose and little stress

It is often said that important factors for us to live long are meals, physical activity, aims of living and little or no stress, and I agree with them. All four factors seem to be really important, and among them the **aims of living** may be the most important. If you think you do not have an aim, I would recommend you to find something which you like or think important, and to make it your aim. As for a **stress**, if it is of your body and continues for a long time, it will lead to a disease or injury and finally shorten your lifespan. A mental stress is also thought to shorten the lifespan if it is strong. In contrast, since no stress condition is said to lead to dementia, moderate stress may be good for health and a long lifespan.

Meanwhile, there are several other expressions of factors for a long lifespan. It is written in a Japanese book on principles of nutrition (渡邊, 2009, 276) that a nice sleep, a nice meal and healthy bowel movements are the important factors to keep mind and body in a good condition. The Ministry of Health, Labor and Welfare in Japan announced a slogan for Health Frontier, "Physical activity first, meal second, strict no smoking and drugs last" (渡邊, 2009, 276). It was described before that sleep and no smoking are important factors for the lifespan, along with meals and physical activities. In this chapter, I will summarize the important factors for lifespan extension, including some of those described in Chapter 4.

Meals

1) Calories

It is important not to eat an excess of calories since it leads to obesity which leads to a shorter lifespan for the various reasons described in Section 4-1. The amounts of required calories per day based on the outline of standards on food intake by The Ministry of Health, Labor and Welfare in Japan (2020) (https 196) are cited in **Table 8-1**. In this table, calorie amounts required per day are classified by age, gender and three physical activity levels (I, II, III). The **physical activity levels** are supposed to be classified by assuming that in rest equates to 1.0 and are as follows: the low level (I) is 1.40~1.60 times as high, the normal level (II) is 1.60~1.90 times as high and the high level (III) is 1.90~2.20 times as high (https 197). For example, 2,600kcal and 1,950kcal are indicated for men and women of 50~64 years old and in level II, respectively. However, these values are for people with the average Japanese body size (men: 160.8cm tall and 60.0kg in weight; women: 148.0cm and 49.5kg; the BMI is about 23 for both). As a result, they should be higher or lower depending on one's weight. As for the change by age in level II, the highest value is 2,800kcal and 2,300kcal for 15~17 year old men and women, respectively, and the values for the people of the ages older than 17 years are lower.

Table 8-1: Estimated amounts of energy requirement/day in kcal.

Age / Gender	Men			Women		
Phys. activity level	I	II	III	I	II	III
0~5 m	---	550	---	---	500	---
6~8 m	---	650	---	---	600	---
9~11 m	---	700	---	---	650	---
1~2 y	---	950	---	---	900	---
3~5 y	---	1,300	---	---	1,250	---
6~7 y	1,350	1,550	1,750	1,250	1,450	1,650
8~9 y	1,600	1,850	2,100	1,500	1,700	1,900
10~11 y	1,950	2,250	2,500	1,850	2,100	2,350
12~14 y	2,300	2,600	2,900	2,150	2,400	2,700
15~17 y	2,500	2,800	3,150	2,050	2,300	2,550
18~29 y	2,300	2,650	3,050	1,700	2,000	2,300
30~49 y	2,300	2,700	3,050	1,750	2,050	2,350
50~64 y	2,200	2,600	2,950	1,650	1,950	2,250
65~74 y	2,050	2,400	2,750	1,550	1,850	2,100
≧75 y	1,800	2,100	---	1,400	1,650	---
Addition to a pregnant				+50	+50	+50
woman at early,				+250	+250	+250
middle or late stages				+450	+450	+450
Addtion to a nurse				+350	+350	+350

m: month, y: year. Activity level classification is described in the last page. Transferred from https 196.

This standard for food intake was based on the 2010 version. It is written that necessary revisions were made based on the discussions on the 2010 version, but the grounds of the present standard seem to be complex and unclear to me.

2) **Proteins, lipids and carbohydrates**

As for these, **recommended values for the intake of each** are common to both men and women and to all ages in terms of their ratio per caloric intake. The values and their medians (in parentheses) are as follows: 13~20% (16.5%) for proteins, 20~30% (25%) for lipids and 50~65% (57.5%) for carbohydrates. Namely, over 15% for proteins, about 25% for lipids and about 60% for carbohydrates (data from the 2015 standard). Since the calories produced from 1g are 4kcal for proteins or carbohydrates and 9kcal for lipids, the weight ratio for median intake standards of these is 16.5:11:57.5 or about 20%, 13% and 67%.

On the other hand, for **proteins**, the estimated average required amounts per day for an adult (50g or 200kcal for a man and 40g or 160kcal for a woman) are indicated in the table "The **standards for protein intake**". These protein amounts are only about 8% or 10% of the estimated amounts required for an average person of 50~64 years old (2,600kcal for a man and 1,950kcal for a woman). These values are less than 13% which is the lowest desirable value for the ratio of protein intake. Although the estimated energy requirement for a person younger than 70 years old is higher than that for a ≧70 year old person, the required or recommended protein amounts are the same for all the adults, and therefore the protein calorie ratios of the required total calories is less than 10% for most adults, for example 7.5% for a man of 18~29 years old. These ratios are much less than the median value for the desirable ratio of 16.5%. Thus, the food intake standards in 2015 seem to be inconsistent among the individual contents. However, it is written in the explanations of the standards that the "desirable amounts" were set higher than the "recommended amounts" in order for the former to prevent lifestyle-related diseases. **At present, it is not concluded as to how much protein intake is the best for health or a long lifespan, as described in Section 4-3.** There are two kinds of different results: one suggests that a lower amount (about 10%) is better and the other that a higher amount (15~20%) is better.

As stated here, the adequate amount of protein intake is left to each person. Even if there is evidence showing that a higher amount is good, 20% may be dangerous and around 15% seems safer. **I myself think that a lower protein amount is better for a longer life.** One of the grounds for my idea is the result of the experiments done in the USA described in Section 4-3. In the experiments, the mortalities and related indicators were compared among the higher (≧20%), lower (about 10%) and the middle protein intake groups, and the lower group was the best before 65 years old, which I think is important. The other reason is the result showing that **the centenarians in Portugal or Okinawa in Japan eat little meat** (Chapter 5).

Another important point about proteins is their contents. In the few studies introduced in Section 4-3, it was shown in all of them that plant proteins are better than animal proteins. A reason for this may be that foods of an animal origin contain much of the amino acid methionine which is not good for the human body (Kitada et al. 2019, 632-640). Also, meats contain many lipids including saturated fatty acids which are not good for the body. Accordingly, **as for proteins, intake of plant proteins such as soy beans or protein from fish is recommended**. It is said that soy bean proteins contain little methionine (渡邊, 2009, 169). In a table of contents of foods (香川, 2013, 106 & 128), the ratio of methionine in all the amino acids is 1.4% in soy beans and 2.7% in red meat.

As for **lipids**, the ratio of saturated fatty acids, which are not good for the body, in the total calorie intake should be ≦7%, and their ratio in the total lipids should be ≦30%.

3) The other nutrients

In the above standards (for the report and its outline, see: https 196), large tables are included which show the required amounts etc. for various nutrients classified by gender and age. Here, only the standards on dietary fiber, major vitamins and minerals are introduced briefly. **Dietary fiber** mainly represents cellulose, lignin etc. which are not digested by human digestive enzymes. In Japan, chitin and chitosan in foods from an animal are regarded as fiber, but the definition is said to differ among other countries (渡邊, 2009, 114). In the outline of the standards, ≧20g for a male adult and ≧18g for a female adult are given as the desired amounts per day. Dietary fiber seems to be important since it is included in the outline, and it may be for healthy bowel movements. Since we do not know the amounts of such fibers in specific foods, it is difficult for us to determine how much fibrous food should be eaten. **I recommend eating many vegetables in this context.**

Next, recommended or standard amounts for intake of **major vitamins and minerals** per day for an adult are collected in **Table 8-2**. The values written as A~B in the table are due to their difference by age. In such cases, the values are the highest for 30~49 year olds and lower for ≧70 year olds.

Table 8-2: Standard amounts of major vitamins and minerals for intake per day for an adult

Nutrients	Standard amounts		Nutrients	Standard amounts	
	Man	Woman		Man	Woman
Vitamin A	850~900 μg RAE	650~700 μg RAE	Vitamin E	6.0~7.0 mg	5.0~6.5 mg
Vitamin B_1	1.2~1.4mg	0.9~1.1mg	Calcium	750~800 mg	600~650 mg
Vitamin B_2	1.3~1.6mg	1.0~1.2mg	Magnesium	320~370 mg	280~290 mg
Vitamin B_6	1.4 mg	1.1 mg	Phosphorus	1000 mg	800 mg
Vitamin B_{12}	2.4 μg	2.4 μg	Iron	7~7.5 mg	6~6.5 mg
Niacin	13~15 mg NE	10~12 mg NE	Zinc	10~11 mg	8 mg
Pantothenic acid	5~6 mg	5 mg	Copper	0.8~0.9 mg	0.7 mg
Biotin	50 μg	50μg	Manganese	4.0 mg	3.5 mg
Folic acid	240 μg	240 μg	Iodine	130 μg	130 μg
Vitamin C	100 mg	100 mg	Selenium	30 μg	25 μg
Vitamin D	8.5 μg	8.5 μg	Chromium	10 μg	10 μg

RAE: retinol activity unit; NE: niacin unit. From https 160.

Actually, it may be quite laborious or even impossible to see how much of each nutrient is contained in a specific food. Probably, **a balanced intake of various foods may be roughly sufficient to get the required amounts of most vitamins or minerals**.

I myself am rather nervous of vitamin and mineral deficiencies, and take a tablet every day containing half of the recommended amounts of 12 vitamins and 7 minerals. If the reader is also nervous, I recommend a similar routine. By the way, the allowable upper limits for vitamins B6, D, and E, niacin and folic acid are listed separately, as an excess intake of one of these should be harmful. If the reader is interested in the function or necessity of a vitamin or mineral, please refer to a book on nutrition, such as 渡邊, 2009, 1-312.

4) Meals eaten by centenarians in the past, and meals for longevity recommended for the future

I found a recent review in a Japanese version of *National Geographic* which introduced four regions in the world rich in centenarians and the characteristics of their foods (Buettner 2020, 57-73), and I shall summarize it here. The **four regions said to be rich in centenarians** are ① a province of Sardinia (an island in the Mediterranean Sea), ② a district in the Republic of Costa Rica in Central America, ③ Okinawa Island in Japan and ④ a city near Los Angeles in the State of California in the USA. Centenarians in Okinawa and the characteristics of their meals were introduced earlier in this book (Section 5-3). The author of this review made a list of foods eaten in these regions during the past 100 years and surveyed them. Based on the result, **whole particle cereals, leaf-vegetables, nuts, tubers such as potatoes and beans were mainly eaten. Meats were consumed 5 times per month on average, and little cow milk was used**. The meals eaten by the Portugal centenarians introduced in Section 5-3 are similar. These data may be informative to the people who wish to live long lives. However, all these regions are located in subtropical or tropical zones, and therefore it is not certain that those foods are good for a long life in colder regions too.

In the same article, a report entitled "**Healthy Diets from Sustainable Food Systems:** Summary Report" (web 200), which was **issued by EAT-Lancet Committee** in 2019, was introduced. Based on the announcement in 2019 by the United Nations (https 201), the total population in the world is 7.7 billion at present and is expected to increase to 9.7 billion in 2050. Based on this expectation and the environmental and food production problems in the world, this report proposed that changes to meals which are sustainable and good for our health are necessary. As such, it proposed detailed contents of the desirable meals.

Table 8-3 was made by the author based on the recommended meal shown in Table 1 of the Lancet Report. In this table, foods to be eaten often are vegetables (1st), dairy foods (2nd) and whole grains (3rd), and foods containing high calories are whole grains (1st), protein sources (2nd) and added fats (3rd). The estimated calories of proteins or fats in such a meal per day are 294kcal and 739kcal, respectively, and they are 12% and 30% of a total caloric intake of 2,500kcal. Carbohydrates, therefore, comprise 58%.

One of the major characteristics of these meals is that **little animal foods are included (11% in terms of calories)**. Accordingly, 60% in weight and 80% in calories in the foods for protein sources are of plant origins (nuts and beans). The second characteristic is that the protein ratio (12%) is much lower than in the Japanese standards described above (16.5% for protein), and thereby the fat ratio is higher.

Table 8-3 is the most concrete outline of a meal introduced in this book and thereby the indicated meal plan is easy to practice. Also, since this meal plan is stressed as being strong against disease and good for health, it may be valuable information. Furthermore, the Lancet Committee claims that meals like those in the plan can rescue more than 10 million lives globally per year. However, since this report is a summary at present and the evidence for this is not shown, we cannot know how much we should believe it.

The content of this diet is similar to those in the regions rich in centenarians, which may be one of the reasons for the Lancet Committee's claim. The author feels that this meal may be good for old people, but that the animal protein amount may be insufficient for the people of 20~60 years old and especially for hard workers. Consumption of many nuts is included in the plan. However, the fatty acids included in peanuts are said to be bad for our health, and there may be difficulties in the supply of a large quantity of nuts.

Table 8-3: Healthy diets recommended by EAT-Lancet Commission for an intake of 2,500kcal/day (based on Table 1 of web 200).

Food		Intake g/day	Calorie kcal/day	Food		Intake g/day	Calorie kcal/day
Whole grains (rice, wheat, corn)		<u>232</u>	<u>811</u>	Added fats	Un-satur.	40 (20-80)	354
Protein sources	Beef, lamb, pork	14 (0-28)	30		Satu-rated	11.8 (0-11.8)	96
	Chicken etc.	29 (0-58)	62		Total		450
	Eggs	13 (0-25)	19	Dairy foods		250 (1-500)	153
	Fish	28 (0-100)	40	Fruits		200 (100-300)	40
	Legumes	75 (0-100)	284	Added sugars		31 (0-31)	120
	Nuts	50 (0-75)	291	Vegetables		300 (200-600)	78
	Total	209	<u>726</u>	Starchy veg. (potatoes etc.)		50 (0-100)	39

The three underlined values indicate high intakes or calories.

The reasons to decrease meats which are representative animal foods are not only those related to health. The results of the analyses are described in this Lancet Committee Report (web 200), which indicates that deforestation is advancing and vast amounts of fertilizers containing phosphorus and nitrogen are used and that these are important causes of the earth's environment being destroyed, since vast amounts of grains such as corns are consumed and farms of a large area are used for feeding cattle for meat. **In this report, to reduce wastes in the world by half and to reduce exhausts of greenhouse gas are proposed to be important. Thus, these proposals in the report constitute a comprehensive future plan across the whole world. It argues that the change in meals is the key of the plan.** If you are interested, please look at it online. It's likely that the details of the plan, rather than the summary, will be reported sometime in the future.

Obesity

Obese people are not in the majority in Japan, but **obesity is a large negative factor for human lifespans in many parts of the world**. It causes a **high blood pressure** and **vascular sclerosis** etc. as direct effects and it frequently leads to **diabetes** indirectly by accumulation of fats in the internal organs. As was shown in Table 4-2, **the hazard ratio for mortality becomes ≧1.2 in people with a BMI of ≧27.5** (in overweight class 2 or obesity grades), which means a reduction in lifespan. These people should reduce their BMI to about 25 by reduction of caloric intake and by practice of adequate physical activity.

Physical activity

Physical activity is a very important factor for a long lifespan, as much as healthy meals. As was shown in Fig. 4-8, **by practice of adequate physical activity every week, mortality risk can be reduced to 60-70% of that in the case of no physical activity**. The amount of physical activity or exercise can be measured scientifically in **MET** units, and the amount of physical activity is expressed by multiplication of it by time in hours into **MET h** units. The actual physical activity values can be seen, for example in Table 4-4. Even usual behaviors at home are light physical activities. If light activities such as walking and light physical exercise are practiced every day, the activity amounts become 20~40 MET h and they can bring the risk of mortality down to its lowest level. When commuting by **walking** or by **bicycle** is practiced every day, such physical activity is sufficient and in accordance with the recommended amount.

If physical activity every day is difficult, **jogging**, cycling or a long walk at the week end may be good enough. Continuous sitting is troublesome, and **a person who is usually sitting should improve their blood flow by a brief walk or moving the body lightly once per hour**. Mood change may also be good for working efficiency. Especially, a person who is sitting for a long time every day needs physical activity (Fig. 4-9). The reason why **physical activity** is effective for a long lifespan is that it **greatly decreases mortality by cardiovascular disease or cancer due to a decrease in the concentrations of blood sugar and insulin after a meal** and by making blood pressure and hyperlipidemia better.

Sleep

As it is said that good sleep is one of the three big factors for health, sleep is important for the lifespan. Based on Fig. 4-5 showing the relationship between sleep duration and mortality, 5~8h sleep durations are recommended. One result of a survey in Japan showed that **sleep durations ≦ 5h more than doubles the risk of mortality and dementia** (Section 4-4 [3]). Sleeping for 6~7h on average is likely to be the best. When sleep is insufficient, sleep for 6h or more is required. As for sleep, its quality is also important, but that was not described in this book. **Walking or light physical exercise in the evening, around 80% saturation in terms of supper, taking a bath and no severe stress are recommended for a good sleep.** As for sleep quality, drugs for sleep or important points for good sleep, reading an adequate book such as 大川, 2019, 1-160 is recommended.

Bowel movements

Although this was not mentioned in Chapter 4, it may be important for maintenance of the health and longevity as it is said that "good sleep good meal and healthy bowel movements are keys for a good body and mind". A medical encyclopedia (伊藤 et al. 2003, 2253-54) states that the frequency of bowel movement of a healthy person is usually once or twice per day and that once per three days or a week is frequent in **constipation**. Also, even if the frequency is normal, if the amounts of feces are small or they are very hard, those states are also said to be due to constipation. If constipation is severe, it leads to an important abnormality in the intestines. Even if constipation is not severe, it leads to a stomach ache or poor appetite, and is not good for the health. **Constipation is said** to be habitual or functional and **to be caused by an intestinal strain or a low level of physical activity** (高久 et al. 2004, 1954). Since the activity of the large intestine is activated by a stimulus from a meal, it is said that trial of bowel movement after a meal, especially after breakfast, is recommended. **Intake of much fibrous food is effective to stop constipation**, and a kind of laxative such as magnesium oxide is also effective if needed (Ibid.). The author thinks that shower by a shower toilet is very effective for bowel movements and recommends it.

Cancer

Based on the Dynamic Population Statistics in 2017 in Japan (https: 204), **five important causes of death in Japan were cancer (27.9% 1st), heart disease (15.3%, 2nd), cerebrovascular disease (8.2%, 3rd), senility (7.6%, 4th) and pneumonia (7.2%, 5th)**. As shown here, **cancer is the top** among the important causes of death. The ratios of cancer death by its location were: in men, **lung** 1st, **stomach** 2nd, **liver** 3rd, **colon** 4th, and pancreas 5th; in women, lung 1st, colon 2nd, **pancreas** 3rd, stomach 4th, **breast** 5th. The colon indicates most of the large intestine except for the rectum located just before the anus. **Ranking highest in cancer positions is the lung in both men and women**, and the stomach and colon are also common to both. As for changes in the rank for mortality risk from the year before, in men and women together pneumonia went from the 3rd to 5th, and both cerebrovascular disease and senility came up by a rank.

Now it is clear that most cancers arise when mutations have occurred in all of three or four genes. Probably there are several tens of such genes, and they are called **oncogenes or proto-oncogenes**. Several Ras genes, Myc genes and the p53 gene are representative oncogenes. Therefore, reduction of mutations is the way to reduce cancer incidences. Gene mutations arise naturally by various mechanisms, and the mutation frequency increases due to the induction of a mutation by various substances. It is thought that the most important problem in oncogenesis is the **oncogenic substances in the smoke** which are incorporated into the lungs etc. due to smoking and are absorbed. Incidences of lung cancer increase of course due to this fact, and the same is true for other cancers. It is said that as many as 70 kinds of oncogenic substances such as benzo(a)pyrene and dimethylnitrosamine are present in cigarette smoke. For example, likely the most harmful substance, benzo(a)pyrene binds to gene DNA and causes mutations after being activated in the body. No smoking and the discovery and medical treatment of a cancer in its early stages by physical examination (to be described below) may be effective for cancer prevention. As for stomach cancers, most of them are said to be due to the bacterium *H. pylori* and its elimination is effective against stomach cancers.

Smoking

As described in Section 4-6 in detail, the mortality risk of a person who has continued smoking from a young age is about twice as high as that of a never-smoker, and **the expected survival life of the smoker is about 10 years less**. Therefore smoking is an important factor for a shorter lifespan.

One of the reasons for this is that oncogenic substances contained in the cigarette smoke induce gene mutations and thereby cause a cancer such as lung cancer as described in the previous section. The other important reason is that cigarette smoke increases the risk of cardiovascular diseases by promoting arteriosclerosis and by the constriction of blood vessels by nicotine (http 206). It is very good that the ratio of smokers among Japanese people has decreased much during the past 50 years. As stated in Section 4-6, since stop of smoking leads to a mortality decrease even in long time smokers, to stop smoking is recommended.

Hypertension and diabetes

Recently in 2019, the change of the criterion for **hypertension** (high blood pressure) to ≧ 130mmHg of systolic blood pressure was proposed by a related academy, however the previous criterion had been ≧140mmHg. A person whose daily systolic B. P. is ≧140 is thought to be really suffering from hypertension. As shown in Fig. 4-17 (Section 4-8), **the mortalities of people showing a systolic B. P. of 140~159mmHg (grade 1 hypertension) or ≧160mmHg (grade 2 or 3 hypertension) are twice or three times as high as those of people with levels less than 120mmHg**. This is because hypertension leads to higher incidences of cardiovascular or cerebrovascular diseases which are 2nd or 3rd causes of death. The **three main points to prevent hypertension** are as follows: 1) Prevent an increase in blood pressure by reducing the salt in meals (to less than 7~8 g/day); 2) Prevent obesity by not eating too many calories, and for an obese person, lose weight; and 3) Improve blood flow and prevent obesity by adequate physical activity.

If one's blood sugar level is $\geqq$126 mg/dl in hunger or $\geqq$200 mg/dl at any time, diabetes is suspected. If these are observed twice or HbA_{1C} is $\geqq$6.5% and so on for a person, he or she is diagnosed as a diabetes patient. In Japan, $\geqq$95% of diabetes patients are type II, and type II diabetes is a typical life style-related disease in adults. Diabetes is a risk factor for arteriosclerosis and for various kinds of diseases such as nephropathy, retinopathy and neuropathy (Section 4-7). The causes for type II diabetes are said to be intakes of excess calories, obesity, insufficient physical activity and stress (http 207). **The main points to prevent type II diabetes are following recommended calorie guidelines and doing an adequate amount of physical activity.**

Pneumonia

As stated in the cancer section, pneumonia is the 5th biggest cause of death for Japanese people in recent years. However, **for the people $\geqq$70 years old, the rank of the risk goes up from 4th to 3rd to 2nd as their age increases**. One of the reasons for this is thought to be a decrease in self-immunity level. If one's self-immunity is decreased, a patient may often die even if treated with an antibiotic. In the case of my brother who was 17 years older than I, pneumonia may have been the direct cause of his death. If pneumonia is suspected for an old person based on coughs or fever, early treatment is the key. For prevention, it is recommended to keep in good health by adequate meals and physical activity etc.

Physical examination

To live long in a healthy state, prevention of obesity, hypertension and diabetes etc. and no smoking are important. No smoking is important for prevention of cancer in general, and elimination of bacterium *H. pylori* is effective for prevention of stomach cancer. However, cancers can arise everywhere and in every person. **To find and treat various diseases including cancer at an early stage is important to live long. For the early detection of a disease, having an adequate physical examination periodically is necessary.**

The author had an extensive physical examination called a "human dock" in Japanese every 2 years from the age of about 50 to 70. One of the early results was the detection of a polyp in the rectum, and an endoscopy of the entire large intestine was recommended. Then, plural polyps were found in the intestine by endoscopy, which were excised. The doctor said that one of the excised polyps would possibly have become cancerous, and I think that my lifespan was extended by more than several years by these examinations and operations. Based on this experience, I underwent several endoscopic examinations of the intestine and excision of polyps when found thereafter. Recently, I have been going for a general physical examination including an electrocardiogram and a PSA test every year.

The cost for a general physical examination such as a human dock may be around $700 (in Japan) which could possibly be shared by a mutual-aid association if you join one. **The author recommends the reader to take the first one as early as around 40 years old, once per every 3~5 years**

until about 60 years old and once every 2 years after that. The lifespans of many people are thought to be extended by more than several years by such examinations and treatments based on the examination results.

CHAPTER 9

THE BIOLOGICAL SIGNIFICANCE OF A LIFESPAN

In the other chapters, almost all the sentences are English translations from the original Japanese book published in Japan (大島, 2020, 1-238). This short chapter, however, is new to the English version. I think that "the biological significance of a lifespan" indicates the following two meanings which are quite different from each other.

(1) An important indicator in biology

Of course, lifespan represents how long an organism lives in general, and it may be the most important indicator in biology. The actual lifespan of an organism can in principle be measured and shown exactly in a specific numeral in days, months or years, and so is a quite objective indicator of life.

Two kinds of lifespan are usually used, and also in this book: a longest lifespan and an average lifespan. The former, the **longest lifespan**, is more important in biological significance since it is rather independent of environmental conditions and more closely related to genes. In contrast, an **average lifespan** varies greatly depending on environmental conditions.

Table 9-1: Average lifespans and longest lifespans

Animal/ plant	Classification/Species	Average lifespan	Longest lifespan	Reference
Animal	Invertebrate:			
	Nematode *C. elegans*	21 d	36 d, 26 d	Table 1-3, 220
	Insect *D. melanogaster*	~20 d?	46 d	Table 1-3
	Fish: salmon	3~5 y	13 y	17, Table 1-1
	carp	15~20 y	70~100 y	17, Table 1-1
	eel	20~30 y	88 y	17, Table 1-1
	whale shark	100 y	70 y, 150~y	17, Table 1-1
	Bird: sparrow	20 y	40 y	16
	hen	10 y	30 y	16, Table 1-1
	stork	35 y	70~100 y	16, Table 1-1
	Mammal: mouse	196 d	4 y=1,460 d	220, Table 1-1
	dog	14.4 y	34 y	Sec. 1-1, Table 1-1
	human	72 y	122 y	Sec. 1-1, Table 1-1
Plant	Gymnosperm:			
	Thuja occidentalis	~200 y	~700 y	Sec. 6-2
	spruce (Sweden)	300~350 y	9,550 y	Table 6-2, 2-1
	Angiosperm:			
	Dicotylenodopsida beech	230~260 y	435 y	Table 6-2, 2-1
	Mongolian oak	230~260 y	444 y	Table 6-2, 2-1
	Monocotylenodopsida			
	spider orchid	~4 y	26 y	Sec. 6-1

y: year, d: day. References: 17 (https 17), 16 (http 16), 220 (https 220).

Good examples of this may be the changes in the human average lifespan in human history and the varieties among the countries in the world (Section 1-2). Also, an average lifespan is harder to measure, and reliable data are few. Longest lifespan data are much more present than average lifespan data in this book, too.

As for the longest lifespan records of the organisms described in this book, the shortest is the 14 days of the saline rotifer (Table 1-3) and the longest is the 43,600 years or more of *L. tasmanica* (Table 2-1), the latter being about 10^6 (1 million) times as long as the former. **Table 9-1** shows comparisons between both lifespans in various animals and plants. Most of the longest lifespan data in the table were described earlier in this book. The average lifespan data can vary much depending on the living place and the era, and so the data in the table are the available examples. Based on this table, the longest/average ratios vary from less than 2 to about 30 and their average seems to be 3~4.

(2) Possible positive functions in the survival and evolution of an organism

I have read descriptions on the biological significance of a lifespan or ageing in several books, and I think that most people including the authors of these books believe the following hypothesis (for our purposes, **hypothesis A): A limited lifespan has a positive function important for an organism, and is necessary for the survival and evolution of a species.** The main reason for this hypothesis seems to be that long lives of many old and non-reproductive individuals are harmful for the existence and evolution of that species since, for example, they take away much food and many bed sites etc. from young people. I think that a sentence written in the summary of the Japanese book 小林 (2016, 189) is a most concise and clear expression of this hypothesis. Another Japanese book (本川, 2016, 242-244) describes that a limited lifespan sets us free from a painful life in old age. These may be representative opinions which favor this hypothesis.

However, I now think that this hypothesis is doubtful, and greatly favor a second **hypothesis (B): A limited, specific lifespan has no positive or important function for an organism.** I think that a limited, specific lifespan is determined by inevitable **ageing** of the organism and by several **environmental or biological conditions** such as climate, foods or nutrients, competition, being captured or eaten, being infected with a pathogen, or suffering an accident, as well as by the organism's **genes**.

As for the **role of genes in the lifespan**, I described many genes which control the lifespan. Also, I wrote in Chapter 7 that the factors which determine the lifespan and are common to animals and plants are body sizes and genes, and that the body size is determined ultimately by genes. It is certain that genes are included in the important determinants in various degrees. More advanced animals are said to have the highest possibility for a genetically programmed lifespan. However, let us think of the human lifespan. As described in Section 1-2, the **average human lifespan** Before the Common Era was likely to be around 20 years, and this lifespan probably represents that of primitive human beings before civilization. Since the recent average human lifespan in the world is 72 years (Section

1-2), the average human lifespan has increased more than three-fold. This increase is certainly due to the civilization in the world and not related to the biological or genetically programmed lifespan. As for the longest human lifespan, it likely increased from 40~50 years to 122 years or two to three-fold. These facts on the human lifespan show that **the lifespan greatly depends on the environment and that the role of genes is not so high even in humans**.

I think that hypothesis (A) is based on the assumption that an organism lives really eternally without a specific lifespan, which is impossible since both animals and plants must die due to ageing and unfavorable environmental conditions as stated above.

Ageing cannot be prevented in any organism or cell since every organism or cell is not perfect and since toxic wastes and genetic mutations are accumulated.

Also, I feel that hypothesis (A) is based on the assumption that the lifespan is genetically programmed, which may not be right in general since, for example, trees can live for a very long time, up to several thousand years. In such trees, although a specific lifespan partly depends on the genes of the organism, it is hard to say that the lifespan is genetically programed since there is a great variety in the actual lifespan.

I rather favored hypothesis (A) and wrote as such in several parts of this book. I thought that lifespan is genetically programmed in most animals, especially in more advanced animals. This thought is highly related to hypothesis (A). However, in adding a new chapter to the English version, I have come to think about the biological significance of a lifespan again, and deeply. As a result, **I now greatly favor hypothesis (B)**. I find that the lifespans of most organisms (except for the clonal lifespan of unicellular organisms) can mostly be explained by ageing and environmental conditions as stated above. I think this is much better than (A) since it is simple and quite universal.

As for the ageing which is intimately related to the lifespan, many studies have been done, too. Here, I cite only a recent and comprehensive book by Sinclair and LaPlante (2020, 1-491).

CHAPTER 10

METHODS FOR THE MEASUREMENT OF AGES AND LIFESPANS

As stated in the section on "Lifespan ranking of vertebrates" (1-1), it is difficult in general to precisely determine the age at death or the lifespan of an animal. Here, methods to measure or estimate the age of an animal such as a vertebrate and a plant are described. As for a plant, measurement of the age is difficult in general, too. New methods have been created also in the measurement of an age by development of molecular biology etc.

Breeding and cultivation

Continuous breeding or cultivation of an animal or a plant from birth is the most certain and accurate method to measure the age or the lifespan in days. This is possible for an animal bred in a zoo or at home. Otherwise, if precise records of the dates of birth and death are available, the precision of the measurement is the same. Methods like these are the most general ones which could be applied to all animals and plants. However, application of such a method to an animal or plant which lives for more than 100 years is likely to be quite difficult. Also, the lifespan of an organism under breeding or culture is probably different from and longer than that of a wild one.

Catch and labelling

If a wild animal was caught at a young age and if the age was estimated and again caught after labelling, the age can be estimated. As for animals such as insects or fish, this kind of survey is done for various purposes.

Ages of a tooth, a bone or a horn

The best measure of the age of a vertebrate seems to that based on annual rings of a tooth (a stratified structure). This structure is formed in the cementum parts at the tooth base shown in **Fig. 10-1** by the difference in the growth speed between a spring-summer season and a winter season. An example is shown in **Fig. 10-2**. This figure shows a tooth in the lower jaw of a Japanese deer, which is stained with hematoxylin after removal of calcium with an acid and cut into thin sections. The parts stained dark are the layers formed during winter, from which the age is estimated to be 6 years old (三浦, 1996, 50).

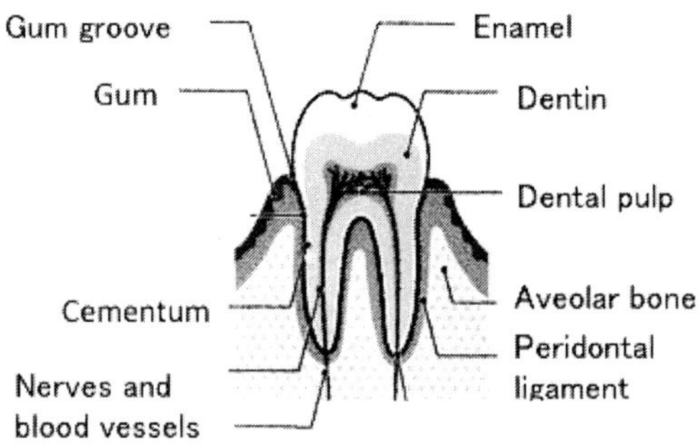

Fig. 10-1: Structure of a mammalian tooth (adapted from Fig. 9-1 of 大島, 2020, 218).

Such a stratified structure or an annual ring is observed in the teeth of many mammals and is used as a means of age determination. Similar annual rings are also observed in the tooth dentin of a toothed whale or a seal and in the bones of a rabbit or a bird, which are also used for age determination. A similar stratified structure is formed also in a human tooth, but it is not an annual ring because human beings lack a seasonal change in metabolism, and so the stratified structure cannot be used for age determination.

Fig. 10-2: Annual rings in a tooth in the lower jaw of a Japanese deer

(三浦, 1996, 50).

Annual rings on a shell

Annual rings are formed also on a shell of a reptile tortoise or turtle due to a change in the growth speed, and they can be used to estimate their age (http 210).

Annual rings in an otolith, a scale etc.

In fish, annual ring-like structures are formed in the otolith (stone in the inner ear), scale, spine etc. Especially, annual rings in an otolith are easier to identify, and they are used for determining the age of fish (**Fig. 10-3**). An **otolith** is like a bone made of a calcium carbonate crystal, exists at the right and left sides of a head as a pair, and is involved in the sense of equilibrium and in hearing. Such an annual ring is sometimes difficult to identify depending on the fish species, and especially difficult in an individual older than 10 (http 211).

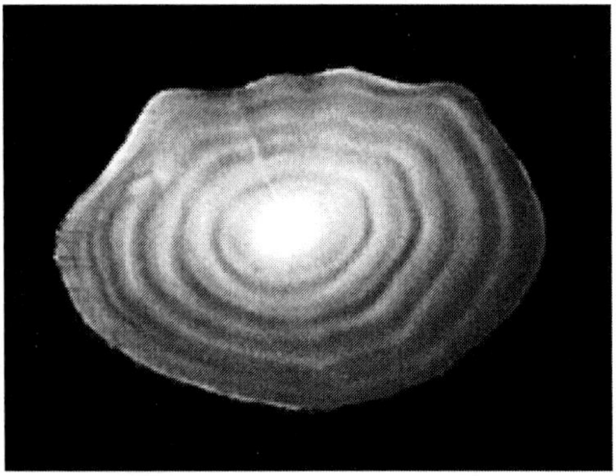

Fig. 10-3: Annual rings seen on an otolith of a kind of flatfish (http 211).

An example of annual rings on a **scale** of a fish is shown in **Fig. 10-4**. Also for an annual ring on a scale, it cannot always be counted, and we should be cautious since sometimes two annual rings are formed per year (http 212).

Racemization of an amino acid

Most of the organic compounds in a body exist only as one of the two optical isomers (**D or L body**). This phenomenon arises because the enzymes, which catalyze the synthesis of the compounds, strictly distinguish between D and L forms which entirely differ in structure, both as materials and products. After the death of or release from an organism, D to L and L to D changes occur non-enzymatically, and finally an equilibrium occurs in which D and L exist in equal amounts. This phenomenon is called "**racemization**".

Fig. 10-4: A scale of a yellowback seabream. The arrow indicates an annual ring (http: 212).

Amino acids exist in large quantities in a body as structural components for a protein etc. and all of them are in L forms. The speed of racemization differs by the temperature in general and by the kind of amino acids. Complete racemization of all the amino acids present in a body takes about 100,000 years. For this reason, the ratio of racemization of an amino acid has been used to estimate the era of a sediment or a shell etc. and the temperature of the environment in which they existed. **Aspartic acid** is likely to have the fastest speed of racemization among all the amino acids. Therefore, measurement of the ratio of racemization of aspartic acid is the best method to estimate the age of a living animal, whose lifespan is at most several hundred years, or to estimate the age of an animal just after death (Helfman and Bada 1975, 2891-2894). The method of estimating an age based on the racemization of an amino acid has a high generality, namely it can be applicable to all animals and plants.

Based on these facts, if the racemization ratio of aspartic acid contained in a tissue which is not at all metabolized after its formation in a body is measured, the age of the tissue after formation can be estimated. The authors of the above paper examined racemization ratios (0.045~0.112) of enamels in the teeth (Fig. 10-1) of the living people of various ages, and found that the ages of the teeth estimated from racemization ratios were nearly the same as those estimated from the real ages of the people. This method is used in medical jurisprudence as the most reliable method to estimate the age of a dead body without an identity, and is thought to be used also to estimate the age of an individual wild animal. By the way, the racemization rate of aspartic acid in the enamel of a human tooth was 8.29×10^{-4}/year (Helfman and Bada 1975, 2891-2894).

An important example of this method using aspartic acid racemization was the measurement of the age of the Arctic whale (211+/-35 years), which is ranked second in terms of the longest lifespan records of vertebrates. In this case, an eye lens was used as the tissue which had no metabolism after the birth, and the measurement was based on the racemization rate of a man whose body temperature was 37℃ and that of a fin back whale whose temperature in the deep body part was 36℃. There is a standard error range of +/-35 years due to various factors for the estimation of an age.

Radioactive carbon

As stated in Section 1-1, the vertebrate which has the longest lifespan record (392+/-120 years) is a kind of shark called the Greenland shark living in the Arctic Ocean. The estimation of this lifespan is based on the ratio of the radioactive carbon (C^{14}) contained in a certain amount of carbon of the eye lens nucleus, which is formed in the body of the mother before the birth and is thought to be not metabolized at all after birth.

Most parts of the radioactive carbon in the biological zone on the earth are formed by a collision between neutrons in the secondary cosmic rays and nuclei of nitrogen atoms. The amount of products by this reaction changes, and the average ratio of C^{14} over the total carbon is about 10^{-12}. Formed C^{14} immediately changes to CO_2, which spreads into the atmosphere and seawater. A part of the CO_2 is incorporated into plants by photosynthesis, and the products of photosynthesis are incorporated into various animals through a food chain. While an organism is alive, metabolism functions in many tissues and the ratio of C^{14} is almost constant. After the death of an organism, metabolism does not function and the ratio of C^{14} declines logarithmically with a half-life of 5,730 years. Based on this principle, the era of the death of an organism can be estimated from the measured radioactivity of C^{14} in the dead body. Even for a tissue of a living organism, the era of its formation can be estimated if it is not metabolized. This is the principle of the estimation of the era of the birth of an organism or of the formation of a tissue (八杉 et al., 1996, 221). This is a highly general method applicable to all animals and plants, similar to amino acid racemization. The ages of *Lomatia tasmanica*, which ranks first among the longest lifespan records of plants (43,600 years old), and of the long-living tree spruce (9,550 years old) described in Chapter 2, were both measured by C^{14}.

In the case of the Greenland shark, the measurement of tissue not metabolized after birth was required to know the birth date and so C^{14} of the eye lens was measured. Actually, several necessary adjustments were done to get a result as accurate as possible, and the age of the largest individual of 502cm long was estimated to be 392+/-120 years old (Nielsen et al. 2016, 702-704). This method using an eye lens is used also in the medical jurisprudence field as one which estimates human age with a high accuracy (Lynnerup et al. 2008, e1529).

Measurement of the lifespan of a tree

(1) Measurement by **annual rings**: In trees growing in a temperate zone, large cells with thin cell walls are formed in the xylem around summer when the growth is fast, and small cells with thick cell walls are formed around winter when the growth is slow. As a result, growth rings or annual rings are formed in the trunk of a tree. In tropical or subtropical zones, such annual rings are also formed in pines. If the number of annual rings are

counted, the period required for the growth of that part of the tree can be estimated. If the trunk part near the root is cut, the age of the entire tree can be estimated. However, it is said that annual rings are not always clear, when staining or dipping in water is said to make annual rings clearer. Also, counting the annual rings in several directions will lead to a more accurate estimation.

To examine annual rings without cutting the tree, a "**growth gimlet**" is used. This is a T-shape appliance, whose vertical part is driven into the center of the trunk. A cylindrical xylem of about 5mm diameter is then taken out, and its annual rings are counted. If measurement down to the center of the trunk is difficult, the age is estimated by proportion of the measured depth to the radius of the trunk. Usually, a growth gimlet is used at the height of a man at which a gimlet is easy to handle, with the estimated ages up to that height being added to the obtained value (加茂 1999, 49).

(2) Methods based on **the growth speed or the growth amount**: If the diameters of the trunks of all the subject trees in the survey area are measured once per several years or every year for several years, growth speeds can be calculated and the ages at present estimated by the present trunk diameters (加茂 1999, 49). If the dying probability of a specific tree species (mortality) is examined in the same way, the half-life of that tree can be calculated as the reciprocal of the mortality. The lifespans of the trees on Yakushima Island shown in Section 6-2 or Table 6-1 were estimated in such a way.

The age and the lifespan of grass

It is thought that there is no general method to determine the age or lifespan of grass (herb) except for continuous observation after budding. As for the spider orchid and *P. lanceolata* described in Section 6-1, they were observed every year to determine the age for a long time, (32 years and $\geqq$10 years). In the case of the perennial herb *B. pyrenaica* also described in that section, its age could be exactly determined since an annual scar is left in the tuber every year. This was the special case in which the longest lifespan of over 300 years was shown.

DNA methylation and telomere length

Various modifications of DNA such as methylation have been actively studied recently, and their possibly important functions are becoming clear. Related to this, many studies have been reported which indicate that the ratio of methylation of **CpG sequences** in a specific position of the genome is related to age in humans and animals (Paoli-Iseppi et al. 2017, Article 106). For example, when the methylation of seven specific positions were examined using human saliva samples, the **methylation showed a 95% association with the age as a whole** and was reported to be valuable in medical jurisprudence (Hong et al. 2017, 118-125). It is anticipated that estimations of the ages of various animals in a similar high reliability will become possible by analysis of DNA methylation. This method has a high generality, too.

A **telomere** is a structure containing DNA which exists generally at the ends of DNA in the chromosomes of eukaryotes. Its function is to reverse the shortening of DNA accompanied by a duplication of DNA. However, this function is not necessarily perfect, and it is known that the length of a telomere decreases as the DNA duplication increases or due to ageing. When the degree of telomere shortening was examined on human teeth, telomere shortening showed a meaningful relationship with age, but the precision in the estimation of the age was not good enough (Marquez-Ruiz et al. 2018, 353-359). This method may also advance to be a useful one to estimate animal ages.

Bibliography

(1) Journal articles and books in an alphabetical order

Aiba, Shin-Ichiro, Kohyama, Takashi. 1996. Tree species stratification in relation to allometry and demography in a warm-temperate rain forest. *J. Ecol.*: 84, 207-218.

Ainsworth, Barbara E., Haskell, William L., Herrmann, Stephen D. et al. 2011. Compendium of Physical Activities: A Second Update of Codes and MET Values. *Med. Sci. Sports Exerc..*: 43, 1575-1581.

赤木優也 (Akagi), 神出計. 2018. 長寿の遺伝素因：百寿者研究、高齢者疫学研究から得られた知見より. *日老医誌*: ５５,５５４−５６１.

Akerrstedt, Torbjorn, Ghiilotti, Francesca, Grotta, Alessandra et al. 2017. Sleep duration, mortality and the influence of age. *Eur. J. Epidemiol.*: 32, 881-891.

Alberts, Bruce, Johnson, Alexander, Lewi, Julian et al. 中村桂子・松原謙一監訳. 2010.「*細胞の分子生物学*」第５版. 東京：ニュートンプレス. Original: 2008, 2002. *Molecular Biology of the Cell.* New York: Garland Science.

Alves, Ruy J. V., Da Silva, Nilber G., Fernandes Jr., Aluisio J. et al. 2013. Longevity of the Brazilian underground tree *Jacaranda decurrens* Cham. *Anais da Academia Brasileira de Ciencias* 85: 671-677.

Arabidopsis Genome Initiative. 2000. Analysis of the genome of the flowering plant Arabidopsis thaliana. *Nature*: 408: 796-815.

Arai, Yasumichi, Sasaki, Takashi, Hirose Nobuyoshi. 2017. Demographic, phenotypic, and genetic characteristics of centenarians in Okinawa and Honshu, Japan: Part 2 Honshu, Japan. *Mech. Ageing Dev.*: 165, 80-85.

新井康通 (Arai)、広瀬信義. 2018. スーパーセンチナリアンの医学生物学的研究. *日老医誌*: 55, 578-583.

Arem, Hannah, Moore, Steven C., Patel Alpa et al. 2015. Leisure Time Physical Activity and Mortality: A Detailed Pooled Analysis of the Dose-Response Relationship. *JAMA Intern. Med.*: 175, 959-967.

Armenteros-Yeguas, Victoria, Garate-Echenique, Lucia, Tomas-Lopez, Maria Aranzazu et al. 2017. Prevalence of difficult venous access and associated risk factors in highly complex hospitalised patients. *J. Clin. Nurs.*: 26, 4267-4275.

Ashton, Peter S., Hall, Pamela. 1992. Comparisons of structure among mixed dipterocarp forest of north-western Borneo. *J. Ecol.*: 80, 459-481.

Aune, Dagfinn, Sen, Abhijit, o'Hartaigh, Briain et al. 2017. Resting heart rate and the risk of cardiovascular disease, total cancer, and all-cause mortality - a systematic review and dose-response meta-analysis of prospective studies. *Nutr. Metab. Cardiovasc. Dis.*: 27(6), 504-517. Doi: 10.1016.

Bartke, Andrzej, Wright, J. Chris, Mattison, Jurie A. et al. 2001. Extending the lifespan of long-lived mice. *Nature*: 414, 412.

Bauer, Joseph A., Pearson, Kevin J., Price, Nathan L. et al. 2006. Resveratrol improves health and survival of mice on a high-calorie diet. *Nature*: 444, 337-342.

Benigni, Ariela, Corna, Daniela, Zoja, Carla et al. 2009. Disruption of the Ang II type I receptor promotes longevity in mice. *J. Clin. Invest.*: 119, 524-530.

Bigler, Christof. 2016. Trade-Offs between Growth Rate, Tree Size and Lifespan of Mountain Pine (*Pinus montana*) in the Swiss National Park. *PLoS ONE* : 11(3), 1-18, e0150402.

Brandhorst, Sebastian, Choi, In Young, Wei, Min et al. 2015. A Periodic Diet that Mimics Fasting Promotes Multi-System Regeneration, Enhanced Cognitive Performance, and Healthspan. *Cell Metabolism*: 22, 86-99.

Brown-Borg, Holly M., Borg, Kurt E. 1996. Dwarf mice and the aging process. *Nature*: 384, 33.

ダン・ビュートナー (**Buettner**). 2020.「長寿の食卓を巡る旅」. *ナショナルジオグラフィック日本版*:２０２０年１月号，５７—７３.

Burian, Agata, Barbier de Reuille, Piere, Kuhlemeier, Cris. 2016. Patterns of Stem Cell Divisions Contribute to Plant Longevity. *Current Biology*: 26, 1385-1394.

Butler P. G., Wanamaker A. D., Scource, J. D. et al. Variability of marine climate on the North Icelandic Shelf in a 1357-years proxy archive based on growth increments in the bivalve *Arctica Islandica*. *Palaeogeogr. Paleocl.* 2012.

Chastin, Sebastien F. M., Craemer, Marieke De, Coccker, Katrien De et al. 2019. How does light-intensity physical activity associate with adult cardiometabolic health and mortality? Systematic review with meta-analysis of experimental and observational studies. *Br. J. Sports Med.*, 53: 370-376.

Colman, Ricki J., Anderson, Rozalin M., Johnson, Sterling C. et al. 2009. Caloric restriction delays disease onset and mortality in rhesus monkeys. *Science*: 325, 201-204.

Conti, Bruno, Sanchez-Alavez, Manuel, Winsky-Sommerer, Raphaelle et al. 2006. Transgenic Mice with a Reduced Core Body Temperature Have an Increased Life Span. *Science*: 314, 825-828.

D'Antona, Giuseppe, Ragni, Maurizio, Cardile, Annalisa et al. 2010. Branched-Chain Amino Acid Supplementation Promotes Survival and Supports Cardiac and Skeletal Muscle Mitochondrial Biogenesis in Middle-Aged Mice. *Cell Metabolism*: 12, 362-372.

Dato, Serena, Soerensen, Mette, Rango, Francesco De et al. 2018. The genetic component of human longevity: New insights from the analysis of pathway-based SNP-SNP interactions. *Aging Cell*: 17, 1-12: e12755.

Deng, Qucheng, Wei Yongping, Zhao, Yan et al. 2018. Understanding the Natural and Socioeconomic Factors behind Regional Longevity in Guangxi, China: Is the Centenarian Ratio a Good Enough Indicator for Assessing the Longevity Phenomenon? *Int. J. Environ. Res. Public Health*: 15, 938, 1-16; doi:10.3390

de Witte, Lucienne C., Stocklin, Jurg. 2010. Longevity of clonal plants: why it matters and how to measure it. *Annals of Botany*, 106: 859-870.

de Witte, Lucienne C., Armbruster, G. F., Gielly, et al. 2012. AFLP markers reveal high clonal diversity and extreme longevity in four key arctic-alpine species. *Mol. Ecol*. Mar: 21(5): 1081-97.

Doll, Richard, Peto Richard, Boreham, Jillian, Sutherland, Isabelle. 2004. Mortality in relation to smoking: 50 years' observation on male British cohorts. *BMJ*: 328, 1519-28.

Fanson, Benjamin G., Weldon, Christopher W., Perez-Staples, Diana et al. 2009. Nutrients, not caloric restriction, extend lifespan in a Queensland fruit flies. *Aging Cell*: 8, 514-523.

Flindt, Rainer 著、浜本哲郎訳. 2007.「*数値で見る生物学*」. 東京：シュプリンガー・ジャパン. Original: Flindt, Rainer. 2002. *Biologie in Zahlen*. Heidelberg: Spectrum Akademischer Verlag.

Garcia, Maria B., Antor, Ramon J. 1995. Sex-ratio and sexual dimorphism in the dioecious *Bordera pyrenaica* (Dioscoreaceae). *Oecologia*: 101, 59-67.

Garcia, Maria B., Dahlgren, Johan P., Ehrlen, Johan. 2011. No evidence of senescence in a 300-year-old mountain herb. *J. Ecol.* 99: 1424-1430.

GBD 2015 Tobacco Collaborators. 2017. Smoking prevalence and attributable disease burden in 195 countries and territories, 1990–2015: a systematic analysis from the Global Burden of Disease Study 2015. *Lancet*: 389, 1885-1906.

George, John C., BADA, Jeffrey, Zeh, Judith et al. 1999. Age and growth estimates of bowhead whales (*Balaena mysticetus*) via aspartic acid racemization. *Can. J. Zool.* 77: 571-580.

権藤恭之 (Gondo). 2018. 百寿者の国際共同研究の目的と成果. *日老医誌*: 55, 570-577.

Goto, Atsushi, Takao, Toshiko, Yoshida, Yoko et al. 2019. Causes of death and estimated life expectancy among people with diabetes: A retrospective cohort study in a diabetes clinic. *Journal of Diabetes Investigation*: 10:25, 1-9.

Harrison, David E., Strong, Randy, Sharp, Zelton Dave et al. 2009. Rapamycin fed late in life extends lifespan in genetically heterogeneous mice. *Nature*: 460, 392-395.

Helfman, Patricia Masters, Bada, Jeffrey L. 1975. Aspartic acid racemization in tooth enamel from living humans. *Proc. Natl. Acad. Sci. USA*: 72, 2891-2894.

Hippisley-Cox, Julia, Coupland, Carol, Vinogradova, Yana et al. 2008. Predicting cardiovascular risk in England and Wales: prospective derivation and validation of QRISK2. *BMJ*: 336, 1475-1482.

Hofmann, Jeffrey, Zhao, Xiaoai, De Cecco, Marco et al. 2015. Reduced Expression of MYC Increases Longevity and Enhances Healthspan. *Cell*: 160, 477-488.

Hong, Sea Rom, Jung, Sang-Eun, Lee, Eun Hee et al. 2017. DNA methylation-based age prediction from saliva: High age predictability by combination of 7 CpG markers. *Forensic Sci. Int. Genet.*: 29, 118-125.

Hozawa, Atsushi, Ohkubo, Takayoshi, Kikuya, Masahiro et al. 2004. Prognostic Value of Home Heart Rate for Cardiovascular Mortality in the General Population. *American Journal of Hypertension*: 17, 1005-1010.

Hutchings Michael J. 2010. The population biology of the early spider orchid *Ophrys sphegodes* MiII. III. Demography over three decades. *J. Ecol.*: 98, 867-878.

伊藤正男 (Ito)、井村裕夫、高久史麿編. 2003.「*医学書院　医学大辞典*」. 東京：医学書院.

今堀和友 (Imabori)・山川民夫監修. 2007.「*生化学辞典（第 4 版）*」. 東京：東京化学同人.

Ireland, Kathryn, B., Moore, Margaret M., Fule, Peter Z. et al. 2014. Slow lifelong growth predisposes *Populus tremuloides* trees to mortality. *Oecologia*: 175: 847-859.

Jha, Prabhat, Ramasundarahettige, Chinthanie, Landsman, Victoria et al. 21st-Century Hazards of Smoking and Benefits of Cessation in the United States. 2013. *N. Eng. J. Med.*: 368, 341-350.

Johnson, Simon C., Ravinovitch, Peterr S., Kaeberlein, Matt. 2013. mTOR is a key modulator of ageing and age-related disease. *Nature*: 493, 338-345.

Jones, Owen R., Scheuerlein, Alexander, Salguero-Gomez, Roberto et al. 2014. Diversity of ageing across the tree of life. *Nature*: 505, 169-173.

Joshi, Peter K, Piratsu, Nicola, Kentistou, Katherine A. et al. 2017. Genome-wide meta-analysis associates *HLA-DQA1/DRB1* and *LPA* and lifestyle factors with human longevity. *Nature Commun.* 8: 910, 1-13| DOI: 10.1038.

加茂皓一 (Kamo). 1999.「樹木の年齢」. *森林科学* :27 巻、49.

Kelly, P. E., Larson, D. W. 1997. Dendroecological analysis of the population dynamics of an old-growth forest on cliff-faces of the Niagara Escarpment, Canada. *J. Ecol.*: 85, 467-478.

Kenny, Karen Latchana. 2019. *Extreme Longevity*. Minneapolis, USA: Twenty-First Century Books.

Kenyon, Cynthia, Chang, Jean, Gensch, Erin et al. 1993. A *C. elegans* mutant that lives twice as long as wild type. *Nature* 366: 461-464.

Kenyon, Cynthia J. 2010. The genetics of ageing. *Nature*: 464, 504-512.

Kikuchi, H., Inoue, S., Lee, I. M. et al. 2018. Impact of Moderate-Intensity and Vigorous-Intensity Physical Activity on Mortality. *Med. Sci. Sports Exerc.* 50: 715-721.

Killic, Ulkan, Gok, Ozlem, Erenbeck, Ufuk et al. 2015.: A Remarkable Age-Related Increase in SIRT1 Protein Expression against Oxidative Stress in Elderly: *SIRT1* Gene Variants and Longevity in Human. *PLOS ONE*: 1-19| DOI: 10.1371/journal.pone.0117954.

Kim, Du Hyun. 2018. Extending *Populus* seed longevity by controlling seed moisture content and temperature. *PLOS ONE*: 13(8), 1-16: e0203080.

Kitada, M., Ogura, Y, Monno, I., Koya, D. 2019. The impact of dietary protein intake on longevity and metabolic health. *EBioMedicine*: 43, 632-640.

小林武彦 (Kobayashi). 2016. *寿命はなぜ決まっているのか*. 東京：岩波書店.

Kurihara, Ayako, Okamura, Tomonori, Sugiyama, Daisuke et al. 2019. Vegetable Protein Intake was Inversely Associated with Cardiovascular Mortality in a 15-Year Follow-Up Study of the General Japanese Population. *J. Atheroscler. Thromb.*: 26, 198-206.

Ladiges, Warren, Remmen, R. Strong, Ikeno, Yuji et al. 2009. Lifespan extension in genetically modified mice. *Aging Cell*: 8, 346-352.

Levine, Morgan, Suarez, Jorge A., Brandhorst, Sebastian et al. 2014. Low Protein Intake is Associated with a Major Reduction in IGF-1, Cancer, and Overall Mortality in the 65 and Younger but Not Older Population. *Cell Metabolism*: 19, 407-417.

Li, Yan, Zheng, Guowei, Jia, Yanxia et al. 2014. Acyl Chain Length of Phosphatidylserine Is Correlated with Plant Lifespan. *PLOS ONE*: 9(7), 1-7, e103227.

Lima, Juliana Joice Pereira, Buitink, Julia, Lalanne, David et al. 2017. Molecular characterization of the acquisition of longevity during seed maturation in soybean. *PLOS ONE*: 12(7), 1-25 e0180282.

Liu, Fenghong, Liu, Jian, Dong, Ming. 2016. Ecological Consequences of Clonal Integration in Plants. *Frontiers in Plant Science* 7: Article 770, 1-11.

リヴィーバッチ著、速水・斎藤訳. 2014.「*人口の世界史*」東京: 東洋経済新報社. Original: Livi-Bacci, Massimo. 2012. *A Concise History of World Population*, Fifth Edition. John Wiley and Sons.

Longo, Valter D., Panda, Satchidananda. 2016. Fasting, Circadian Rhythms, and Time-Restricted Feeding in Healthy Lifespan. *Cell Metabolism*: 23, 1048-1059.

Lopez-Otin, Carlos, Galluzzi, Lorenzo, Freije, Jose M. P. et al. 2016. Metabolic Control of Longevity. *Cell*: 166, 802-821.

Lynch, A. J. J., Barnes, R. W., Vaillancourt, R. E. et. al. 1998. Genetic evidence that *Lomatia tasmanica* (Proteaceae) is an ancient clone. *Australian Journal of Botany* 46(1): 25-33.

Lynnerup, Niels, Kjeldsen, Henrik, Heegaard, Steffen et al. 2008. Radiocarbon Dating of the Human Eye Lens Crystallines Reveal Proteins without Carbon Turnover throughout Life. *PLoS ONE*: 3(1), e1529.

Marba, Nuria, Duarte, Carlos M., Agusti, Susana. 2007. Allometric scaling of plant life history. *PNAS*: 104, 15777-15780.

Marquez-Ruiz, Ana Belen, Gonzalez-Herrera, Lucas, Valenzuela, Aurora. 2018. Usefulness of telomere length in DNA from human teeth for age estimation. *Int. J. Legal Med.*: 132(2): 353-359.

Martinez, Daniel E., Bridge, Diane. 2012. *Hydra*, the everlasting embryo, confronts aging. *Int. J. Dev. Biol*. 56: 479-487.

Mattson, Mark P., Allison, David, B., Fontana, Luigi et al. 2014. Meal frequency and timing in health and disease. *PNAS*: 111, 16647-16653.

McCay et. al. 1935. *J. Nutr*. :10, 63-79.

McMahon and Bonner 著、木村武二他訳. 2000.「*生物の大きさとかたちーサイズの生物学*」.東京：東京化学同人. Original: McMahon, Thomas A., Bonner, John Tyler. 1983. *ON SIZE AND LIFE*. New York: W. H. Freeman and Company.

Miller, Richard, A., Buehner, G., Chang, Yayi et al. 2005. Methionine-deficient diet extends mouse lifespan, slows immune and lens aging, alters glucose, T4, IGF-1 and insulin levels, and increases hepatocyte MIF levels and stress resistance. *Aging Cell*: 4, 119-125.

Minina, Elena A., Sanchez-Vera, Victoria, Moschou, Panagiotis, N. et al. 2013. Autophagy mediates caloric restriction-induced lifespan extension in *Arabidopsis*. *Aging Cell*: 12, 327-329.

三浦慎吾 (Miura). 1996.「野生動物の年齢」. *森林科学* : 18, 50.

本川達雄 (Motokawa). 2016. *人間にとって寿命とは何か*. 東京：株式会社 KADOKAWA.

Munro, Saniel, Blier, Pierre. 2012. The extreme longevity of *Arctica islandica* is associated with increased peroxidation resistance in mitochondrial membranes. *Aging Cell* 11: 845-855.

Murakami, Yoshitaka, Ueshima, Hirotsugu, Okamura, Tomonori et al. 2007. Life expectancy among Japanese of different smoking status in Japan. *J. Epidemiol.* 17: 31-7.

長田典之 (Nagata), 及川真平, 宮田理恵 et al. 2013. 環境条件に応じた葉寿命の種内変異:一般的傾向と機能型間の差異. *日本生態学会誌* :６３,１９−３６.

Nguyen, Thu-Phuong, Cueff, Gwendal, Hegedus, Dwayne et al. A role for seed storage proteins in *Arabidopsis* seed longevity. 2015. *Journal of Experimental Botany*: 66, 6399-6413.

Nielsen, Julius, Hedeholm, Rasmus B., Heinemeier, Jan et al. 2016. Eye lens radiocarbon reveals centuries of longevity in the Greenland shark (*Somniosus microcephalus*). *Science* 353, 702-704.

Ohara, Tomoyuki, Honda, Takanori, Hata, Jun et al. 2018. Association Between Daily Sleep Duration and Risk of Dementia and Mortality in a Japanese Community. *J. Am. Geriatr. Soc.*: 66, 1911-1918.

大島靖美 (Ohshima). 2013.「*生物の大きさはどのようにしてきまるのか*」. 東京：化学同人.

大島靖美 (Ohshima). 2015.「*線虫の研究とノーベル賞への道*」. 東京：裳華房.

大島靖美 (Ohshima). 2020.「*４００年生きるサメ、4万年生きる植物 生物の寿命はどのように決まるのか*」. 東京：化学同人.

及川真平 (Oikawa), 長田典之, 宮沢良行 et al. 2013. 葉寿命研究の歴史と近況. *日本生態学会誌*：６３、１１−１７.

大川匡子 (Okawa)・高橋清久監修. 2019.「*睡眠のなぜ？に答える本*」. 東京:（株）ライフサイエンス.

大田秀隆 (Ota). 2010. 長寿遺伝子 Sirt 1 について. *日老医誌*: 47, 11-16.

Ozasa, Kotaro, Katanoda, Kota, Tamakoshi, Akiko et al. 2008. Reduced life expectancy due to smoking in large-scale cohort studies in Japan. *J Epidemiol*: 28, 111-8.

Paoli-Iseppi, Ricardo De, Deagle, Bruce E., Mcmahon, Clive R. et al. 2017. Measuring Animal Age with DNA Methylation: From Humans to Wild Animals. *Frontures in Genetics*: 8| Article 106.

Pereira da Silva, A., Valente, A., Chaves, C. et al. 2018. Characterizattion of Portugese Centenarian Eating Habits, Nutritional Biomarkers, and Cardiovascular Risk: A Case Control Study. *Oxidative Medicine and Cellular Longevity*: 2018, 1-10, Article ID 5296168.

Piraino, S., Boero, F., Aeschbach, B. et al. 1996. Reversing the life cycle: Medusae transforming into polyps and cell transdifferentiation in *Turitopsis nutricula* (Cnidaria, Hydrozoa). *Biol. Bulletin* 190: 302-12.

Preston, Samuel H., Choi, Daesung, Elo, Irma T., Stokes, Andrew. 2018. Effect of Diabetes on Life Expectancy in the United States by Race and Ethnicity. *Biodemography Soc Biol*: 64(2), 139-151.

Revelas, Mary, Thalamuthu, Anbupalam, Oldmeadow, Christopher et al. 2018. Review and meta-analysis of genetic polymorphisms associated with exceptional human longevity. *Mechanisms of Ageing and Development*: 175, 24-34.

Richie, J. P., Leutzinger, Y., Parthasarathy, S. et al. 1994. Methionine restriction increases blood glutathione and longevity in F344 rats. *FASEB J.*: 8, 1302-1307.

Riera, Celline E., Huising, Mark O., Follet, Patricia et al. 2014. TRPV1 Pain Receptors Regulate Longevity and Metabolism by Neuropeptide Signaling. *Cell*: 157, 1023-1036.

Roark, E. Brendan, Guilderson, Thomas P, Dubner, Rober B. et al. 2009. Extreme longevity in proteinaceous deep-sea corals. *PNAS* 106: 5204-5208.

Ravussin, Eric, Redman, Leanne M., Rochon, James et al. 2015. A 2-Year Randomized Controlled Trial of Human Caloric Restriction: Feasibility and Effects on Predictors of Health Span and Longevity. *J. Gerontol. A. Biol. Sci. Med. Sci.*: 70, 1097-1104.

Robine, Jean-Marie, Herrmann, Francois R., Arai, Yasumichi et al. 2012. Exploring the impact of climate on human longevity. *Exp. Gerontol.*: 47(9), 660-71.

Sakata, R., McGale, P., Grant, E. J. et al. 2012. Impact of smoking on mortality and life expectancy in Japanese smokers: a prospective cohort study. *BMJ*: 345: 1-12, e7093.

佐竹義輔 (Satake)、大井次三郎、北村四郎他. 2005.「*フィールド版日本の野生植物　草本*」. 東京：平凡社.

Schaible, Ralf, Scheuerlein, Alexander, Danko, Maciej, et al. 2015. Constant mortality and fertility over age in *Hydra. PNAS* 112: 15701-15706.

Sharabi-Schwager, Michal, Lers, Amnon, Samach, Alon et al. 2010. Overexpression of the *CBF-2* transcriptional activator in Arabidopsis delays leaf senescence and extends plant longevity. *Journal of Experimental Botany*: 61, 261-273.

椎野季雄著 (Shiino). 1969.「*水産無脊椎動物学*」. 東京：培風館.

Shefferson, Richard P., Roach, Deborah A. 2013. Longitudinal analysis in *Plantago*: strength of selection and reverse age analysis reveal age-indeterminate senescence. *J. Ecol.*: 101, 577-584.

Shen-Miller, J., Mudgett, Mary Beth, Schopf, J. William et al. 1995. Exceptional seed longevity and robust growth: ancient Sacred Lotus from China. *American Journal of Botany*: 82, 1367–1380.

Shin, Woo Young, Lee, Taehee, Jeon, Da-Hye et al. 2018. Diabetes, Frequency of Exercise, and Mortality Over 12 Years: Analysis of National Health Insurance Service-Health Screening (NHIS-HEALS) Database. *J. Korean Med Sci.*: 33: e60, 1-9.

Shriner, Samuel E., Linford, Nancy J, Martin, George M. et al. 2005. Extension of Murine Life Span by Overexpression of Catalase Targeted to Mitochondria. *Science*: 308, 1909-1911.

Sinclair, David, A., LaPlante, Mathew D. 梶山あゆみ訳. 2020. *LIFESPAN 老いなき世界*. 東京：東洋経済新報社 (Original: *Lifespan*. 2019. New York: Park & Fine Literary and Media).

Solon-Biet, Samantha, M., Mcmahon, Aisling, C., Ballard, J. William O. et al. 2014. The Ratio of Macronutrients, Not Caloric Intake, Dictates Cardiometabolic Health, Aging, and Longevity in Ad Libitum-Fed Mice. *Cell Metabolism*: 19, 418-430.

Song, Mingyang, Fung, Teresa, T., Hu, Frank B. et al. 2016. Association of Animal and Plant Protein Intake with All-Cause and Cause-Specific Mortality. *JAMA Intern. Med.*: 176, 1453-1463.

Stamatakis, Emmanuel, Gale, Joanne, Bauman, Adrian et al. 2019. Sitting Time, Physical Activity, and Risk of Mortality in Adults. *J. Am. Coll. Cardiol.*: 73, 2062-2072.

Sussman, Rachel. 2014. *The Oldest Living Things in the World*. Chicago: The University of Chicago Press.

鈴木英治 (Suzuki). 2002.「*植物はなぜ５０００年も生きるのか*」. 東京: 講談社.

鈴木基夫 (Suzuki)、横井政人監修. 1995. *「山渓カラー図鑑　園芸植物」*. 東京：山と渓谷社.

Swindell, William, R. 2012. Dietary restriction in rats and mice: A meta-analysis and review of the evidence for genotype-dependent effects on lifespan. *Aging Res. Rev.*: 11, 254-270.

高橋勝男 (Takahashi)、長野伸江. 2018.「*山渓名前図鑑　樹木の名前*」. 東京：山と渓谷社.

Takahashi, Mizuki K., Horner Liana M., Kubota, Toshiro, et al. 2011. Extensive clonal spread and extreme longevity in saw palmetto, a foundation clonal plant. *Mol. Ecol*. Sep: 20(18): 3730-42.

The Global BMI Mortality Collaboration. 2016. Body-mass index and all-cause mortality: individual-participant-data meta-analysis of 239 prospective studies in four continents. *Lancet*: 388, 776-786.

Tuscan, G. A., Difazio, S., Janssson, S. et al. 2006. The genome of black cottonwood, *Populus trichocrpa* (Torr. & Gray). *Science*: 313, 1596-1604.

Ungvari, Zoltan, Ridgway, Iain, Philipp, Eva E. R. et al. 2011. Extreme longevity is associated with increased resistance to oxidative stress in *Arctica islandica*, the longest-living non-colonial animal. *J. Gerontol. A Biol. Sci. Med. Sci.* 66A (7): 741-750.

Vasek F. C. 1980. Creosote Bush: Long-Lived Clones in the Mohave Desert. *American Journal of Botany* 67: 246-255.

渡邊昌 (Watanabe). 2009.「*栄養学原論*」. 東京：南江堂.

Wei, Yu-Chang, George, Nysia, Chang, Ching-Wei, Hicks, Karen A. 2017. Assessing Sex Differences in the Risk of Cardiovascular Disease and Mortality per Increment in Systolic Blood Pressure: A Systematic Review and Meta-Analysis of Follow-Up Studies in the United States. *PLOS ONE*:1-15|DOI: 10.1371/journal.pone. 0170218.

Willcox, Bradley J., Willcox, Donald Craig, Suzuki, Makoto. 2017. Demographic, phenotypic, and genetic characteristics of centenarians in Okinawa and Japan: Part 1- centenarians in Okinawa. *Mech. Ageing Dev.*: 165, 75-79.

Wright, Ian, Reich, Peter, Westoby, Mark et al. 2004. The worldwide leaf economics spectrum. *Nature*: 428, 821-827.

渡辺典博 (Watanabe). 1999.「*巨樹・巨木*」. 東京：山と渓谷社.

Yamagishi, Kazumasa, Sawachi, Shinobu, Tamakoshi, Akiko, Iso, Hiroyasu. 2019. Blood pressure levels and risk of cardiovascular disease mortality among Japanese men and women: the Japan Collaborative Cohort Study for Evaluation of Cancer Risk (JACC Study). *J. Hypertens.*: 37, 1366-1371.

Yang, Jae Jeong, Yu, Danxia, Wen Wanqing et al. 2019. Tobacco Smoking and Mortality in Asia: A Pooled Meta-Analysis. *JAMA Network Open*: 2(3), 1-14, e191474.

Yang, Jae Jeong, Yu, Danxia, Wen, Wanqing et al. 2019. Association of Diabetes with All-Cause and Cause-Specific Mortality in Asia: A Pooled Analysis of More Than 1 Million Participants. *JAMA Network Open*: 2(4), 1-14, e192696.

矢野恒太記念会 (Yano). 2014.「*世界国勢図会* 2014/15 年版」. 東京：矢野恒太記念会.

八杉龍一 (Yasugi), 小関治男, 古谷雅樹, 日高敏隆編. 1996.「*岩波生物学辞典*」第 4 版、東京：岩波書店.

Yin, Jiawei, Jin, Xiaoling, Shan, Zhilei et al. 2017. Relationship of Sleep Duration with All-Cause Mortality and Cardiovascular Events: A Systematic Review and Dose-Response Meta-Analysis of Prospective Cohort Studies. *J. Am. Heart Assoc.*: 6, 1-13. DOI: 10.1161.

Yu, Winnie, W., Randhawa, Arshdeep, K., Blair, Steven N. et al. 2019. Age-and sex-specific all-cause mortality risk greatest in metabolic syndrome combinations with elevated blood pressure from 7 U.S. cohorts. *PLOS ONE*: 1-10| https://doi.org/ 10.1371/journal.pone. 0218307.

Zeng, Yi, Feng, Qiushi, Gu, Danan, Vaupel, James W. 2017. Demographics, phenotypic health characteristics and genetic analysis of centenarians in China. *Mech. Ageing Dev.*: 165, 86-97.

Zha, Ling, Sobue, Tomotaka, Kitamura, Tetsuhisa et al. 2019. Changes in Smoking Status and Mortality from All Causes and Lung Cancer: A Longitudinal Analysis of a Population-based Study in Japan. *J. Epidemiol.*: 29(1), 1-17.

(2) News

183 歳のカメのジョナサン元気に、最高齢の動物. *National Geographic News*, 1/15, 2016. natgeo.nikkeibp.co.jp/actl/news/16/011400012/

(3) Web information

https 6: Wikipedia. 2019. ジャンヌ・カルマン (Jeanne L. Calment). n.d. https://ja.wikipedia.org/wiki/ジャンヌ・カルマン.

https 8: Wikipedia. 2019. ニシオンデンザメ (Greenland shark). n.d. https://ja.wikipedia.org/wiki/ニシオンデンザメ.

https 9: Wikipedia. 2019.ホッキョククジラ(Arctic whale). n.d. https://ja.wikipedia.org/wiki/ホッキョククジラ.

http 11: Wikipedia. 2019. アルダブラゾウガメ (Aldabra giant tortoise). n.d. http://ja. wikipedia.org/wiki/アルダブラゾウガメ.

https 13: 2022. Jeanne Louise Calment: The world's oldest person. n.d. https: //anson.ucdavis.edu>~wang>calment.

https 14: Wikipedia. 2019. シロエリハゲワシ (griffon vulture).

n.d. https://ja.wikipedia.org/wiki/シロエリハゲワシ.

https 16: 日本ペットフード　小動物の基礎知識. 2019. 種類別の小鳥寿命表 (age of a bird). n.d. https://www.npf.co.jp/kisoaqua bird/kop4-03.html.

https 17: 魚類図鑑/魚の寿命. 2019. 魚の年齢と寿命 (age of a fish). n.d. https://aqua.stardust31.com/jyumyou.shtml.

https 23: Wikipedia. 2019. ベニクラゲ. n.d. https://ja.wikipedia.org.wiki/ベニクラゲ

https 24: Wikipedia. 2019. シオミズツボワムシ (saline rotifer). n.d. https://ja.wikipedia.org/wiki/ シオミズツボワムシ.

https 26: Wikipedia. 2019. アイスランドガイ (ocean quahog). n.d. https://ja.wikipedia.org/wiki/アイスランドガイ.

https 28: NAVER まとめ. 2019. 人間より長生き！？長寿の昆虫ベスト５. n.d. https://matome.navor.jp/odai/2137949300502513301.

http 29: 2019. １００年生きるシロアリ女王. n.d. http://www10.plala.or.jp/kasuga3/insect/100nen.htm

https 30: Wikipedia. 2019. サンゴ (choral). n.d. https://ja.wikipedia.org/wiki/サンゴ.

https 31: Wikipedia. 2019. Hydra vulgaris. n.d. https://en.wikipedia.org/wiki/Hydra_vulgaris.

http 39: 2019. 世界自然遺産屋久島. http://www.tabian.com. /tiikibetu/kyushu/kagosima/yakusima/2.html

https 41: Wikipedia. 2019. https://ja.wikipedia.org/wiki/樹齢. n. d.

https 48: 2019. *Lomatia tasmanica*. n.d. https://gardens.rtbg.tas.gov.au/lomatia_tasmanica/.

https 49: Wikipedia. 2019. King_Clone. n.d.
https://en.wikipedia.org/wiki/King_Clone.

https 50: Wikipedia. 2019. Old Tjikko. n.d.
https.//en.wikipedia.org/wiki/Old_Tjikko.

https 52: Wikipedia. 2019. Britlecone_pine. n.d.
https://en.wikipedia.org/wiki/Bristlecone_pine.

https 53: Wikipedia. 2019. 縄文杉. n.d. https://ja.wikipedia.org/wiki/縄文杉.

Web 55: 林野庁業務資料. 2019. スギ・ヒノキ林に関するデータ. n.d.
https://www.rinya.maff.go.jp › sin_riyou › kafun › data スギ・ヒノキ林に関するデータ

https 57: Wikipedia. 2019. n.d. https://ja.wikipedia.org/wiki/ 1 年生植物

https 58: Wikipedia. 2019. n.d. https://ja.wikipedia.org/wiki/二年生植物

https 59: Wikipedia. 2019. n.d. https://ja.wikipedia.org/wiki/多年生植物

https 61: Wikipedia. 2019. Pando (tree).
https://en.wikipedia.org/wiki/Pando.

https 62: Wikipedia. 2019. n.d.
https://en.wikipedia.org/wiki/Clonal_colony#Examples

https 64: kotobank. 2019. タケ (bamboo). n.d.
https://kotobank.jp/word/タケ-1558724

http 65: 農林水産省. 2019. 竹のお話（2）(bamboo). n.d.
http://www.maff.go.jp/j/pr/aff/1301/spe1_02.html.

https 87: Wikipedia, 2019. ラパマイシン (rapamycin).
https://ja.wikipedia.org/wiki/ラパマイシン.

https 104: （独）国立健康・栄養研究所. 2012. 改訂版「身体活動のメッツ (METs) 表」2012 年 4 月 11 日改訂. n.d.

https://www. nibiohn.go.jp>programs>2111mets.

https 105: 2019. 代謝当量 METs とその場運動. n.d. https://47819157.at.webry.info/201511/article_5.html.

https 107: 身体活動量と死亡との関連について. 2019. 多目的コホート研究（JPHC. n.d. https://epi.ncc.go.jp>jphc>outcome.

https 110: 厚生労働省. 2019.「平成 28 年国民健康・栄養調査報告」. n.d. https://www.mhlw.go.jp>stf>houdou.

http 113: 2019. タバコの害について. n.d. http://www.hokenkai.or.jp/3/3-5/3-55-03.html.

http 119: 厚生労働省の最新たばこ情報. 2019. 成人喫煙率（JT 全国喫煙者率調査）. http://www.health-net.or./jp/tobacco/product/pd090000.html.

https 121: World Health Organization. 2019. WHO Report on the Global Tobacco Epidemic, 2017. n.d. https://www.who.int/tobacco/global_report/2017/en/

https 123: 糖尿病ネットワーク (diabetes). 2019. 糖尿病の調査・統計・数字２０１７年９月. n.d. https://dm-net.co.jp/calendar/chousa/population.php.

http 130: 日本生活習慣病予防協会. 2019.「高血圧の予防と治療」(prevention and treatment of hypertension). n.d. http://www.seikatsushukanbyo.com/guide/hypertension.php.

https 138: Wikipedia. 2019. センテナリアン. n.d. https://ja.wikipedia.org/wiki/センテナリアン

https 150: Wikipedia. 2019. *Ophrys sphegodes*. n.d. https://en.wikipedia.org/wiki/Ophrys_ sphegodes.

https 152: Wikipedia, 2019. *Plantago lanceolata*. n.d. https://en.wikipedia.org/wiki/Plantago_lanceolata.

http 155: 岩手県立大学. 2019. ヤマノイモの会. n.d. http://p-www.iwate-pu.ac.jp/~hiratsuku/yamanoimo /Borderea/photos.html

https 159: Wikipedia. 2019. *Thuja oxidentalis*. n.d. https://en.wikipedia.org/wiki/Thuja_occidentalis.

http 162: 野崎造園新聞. 2019. 植物の寿命. n.d. http://www.nozaki-zoen.co.jp.

https 164: yahoo. 2019. 樹種別の寿命と樹高、直径成長. n.d. https://blogs.yahoo.co.jp/freiburgshuji/18140211.html.

https 165: Wikipedia. 2019. ブナ (beech). n.d. https://ja.wikipedia.org/wiki/ブナ.

https 168: 木材博物館. 2019. 木材の比重. n.d. https:// www.wood-museum.net/specific_gravity.php.

https 172: 森林綜合研究所. 2012. ヒノキの葉の寿命は寒冷な地ほど長い. n.d. https://www.ffpri.affrc.go.jp /research/saizensen/2012/20120528-02.html.

https 173: Wikipedia. 2019. 大賀ハス (Oga lotus). n.d. https://ja.wikipedia.org/wiki/大賀ハス.

http 176: 2019. 種の寿命. n.d. http://www.pixino.com/salen/koukannilyo.htm

https 189: 健康長寿ネット. 2019. ウェルナー症候群 (Werner syndrome). n.d. https://www.tyojyu.or.jp/net/byouki/werner.html.

https 190: Wikipedia. 2019. ハッチンソン・ギルフォード・プロジェリア症候群 (Hutchinson-Gilford syndrome). n.d. https://ja.wikipedia.org/wiki/ ハッチンソン・ギルフォード・プロジェリア症候群.

https 193: 魚類図鑑. 2019. 魚の寿命 (lifespan of fish). n.d. https://aqua.stardust31.com/jyumyou.shtml.

https 196: 厚生労働省. 2015. 日本人の食事摂取基準（２０１５年版）の概要. n.d. https://www.mhlw.go.jp/stf/houdou/0000041733/0000041733.html.

https 197: 厚生労働省, 2010.「日本人の食事摂取基準」（２０１０年版）、各論 エネルギー栄養素 1 エネルギー、p５４の表９. n.d. https://www.mhlw.go.jp/shingi/2009/05/s0529-4.html.

Web 200: Eat-Lancet Commission, 2020. Healthy Diets From Sustainable Food Systems: Summary Report of the EAT-Lancet Commission. *thelancet.com/commissions/ EAT.*

https 201: 国際連合広報センター. 2019. 世界の人口 (world population). 国連報告書プレスリリース日本語訳. n.d. https://www.unic.or.jp/news_press/info/33789.

https 204: 2019. シニアガイド. n.d. https://seniorguide.jp/article/1019204.html.

https 205: 禁煙サポートサイト. 2019. いい禁煙 (No smoking). n.d. https://www.e-kinen.jp/harm/ poison.html.

http 206: 喫煙の健康影響. 2019. 禁煙の効果. n.d. http://www.j-circ.or.jp/kinen/iryokankei/eikyo.htm.

http 207: DM TOWN. 2019. 糖尿病がよくわかる. n.d.

http://www.dm-town.com/oneself/yobou01.html.

http 210: ののちゃんの DO 科学. 2019. 動物の年齢、どう数えるの? n.d. http://www.asahi.com/edu/nie/tamate/kiji /TKY200703260240.html.

http 211: 京都府農林水産技術センター海洋センター. 2019. 研究こぼれ話. 魚の年齢を調べる. n.d. http://www.pref.kyoto/krnkyukoborebanashi-nenrei.html.

http 212: 京都府農林水産技術センター海洋センター. 2019. この魚は何歳？（年齢調査）. n.d. http://www.pref.kyooto.jp/kaiyo/job0103.html.

https 220:東邦大学　Dr. Goto の老化研究　健康長寿 老いとは何か. n.d. https://www.mnc.toho-u.ac.jp › aging › doc1 › doc1-02.